Mary and Paddy

'Peter Carton is a wonderful story teller. He has published a book in memory of his parents entitled *"Mary and Paddy-Joy Wrapped in Tears"*, recounting the story of the brave journey undertaken by them when they emigrated to the UK in search of a better life for their young family.

Paddy from County Carlow and Mary who hailed from Wexford, took their first steps into the unknown when they and their seven children boarded the ferry to England in November 1958.

They settled in Oxford and Peter's meticulous research makes this happy and sometimes sad account of life for the cartons in the City of Dreaming Spires a great read.

Anybody who grew up in the "swinging sixties" will be familiar with a lot of the events depicted as Peter takes us on his closely knit family's journey over the years.

Being a friend of the Carton family greatly added to my interest in the story, but this is a book which will be enjoyed by everybody.

It's not alone a lovely tribute to his parents but is also an absorbing and sometimes traumatic account of the life and times of his family over the past 100 years to the present day.'

Mikie Carthy, former (retired) journalist
with the *Wexford Echo* Newspaper.

Mary and Paddy

The Legacy
Joy wrapped in tears

Peter Carton

Matador
Unit E2 Airfield Business Park,
Harrison Road, Market Harborough,
Leicestershire. LE16 7UL
Tel: 0116 2792299
Email: books@troubador.co.uk
Web: www.troubador.co.uk/matador
Twitter: @matadorbooks

ISBN 978 1803136 233

British Library Cataloguing in Publication Data.
A catalogue record for this book is available from the British Library.

Printed and bound in Great Britain by 4edge Limited
Typeset in 11pt Minion Pro by Troubador Publishing Ltd, Leicester, UK

Matador is an imprint of Troubador Publishing Ltd

Contents

A Personal Note

I discovered my Irish family history contained hidden secrets, stretching back 100 years, involving religious prejudice that divided family members; bravery in service with the British Army; a presence at a Dublin massacre; an ambush by the IRA; elopements and hastily arranged marriages and, personal to myself, a startling revelation of the birth and burial of two twins. Together with my older brothers' we encountered the, sometimes, rather harsh discipline of a Catholic education before discovering the joy and beauty of the City of Oxford.

This is the story about my parents, Mary and Paddy. Commencing with their own background and lives in the rural counties of Wexford and Carlow, in Southern Ireland, it follows them on their journey, beginning with their momentous and life changing decision in 1958, to emigrate from Ireland. Determined to start a fresh life in England to secure a better future for their eight young children, this is informative of their day-to-day struggles to feed, clothe and educate us all in frequently difficult circumstances that required them to work so long and hard all their lives before the toil and stress eventually took its toll.

On behalf of myself, and my sisters and brothers, this book is written as a tribute and a thank you to them both, for a joyous childhood and a more prosperous adulthood bequeathed to ourselves and our own children.

Recollections

This book is not intended as a purely factual history of the Cartons. It is a story about my parents, based on personal memories of myself, siblings, aunts and uncles, cousins and the wider family and friends who knew them. Given the time span covers over 100 years, from their birth to compilation of this book, it is fair to say that recollections, of some events and dates, do vary. I believe that the book provides a comprehensive and substantially accurate account of their lives. I fervently hope that you obtain as much enjoyment reading the book, as much as I have in researching and writing it.

Mary and Paddy

Introduction

November 1958. My ginger-red hair is hidden under a dark grey woollen hat with an ill matching green scarf and my upper body wrapped up in a heavy grey coat, that matched the damp, misty and foggy mood of the Dublin skyline that evening. Stretching down to greet the bottom of my short navy trousers I was afforded some protection from the biting cold wind that tore across the open deck onto my skinny white legs, in that gap before my woollen socks intervened cemented as they were in black leather shoes purchased for this extra special occasion. On the brink of my tenth birthday, I was with my parents and six brothers and sisters, and we were on the second leg of our journey into the unknown. Earlier that day we had left behind the family home in Bagenalstown and cramped into a white delivery van owned by Dad's friend Mr Nolan, a grocer and store owner, who had very kindly agreed to drive us some seventy miles to Dublin.

I recall my father Paddy ushering us from our triple bunked cabin in groups of two or three onto the deck of the Holyhead bound boat. None of us had ever been on a boat this size before so this allowed us briefly to glimpse the noisy bewilderment as we awaited our departure. Leaving behind the land of our birth, we were on a journey across the sea to a place called England.

Nevertheless, this was the defining moment in the lives of us children, ranging in age from one to thirteen years, but especially so for our parents. They had made what must have been a momentous decision to pursue a dream, uproot themselves, forsake family and friends and, in my father's case, leave his job as a respected postman to seek a better future, one that would provide opportunities for their large family. There must have been some degree of anguish and doubt about the challenges ahead, although my father had set out for England two months earlier and had found work as well as securing a temporary home to be shared with his brother Michael and his wife Margaret in Oxford, but no such doubts were ever expressed in my presence that I recall.

Fast forward to 2023. Since that memorable day my pioneering parents have now departed. Much has happened to us all in the intervening years and all of it locked away in individual and collective minds. It is time, I believe, to tell the story of this great adventure. A journey of tears, uplifting joy, difficulties and unbearable sadness borne with humour, grim determination and of ultimate success.

This is a story dedicated primarily to our parents, Mary and Paddy, a record of their legacy arising from that momentous November day in 1958.

Part One

Life in Ireland

Chapter One

Mary Enters the World, Joy Wrapped in Tears

The Quirkes' family home at Kilcorral, a small community close to Wexford town in South East Ireland, comprised a large two-storey home, possibly sporting a thatched roof with a single chimney at its eastern end. Three sets of upstairs laced curtained windows denoted at least three large bedrooms facing the front with another three to the south-facing rear. Downstairs, stood a matching sequence with reception, living room and large kitchen located on the eastern side beneath the imposing single chimney, spewing clouds of steam into Wexford skyline.

Outside there was ample space within a garden bordered by a concrete wall and a large shed to the side of the house. To the rear a few scrawny egg producing hens would most likely wander freely amongst the tall grass and wildly scattered nettles, weeds and thorn bushes. Potatoes, carrots and cabbages lined up formally in well-tended drills ready to provide a supply of fresh food for their attendant carers.

My Grandmother, Elizabeth Quirke, was a member of the Flood family, who appeared genetically prone to gangrene, a disease that accounted for a number of deaths and illness. Her sister, Mary, lost a leg to the disease at a young age and the story goes that the chopped off leg was buried to lie with one of her sons and his grandparents. Displaying renowned family grit and determination she survived her lost leg by many years, happily using a wooden crutch and propelling herself around on this better than most people with two legs until her death at the then ripe old age of 78.

Elizabeth, a tall angular and bespectacled woman, dressed in widow black from head to toe had herself borne nine children, many of them in consecutive years, including a set of twins one of whom died at birth. Accustomed to dealing with hardship and difficulties, even she must have been bewildered at the turn of events now facing her. In early spring of 1918 with warming westerly winds blowing in from the Atlantic across the green landscape of Kilcorral, she would have shared the news that her tenth child would be born at the beginning of the holy season of advent in early December.

By the time the festive season had announced itself a very unholy disaster had cursed itself on the family and all sense of Christmas joy had been displaced. Just three months earlier, her youngest child, the once lively three-year old Ellen, stricken with TB and surrounded by her heart broken family, had passed away at home. Barely recovering from this blow, fate cruelly struck again when her husband Nicholas (Nick) died on 13th November to be followed just three days later by sixteen-years old Mary, both having succumbed, in the Wexford Fever Hospital, to the Spanish-flu, an epidemic that had spread across the world and was now devastating the country, killing an estimated twenty thousand with another eight hundred thousand suffering serious illness. Wexford itself was identified as a national blackspot. According to national research undertaken by Dr Ida Milne, for which I am grateful, newspaper reports and local recollections, early November saw reports of hundreds of cases in the town with several deaths recorded. Within a few days this soon spiralled to well over a thousand, the cinema and schools were closed and dis-infected and shops shut due to staff shortages. There were sadly recalled deaths of several members of the same family, as with Nick and Mary, where the remaining family were advised not to attend traditional wakes for fear of them spreading and catching the disease or because they were themselves too ill to attend the resulting funeral.

The Quirke's home, according to the memories of ageing nieces and nephews, was recalled as being dimly lit, by oil lamps and candles, in what was regarded as the wettest, and most miserable of winters, for many years. Water, collected in buckets from outside supplies via butts or wells for additional use, was boiled over open fires, fuelled by coal, turf and wood that would crackle well into the night. It was in such circumstances that, on 2nd December 1918 and surrounded by family friends and daughters, a mournful Elizabeth (Granny Quirke) gave birth whilst as a cloud of smoke escalated its way upwards through the chimney as if announcing a new papal arrival. A child was born, bringing forth some joyous relief and was named Mary after the daughter who had so recently died. This is how my mother entered this world. *"Joy wrapped in tears."*

*

Mum's early years are largely unrecorded. What is known is that this was a time of great austerity with exceptional levels of poverty and little work, emanating from the First World War, the Easter Rising (1916) and the ensuing Civil War and flu epidemic. Wexford County was at the forefront of rebellion in a divided nation. State troops clashed with an assortment of former army returnees and civilian attired militia and Mum's family, would have been all too aware of local skirmishes. The County of Wexford was placed under martial law followed in 1922 by two years of Civil war. By the end of this period, peace was being restored to a troubled region and Mum, protected and largely oblivious to these external events, was soon to commence her schooling at nearby Screen.

Her father, "Nick" who had died so shortly before her birth was classed as a "Master Thatcher". He supplemented this in less busy times earning a living and decorating entrances to houses using shells. Clearly a man of some ability and earning power his death had implications for the family fortunes. Thomas, the remaining eldest son, took on the role of man of the house to support his stricken mother and his sisters, especially so following the death of the oldest son Patrick, in a point-to-point fall, at least according to local folklore. Officially, the actual cause is given as meningitis. Librarians point out that accuracy in record keeping at this time was commonly flexible. Support for this view is the fact that "Nick's" death certificate recorded his name as Richard instead of Nicholas, requiring the widowed Elizabeth, in timely Irish fashion to correct this on 25th September 1937, some 19 years later.

In the 1930s, Thomas was fully engaged, with his family, working long hours on their own, and nearby neighbours, agricultural holdings. Repetitive daily chores were accepted as a normal part of their lives and, in addition to assisting with indoor tasks of cleaning, washing, and ash removal, Mum may possibly have helped with garden chores such as sowing and weeding and picking any home produced vegetables and perhaps feeding the squawking chickens they may have owned, as well as cleaning and raking-up manure heaps, before being rewarded with a handful of newly laid eggs which were likely to have been an essential part of the daily diet.

Like his father before him, Thomas would also work as a labourer or do whatever was available. Agricultural wages were low and labourers were often paid less than 15 shillings (75 pence in today's world) a week. Accompanied by his good friend Billy Devereux of Poulregan they were both regarded as great characters and became night watchmen on the historic "Barrel Bridge", working on the town side from a small hut, manned around the clock, to ensure that restricted heavy vehicles did not use the bridge to cross the river.

Mum referred to Thomas as "Dad". In later years her handbag always contained a small picture of him, cheery and bushy mopped, which she would proudly reveal to my youngest brother David on a number of occasions. A photo taken on his wedding day in St Alphonsus Church, Barntown, in October 1939, depicts a smiling Thomas sitting alongside his bride Ellen and his best man Will Kinsella. Mum, then a sprightly twenty-year old, would doubtless have participated fully in the celebrations with a night of music, dancing and singing. Such was Mum's attachment and love for Thomas that in August 1963 she was very visibly upset and Dad had to explain to us that she had just received news that her beloved brother, completely unknown to any of us, had died, aged just 63 years.

Mum was also very close to her sisters and especially to Bridget (Bridgie), eight years her senior, who escorted her to school in Screen, with Mum piggy-backing and shrieking with delight. Dressed in school wear they would spend a couple of hours daily trekking the mostly flat terrain of the four-mile round trip, observing the large pastures and hayfields on either side of long slender laneways, being aware of heavy puffing tractors, and stepping briskly onto available field openings or green verges whilst waving the occasionally grumbly-in-a cap farmer on his way. Fields, fenced by trees of varying hues and low broad hedgerows, mixed with spiky blackthorn and hawthorn which would, in their seasons, leave them gasping with joy at the sight of new life, fledging haphazardly from their inner spaces. Whinnying horses, mooing cattle and bleating sheep interspersed with seasonal fields of golden hay and were their companions as they edged and giggled their merry way past intermittent homes to join classmates at the school in Screen.

On other days, filled with more unforgiving skies, the same landscape would unveil a darker, less optimistic mood leaving them bedraggled, heads down and drenched almost to the skin and seeking a refuge from the dampness of the lashing rain and a welcoming opportunity to dry their clothes and soothe their pain. Screen, a village-like community comprised a few shops, a large virgin white Church and an even larger graveyard, each standing loftily on a hillside that afforded the living and dead a heavenly vista, the long lines of those who had passed this way before now resting in deserved peace. Sadly, there are no remaining records of Mum's schooling and little more is known about her time there.

A few photographs survive as a testament to her youth. One, probably taken in her early teens, shows her sporting short dark hair that gives all the impression of having escaped capture in a tight fish-net. Posing on the garden grass in a half sitting position, with a beaming smile and dressed in a long, light coloured half-sleeved dress, she appears a healthy and content young lady.

A more intriguing photo sees her kitted in an army type uniform and bearing a rifle. Her now flowing hair is seen to be springing out erratically from underneath a cadet style V-shape hat. Holding a rifle in an upward position with the heavy butt end held firmly in her right hand next to her waist, her left arm is stretched across from the elbow to reach and clasp the rifle at its mid-point, fingers firmly wrapped around the trigger point displaying poise and confidence. Discussing this photo with family members has aroused speculation as to its origin. Initial thoughts centred on whether Mum may have been a member of the LDF, (Local Defence Force) formed during The Emergency (1939/44) but it is understood that women were not then involved in that organisation. Another suggestion is that this was taken during her time in the WAF Cadet Force and certainly her confident posture with the rifle gives some credence to this, save that the rifle itself in the photo is not recognised as army issue. It may simply be that Mum was friends with a young man in army service, or even a rebellious revolutionary, and they conspired naughtily to produce an enigmatic photo to spark a few wagging tongues. In retrospect, they seem to have achieved their goal.

Two other photos take in her teens appear to have been taken at the same time. Hatless, her short hair is separated to the left with the silent assistance of a slim hairpin giving her a more vibrant look. A short-sleeved v -necked check shirt is tucked into a shiny dark dress, upheld with a wide buckled belt, that daringly finishes just below the knee and in turn reveals a pair of black stockings sat in flat black shoes. There is an indication here of a woman who knows her own mind and using her earnings to dress in a more modern style. Pictured with an older family friend, Anna O' Brien, the setting is formal, standing wide apart from her much more solemn looking friend, with unclenched stiffly placed hands, her eyes and half smile indicate a much more robust sense of determination. More importantly, the scene again emphasises how strong and healthy she looks, a fine testament to all those who cared for and looked after her.

The Quirkes' of Kilcorral were well known for their music and dancing evenings with their cousins the Kinsellas' always holding an open tea house for visitors in search of a cuppa. Will Kinsella was himself an accomplished accordion player encouraging frequent Irish musical evenings (ceilidhs). Given the ancient battles, such as that at Vinegar Hill, and freedom struggles that had been fought around Mum's home county, it is hardly surprising to find so many events reflected in famous ballads. The best known is probably *Boolavogue,* written to record the exploits of Father Murphy, a priest who was provoked into action when British forces burnt his church. He and his rebels had some victories around Wexford but were readily outnumbered and defeated and the poor priest paid the price for his bravery when horribly mutilated after his capture. Mum knew about such history and would most certainly have sung *Boolavogue* and *The Wexford Boys.*

By all accounts Mum possessed a lovely singing voice with her favourite song being "Rose of Tralee", written in the mid-1840s and sung in films and recorded by Bing Crosby amongst others. This was a story about a lost love for a lady, also called Mary, whose beauty was such that she gave her name to the famous Rose of Tralee Festival. Growing up with her mother and a number of sisters she learned many practical skills that would prove invaluable in later years which included baking, mending/sewing and dress making and fire making. There was a wave of emigration across to England in the thirties and forties and this at least had the saving grace of providing more earning opportunity for the remaining population. Food was grown on their own land including an ample supply of veggies and of course the "spud", the national favourite and staple diet.

Mum, accompanied by her siblings and various aunts, uncles and cousins, would look forward to attending the nearby Screen Horticultural Show. This annual event afforded an opportunity for farmers, wives, gardeners and children to dress up at will, display hitherto latent talents to a wider deserving audience, socialise and exchange news and gossip in equal measure. Prizes were awarded by impartial sounding judges to beaming and satisfied winners whilst losers would clap and outwardly congratulate their deserving opponent. *"Sure, I never tasted a soda bread like that before"* was the common refrain, disguising an inwardly competitive edge. Silently, they would be even more determined to prove that next year the judges would finally recognise the error of their ways and award best soda bread to them. I was informed by great aunts and cousins that you should never underestimate the will to win and competition harboured at these events.

One year, three local men named Matt Murphy, Pat Devereux and John Walsh, expressed some disappointment that the Screen show was soon to be closed. Their replacement has morphed into Castlebridge Horticultural and Agricultural Show, established in September 1940, when Mum was twenty. It celebrated its 80th Anniversary in 2022, having lost two years due to the pandemic. Held annually, usually on the second Thursday of each August, it was first held at The Old Schoolhouse before its transfer to Castlebridge Hall, where it now attracts thousands eager to be educated and critically examine the variety of entries for its exhibitions of fruit and flowers, photography and baking classes among others. The Quirke's have been involved in attending and participating since its inception. Indeed, events have turned full circle and my elder brother Nicky, has himself entered the aforementioned soda bread competition. He is confident that nobody can ever bake soda bread to match his, based on his own secret formula. Having tasted his offering and being mindful that he is my older, and bigger brother, I can vouch for its unique taste.

Granny Quirke died at home in May 1941, aged 63 years, due to anaemia and cardiac arrest, in the presence of Thomas, the dutiful son who had carefully looked after her and the family since the death of her husband twenty-three years earlier.

On leaving school Mum had found work at Sinnott's store, in The Ballagh, close to Blackwater. Her sister Bridgie informed us that she would cycle the six miles or so to work and it was here that she was destined to meet our father Paddy, who was working as a relief postman and was a daily visitor to the post office, situated across the road. This was a meeting and a love affair that would change the whole destiny of both their lives.

Chapter Two

War, Bloody Sunday and Paddy at Soldiers Cottage

Named after Walter Bagenal, who had visions of creating a town based on the lay out and structure of the French city of Versailles, Bagenalstown, (Muinea Bheag), is a small mill town set in the scenic Barrow Valley, county Carlow, some 68 miles south-west of Dublin. The river Barrow meanders lazily through the town, from the Royal Oak on the western slopes via now long-lost flour mills and the spire of St. Andrew's church. This central landmark appears bewitchingly from out of the ground and seems almost to caress the often-prevalent white fluffy clouds. South of the town, the river then proceeds on its leisurely way past the outdoor swimming pool and out alongside the open fields towards the county town of Carlow.

The re-routing of the old coach, away from the town, caused the abandonment of all the grand scale plans. A number of his creations including the magnificent Courthouse, now a public library, still stand today as testament to the vision. Access to the river allowed flour mills to flourish and grain, beet, turf and beers were transported via long, narrow river barges, many festooned with pots of flowers. The arrival of the railways in 1846 provided a much-needed impetus for the town and indeed the neo classical railway station, still much the same today, is considered to be one of Ireland's finest.

Granny Carton was christened Mary Ann but became better known as Molly and had an eventful life. Born in 1897 she was first married to Army Private, Henry Bolton, son of an agricultural labourer Jacob and his wife Mary, from Kilgraney. Although little is known about Molly's early life or the marriage, fate decreed that she would be widowed at the tender age of twenty after Henry went to fight in the First World war. He served initially with the Royal Dublin Fusiliers, later subsumed into the Royal Irish Regiment, 2nd battalion and suffered fatal injuries at Flanders in June 1918 before dying of his wounds on 13th November. He lies buried at the beautifully cared for military cemetery at Valenciennes (St Roch) Communal Cemetery, Nord-Pas-de-Calais, France.

My Great Grandfather, Michael Carton, held a license for eight dogs in 1870 so presumably, as a registered farmer, he owned a large plot of land requiring canine assistance and these may also have been used to hunt rabbits to provide food. To add to the general confusion so common in Irish families (and adopted by Irish emigrants to America) he also christened one of his sons Michael.

Grandad Michael and Henry Bolton were firm friends, sharing an interest in army matters. Grandad was himself a Corporal in the 8th London Regiment, having previously been a member of the territorial forces and earned medals for his bravery in service. He lost an ankle when hit by a mortar in a foxhole during the appalling slaughter at The Battle of Passchendaele in 1917. Transported back to Dublin, the remnant of his heel was then fused to his shinbone thus shortening his right leg by two inches. To compensate for this and, his inability to move his toes, the innovative surgeons fitted him with a cork-filled boot which would become his constant life companion.

Grandad was subsequently discharged home to Bagenalstown. Here he met and comforted Henry's widow, Molly and, as friend and widow, they mourned the aching loss of the loved Henry, with Michael able to convey a soldier's reality of a distant war where humour and friendship provided some solace amidst the grimness of death and slaughter. Not unsurprisingly, as they draped their emotions around each other, a shared longing cast its spell like ray of sunshine crashing its way through the dark clouds of grief. Within months they expressed their new found love to their respective families and sought their approval for marriage. However, neither family felt able to give their blessing, expressing the view that it was too soon after Henry's death for them to be able to consent. Faced with this dilemma, Grandad and Molly decided on a bold course of action that would bring them face to face with excitement and death.

They eloped to Dublin where a three week stay ensured that they were able to obtain a licence and were married.

The marriage coincided with a Great Challenge (Gaelic Football) Match between Dublin and Tipperary, at Croke Park Stadium. Following their wedding, they happily paid a shilling each to attend the game. What they had not anticipated was this would bring them face to face with the British Army on what became known as Bloody Sunday, an event on 21st November 1920, that changed history for both nations. On the morning of the game the IRA began a series of co-ordinated attacks against British Intelligence resulting in 14 deaths. The British suspected that a number of the IRA members responsible fled to Croke Park to mingle with the crowd and they dispatched Constabulary Forces and troops from the Black and Tans to locate and arrest suspects. It was not long after their arrival when the forces opened fire on the men, women and children in the crowd resulting in 14 fatalities and many injuries. There were many differing accounts as to what happened although Major Mills, in charge of the Joint Force, criticised his own men for indiscipline. It was also noted, that although the IRA had some of its members within the teams taking part, there were many Irish men attending the game who had fought in the trenches with the British in World War including, of course, our own Grandad. The startling fact was that Molly was pregnant at this time, a taboo subject in a strongly Catholic country. Molly would subsequently become widely known as Granny Carton, the family Matriarch. Mercifully, they returned home safely to Bagenalstown.

Together, Granny and Grandad would form the apex of a new expansive Carton family that would eventually spread its wings across the seas. Lacking the vast oil riches, or indeed any sort of wealth, as depicted in the hugely popular and controversial eighties television drama, Dynasty, that starred Joan Collins, it would become the building blocks for future generations built on hard work, family ties, courage and determination.

They lived initially in Chapel Lane, Kilcarrig Street, in Bagenalstown where Dad was born, before moving a year later, into one of ten Soldiers' cottages, provided for men returning from France, in recognition of their war service. They were not all instantly welcomed as the Dublin Easter Rising of 1916 and subsequent civil war events in Ireland, involving British and rebellious forces, caused some resentment although many of the men found work in the flour mills. Grandad was a strong-minded man and determined that he would return to his pre-war job as a postman. Having previously been well regarded, he was soon reinstated. His "penance" was to be given a difficult route that took him over 2,000 feet high Mount Leinster in the Blackstairs Hills. Fully caped to protect himself and his mail from the typical Irish weather he stoically cycled on his faithful old cycle with his barely working foot.

Grandad himself had three brothers, one being Peter who was employed as a mill hand and married to the well-travelled Alice Edgeworth, who was known to have been in New York in 1913 though her purpose is unclear. One story to emerge from his time as a postie has passed into folklore. Cycling home after a hard day's work he was, he said, ambushed at Sliguffe Bridge. Observing his enhanced foot-boot the armed group of men quickly ascertained that he had fought in the British Army and concluded he should immediately be shot. Given his fighting history it is doubtful he was particularly fearful and most probably would have sought to engage with his captors. At the decisive moment, with guns loaded and pointed, a man stepped out of the shadows and shouted the immortal words "you cannot shoot him, he's my brother". This was Peter. Following a stunned silence and a further brief pow-wow, in deference to their comrade, they agreed not to shoot him. Any immediate relief he may have felt soon evaporated in the grey mood. In a split second a handful of rough hands approached and manhandled him, separating him from his bike and threw him head-first over the old stone bridge onto spiked thorn bushes and nettles, followed immediately by his bike which landed, firmly and painfully, on top of him. They departed and he survived to tell a very tall tale. How he got home remains a mystery but did Peter, now long departed from this world, return to ensure his survival? Remarkably, Grandad had achieved a memorable hat trick of survival: The War, Bloody Sunday at Croke Park and now an ambush.

I have seen a photo of Peter. Certainly, he looked like a man you might not want to mess with, dressed darkly in a long coat, not dissimilar to that favoured by gangsters depicted in old Hollywood films, he wore a criminal smile dressed in a muscular frame and a menacing look. At the time, various armed groups were involved in a raging rebellion against English troops and massacres and brutal treatment had been inflicted by both sides. What cannot be disputed is that the actions of his brother, Peter, saved his life and without his intervention none of us would be alive, either to hear or re-tell the tale. I understand that his grave, in Bagenalstown cemetery, has been annually cleared of weeds over many years by Grandad's son, our gracious uncle Anthony, adding yet another personal twist to this tale.

Grandad persevered for many years until he could no longer persuade his reluctant foot to pedal fast enough to meet his daily round. In later years, he boosted his pedal power with the addition of a small electric motor added to the rear of his bike. With this booster bike he continued until he suffered a heart attack around 1949 and Dr Gavin recommended bed rest. Dogged also by his old war wound he retired years before I was born, with a substantial period of his later life being bedridden.

*

Soldiers Cottage was the hub around which the family associated. It could be classed as a typical country cottage had it been located in the English Cotswolds, let alone in a small town in the Irish midlands. Brick built in a shade of variant reds, with an outer concrete plastered veneer, slate framed and partly thatched, the walls were covered in a mix of ivy and roses of many colours. The frontage was box hedged and inset with displays of geraniums and further roses on either side of a central gravel path, greeting visitors with a visible array of tantalising colour and smell, a sight so welcoming that not even the most curmudgeonly of whom could surely fail to feel uplifted in body and spirit. The path led down past the front, rarely opened brown timbered door, to the rear of the cottage where apple trees and clematis intertwined like embracing lovers lost in a trance. An exotic explanation, perhaps, as why so many children were born here almost annually. Beyond the garden the vista opened out onto a vast field or two where a ready supply of "spuds", carrots and leafy cabbages were growing unhurriedly before giving way to a vast field.

To the rear of the cottage itself a black water butt stood guard on the right- hand side and on entry there was the kitchen with numerous pots and pans that hung around waiting in turn to be dragged into use for the daily routine of cooking. Forking left was the entry to the main lounge with a huge range oven sat cosily in a blackened fireplace. There was a long wooden table, able to accommodate at least a dozen famished souls, surrounded by assorted chairs and stools. Just under the window, offering views over the extensive gardens and fields beyond, was an old pea greenish sofa. In this warm-hearted room there would be musical evenings, with accordion playing and dancing and the obligatory card games involving young and old, with piles of pennies supplied to add to the excitement. This is where we would all discover the art of patience and tactics, jealously guarding our own hand to outwit other players and learning about winning and losing.

Photos of family adorned the walls and a large wooden cased wireless had pride of place on the lounge mantlepiece. One photo in particular stood out for me. It featured two bright and shiny faces of distant cousin, another Michael (Micky) and his wife Mary, both well known in America where they formed a showband in the 1950s and 60s, with Mary as the vocalist. They recorded a large number of record albums for Decca. In the late 1950s Michael returned home and gave Grandad a copy of one of their best-known records, "A little bit of Ireland", now in the safe keeping of my cousin Maureen. In 1956 Micky visited Ireland for the last time to collect royalties for that favourite song before departing for musical heaven in 1992, aged 76.

Leading out from this room, towards the front, you would chance upon a large hall space with a rarely played piano on the left that hid the entrance to a rarely visited downstairs lounge, adorned with glass cabinets and next to this was Grandad's room. An adjacent stairway looped upwards to five bedrooms and an attic where around a dozen people would jostle for sleeping space. All in all, a most wonderful setting for those of us fortunate to have been part of its heritage. It remains in the family hands, having been re-named Kilree Cottage, when purchased from the army after Grandad died and then lived in by uncle Anthony and his wife Eileen, who lovingly cared for, improved and expanded the house and its gardens to reach their current day beauty. The recent loss of Eileen and Anthony means that the cottage is now in the hands of another generation, Marie, Gerard, Sheila, James and Eleanor, their respective family and in-laws ensuring its continued place in the hearts of all Cartons.

*

It was here, in such a crowded but idyllic setting, that Granny and Grandad brought up twelve children, born between 1921 and 1937. The eldest, another survivor of Bloody Sunday no less, was my father born on St Patricks day 1921 so it was hardly surprising that he was named Patrick, after the nations favourite saint, who is said to have banished all snakes, of the animal variety at least, from Ireland. Known throughout his life as Paddy it is doubtful that my father was as equally saintly as his famous namesake

Dad attended Presentation Convent School and latterly the De La Salle Christian Brothers School. During summer months the children would mostly run around in bare feet to save their footwear for the remainder of the year. Leaving school in 1935, aged just 14, he followed in Grandad's footsteps and joined the post office, first as a boy messenger and then as a postman, thus becoming the town's own Postman Pat, albeit it with neither a cat nor a van.

Years later, Dad fortuitously obtained a job as relief postman in Blackwater in county Wexford, where he would meet our mother, Mary Quirke from Kilcorral.

Chapter Three

Mary and Paddy.
Marriage, life and death

Dad was delighted to have acquired his first job as a full postman. He travelled to Blackwater /Oylgate and was housed in a local home. His post route took him around local villages which included the "The Ballagh", a local community with a post office located almost directly opposite Sinnott's Store, where Mum was working. The recollections of nephews and nieces suggest that Dad delivered post to the store and, having seen and conversed with the kindly and attractive Mary, the venue became a routine stop off point regardless of whether there was any actual post to be delivered. From thereon, they met up socially and Dad would be invited to frequent musical nights at Mum's Kilcorral home.

Late in 1944 Dad was recalled to his home town to take up a full-time post. Mum was understandably upset at this turn of events but good fortune would change her mood and her plans. News came that the Bennetts, a wealthy Bagenalstown family, required a live-in housekeeper, a post Mum applied for and obtained. She had made a decision to leave her Wexford home and her family to join her postie sweetheart.

Mum's first sighting of her new home town station would be the signs denoting its name, Bagenalstown, and, underneath, its Irish name of Muinea Bheag. The Carton family, comprising Dad and many of his brothers and sisters, eager to meet the woman that had captured their eldest brother's heart, turned out in numbers to ensure she received a very warm welcome.

Mum could not have failed to notice the irony of a large poster on the station displaying pictures of happy smiling face with a bucket and spade advertising "special train excursions to the seaside", she having spent her life close to the sea with long, sandy stretches of near-empty beaches such as Curracloe, where she and Dad spent such carefree times clasped hand in hand. Bagenalstown, by contrast, could not have been further from such a scene situated as it was in the centre of Ireland.

She would have enjoyed the walk from the station to Soldiers Cottage. All her worldly goods encased in a few battered old cases entrusted to the care of soon to be in-laws, she left the station, with the creamy old façade of the De La Salle Christian Brothers school on her right and the McGrath Hall, the home of dancing evenings, on her left. Meeting a crossroads, she would skirt left past the dark brown walls and rain splattered windows of the Kilree Arms (now closed). where the corner swing doors once enticed the thirsty and the lazy into a darkened room within where drink, good humoured asides and gossip were shared in equal measure. Moving swiftly on past Dan Kelly's grocery shop and the cinema she was escorted beyond a range of homes before taking a right turn along a lane leading to Soldiers cottages, laid out in individual detached plots on either side of a long lane. Midway up the left she was ushered into the Carton family home, to a warm smiling embrace from the Granny and Grandad Carton.

After lunch with all the family, Mum and Dad set off for the short trip back down to the pub corner, this time taking a left turn down The Royal Oak Road, so named like so many Oak trees after King Charles, later to become a Catholic, who was said to have hidden in one in England before making good his escape from chasing Roundheads. Stepping sharply right into Draper Street they arrived at the door of her prospective employers and well-known wealthy landowners, the Bennett family, where she would become a live-in house-keeper.

Dad shared Soldiers cottage with his parents and ten brothers and sisters. Peggy, and her fiancée Tommy Carroll; working teenagers Mary (known as Mae), yet another Michael, plus Lizzie and Anthony; John, Peter, twins Oliver and Liam and the still at school youngest Ado (Ann Dolores), a name derived from the Spanish description of Mary, as mother of sorrows. The Val Delorosa way in Jerusalem is said to refer to the route taken by Jesus on route to his execution at Calvary.

Mum and Dad spent eight months in the town before they were married on 20th October 1944. From Soldiers Cottage it was a straight line down Kilree street, passing The Fair Green, located opposite the cinema, where visiting circuses and carnivals would provide welcome fun and entertainment, and on into Main Street. Here there were a number of shops selling newspapers, groceries and provisions and a pharmacy. At the end of the street was Market Square, with barbers and butchers guarding the route to St Andrews Catholic Church, a huge presence in the town both in terms of stature and culture and influence over the lives of so many.

A wedding day photo of Mum and Dad at the rear of the church in Bagenalstown shows a very happy couple delighted to be in each other's company. Following the service there was the usual family shin-dig at Soldiers Cottage, with a large gathering of family and friends and no doubt some fine music was played and sung well into the evening. They took up residence at 2 Phillip Street, the second in a row of compact terrace houses located heading out of town, beyond the lane leading to Soldiers Cottages, crossing the railway bridge and by passing a large granite block, known as "sliding rock", because it was responsible for many a broken arm and leg among the younger element who insisted on sliding down its bottom-polished surface.

On 14th January 1945, Mum gave birth to their first child, at Soldiers Cottage, where most of her children would be born due to cramped conditions at Phillip Street and the fact that there was an abundance of experience and help at hand. Named Michael, after his Grandad and Great Grandad and to avoid confusion, as Dad also had a brother Michael, he was to be forever known to us siblings as Mehael, the Irish version of Michael. Simpler, perhaps, had he been named Seamus but there we are.

There followed a succession of children each year for the next three years, beginning with Elizabeth (Betty) followed by Nicholas (Nicky) and myself in November 1948. I was born a twin but sadly my brother Patrick lived for barely a week as far as I have been able to ascertain. It must have been very traumatic for Mum, no doubt with some danger to herself and perhaps even recalling the circumstances of her own birth. The experience must have exposed her to such extreme emotional and physical stress that it was almost four years before she gave birth again.

The exact circumstances of the birth were never explained to me. It was by accident that I discovered I ever had a twin when I was in my teens and was playing football in the street with my brother Nicky and a lad called Charlie, when we had a bit of a fall out and Charlie shouted out "you should have died with your twin brother" or words to that effect. The look on my brother's face suggested he was aware of it. I was shocked and simply didn't know what to say. I ran home the few yards to our house asked Mum if it was true. She simply said "yes" and left it at that. We never ever discussed it and nothing more was ever said. Looking back, I assume it must have been too painful to her to recall which is quite understandable.

I was most grateful to my late Aunt Peggy, for providing a lovely descriptive outline of my birth, when I was much older, including details of my twin, Patrick, lying peacefully in his little coffin. The exact cause of death save that I was the stronger has never been explained. I do know that Patrick was born some twenty minutes after myself which in itself suggests all had not gone well.

Thanks to Uncle Anthony, who was present at the burial, I have in recent times visited the unmarked grave of my twin brother in a plot off the Royal Oak Road. It did seem strange at first to find the graves were unmarked and raised some questions in my mind and that of my brother Nicky as to why that should be the case. It is fair to say that it evoked some conspiracy theories between us especially given the secrecy surrounding the births and the reluctance of parents and others to discuss the matter.

Much has been written about child burial customs in Ireland. It appears the souls of unbaptised children were not allowed entry into heaven and thus the tradition of not being laid to rest in consecrated ground then became woven into folklore. *Robin Flower (1881-1946) in "The Western Island" (1944)* eloquently described joining the funeral company of a new born baby, with the men in felt hats and the women with their shawls drawn close to their heads and all in a speechless trance of sorrow and respect.

"We stopped in an unkempt space of dank, clinging grass, with stones scattered over it here and there. A man with a spade had dug a shallow grave, and there, amid the sobs of the women and the muttered prayers of the whole assembly, the father with a weary gesture laid away his

child. The earth was shovelled back, closing with hardly a sound about the little box, a few prayers were said, and then we all turned listlessly away, leaving the lonely, unfledged soul to its eternity".

This is remarkably similar to what aunts and uncles had described to me about my own twin with Uncle Oliver adding, from his memory, that the candle, held I believe by my father and leading the procession behind the little white coffin, had stayed alight and bright despite the wintry night. Thanks to Uncle Anthony and his daughter Marie, I now know that both twins were buried in Killinane Graveyard just outside Bagenalsown. The tradition of the unbaptised being buried alone in un-consecrated ground was overcome by resting them in the company of the graves of previously deceased family members, the identity of whom in this case is unknown. In 1985, a year when there were numerous reports of moving Virgin Mary statues, one such statue was erected at the entrance to the twins' burial place, presumably to stand guard over the poor resting souls.

Discovering the reality of being a twin also brought me back to a short period of dreams I used to have when living in our Parc Muire home. I recall being in the ground twisting around in a circle of wet mud. Recalling it now, I did not find the experience especially scary or disturbing, just strange. Knowing what I do now it seems somewhat uncanny.

A much more inexplicable emotional response is elicited whenever I read a story written by author ***Veronica Breen Hogle***, who once lived with the Fitzpatrick's in one of the Soldiers Cottages. In her story entitled ***"The Other Irish Tenors"***. she recalls the very first Christmas eve carol service presided over by Monseigneur Conway at St Andrews Church in 1948, the year of my birth.

The whole story is beautifully written and highly charged but the paragraph that elicits in me a very strong internal reaction, mystical and spiritual, yet wholly inexplicable is repeated below.

"When the tenors began to sing "A Child is Born in Bethlehem"-Al le lu ia! old women whose silverheads nodded down into their shoulders suddenly shot their heads up and the azure-blue peacock feathers in their hats quivered in the heat. By the fifteenth "al le lu ia!" the candles danced like barley in the wind. Several blew out and the smell of smoking candles spiralled up to the ceiling.

On the last stroke of midnight, the bells of St Mary's Anglican Church joined the bells of St Andrew's in booming out a welcome to the new born babe. The Choir of Angels raised the rafters with "Deck the Halls with Boughs of Holly".

Writing this story, an emotional stirring consumes me, to an extent which is simultaneously joyful and disturbing. I have clearly associated this carol, sung at that time in history, with the story of my own birth and that of my twin, born as we were just a month earlier. It is a joy to reflect that many of the Carton family would have been present at this carol service as well. Alleluia, indeed!!

*

Three and a half years elapsed before Mum gave birth again. Amazingly and unmercifully, history was to repeat itself. Once again, twins were born. Patrick, named after my twin, and Mary. The birth seemed to go well and both children were initially placed in the usual wooden drawers, doubling up as cots, taken from a chest and lined with clean white sheets and blankets. The following day, Mum returned home to Phillip Street with baby Patrick, leaving baby Mary, who was having breathing difficulties, in the care of Granny and her in-laws. A week or so after the birth, Mum asked Nicky, then almost five years old, to visit Granny and enquire about the baby's health. Granny sat him down, gave him the news and sent him back on his way to Mum. Given his tender age and with the belief that this was really good news he skipped smilingly all the way home to be met by Mum. Asked what Granny had said he cheerily blurted out *"Granny said to tell you that the baby has gone to sing with the angels"*, An obviously distraught Mum burst into a flood of tears, leaving poor young Nicky dumbfounded.

Dad was at home and was able to explain the situation to a now upset Nicky. Mehael, then just seven years old, happened to be working on the milk cart this day and part of the round included stopping at Mum's. On arriving at the house, however, he was met by a harassed Dad who told him and, in no uncertain terms it appears, to stop work and go inside immediately to be with his mother as the second baby had died and she was so upset. Six-year-old Betty, meanwhile, was met at the convent school by Uncle Peter who explained what had occurred and then escorted her back home. What had started as a normal spring day had taken a dramatic turn for the worse and left our parents and the young family in a very sad and sorry state. For Mum, coming after the earlier death of my twin, it must have been shattering. Baby Mary was later prepared and laid to rest in the same plot as my twin, presumably following the same process.

Another year passed and Mum gave birth again, this time to a single baby girl without any major problems. A state of relief and blessing was apparent and the child was again called Mary, always known to us as May. Almost four more years rolled by and we had moved house before a final set of twins, Paul and Ann, made their successful appearance to the resounding joy of the whole platoon of Cartons.

Chapter Four

Growing up in Bagenalstown

Our Phillip Street home was very compact with two downstairs rooms, a living room and a tiny kitchen. Additional space was provided via a wooden ladder that led up to the windowless attic. On the opposite side of the road to the home was a pump where water had to be fetched in buckets several times daily and which could have acted as an arm-muscle builder. A rear door led into a small garden overlooking the freight railway line that ran parallel to the neat row of houses. This could be crossed illegally from the rear garden via a flimsy hedge with an appropriately sized hole. On the other side of the line was a sandy slope that doubled as a britches-tearing slide. We would, probably more dangerously and despite parental admonishment, often play on the line itself and on a few occasions at least, one of us would be brave enough, or sufficiently foolhardy, to lend an ear to the iron line, in the belief that we could better hear the sound of any oncoming train. It is miracle that we somehow all managed to survive with ears and head intact to tell the tale.

I recall an incident when a railway inspector, dressed with the full authority of his dark blue uniform jacket set outside his starched white shirt, appeared from out the mist and announced his presence by thumping his gloved fist on the already open rear door. Spotting Mum and without any fanfare, he curtly demanded to know why she had allowed us to play on the line. Frozen with trepidation, I darted behind Mum who brazenly, and in no uncertain terms, admonished the officious inspector for even suggesting her angelic brood would ever do such a thing. The poor man, no doubt taken aback by her ferocious defence, departed with a stern lecture about the dangers, coupled with a warning that anybody caught trespassing would be summonsed. Now, I had never heard the word before and for some reason, got it into my head that it meant we would all be injected with a long needle, a situation that conjured up a sufficient quota of bad dreams to ensure it worked and I, for one, was never caught on the railway again.

Living next door in the end terrace was the Protestant Watkins family, kind and generous neighbours, whose benevolence made a mockery of the all too often sectarian divide in predominantly Catholic Ireland. They had a small holding with chickens and pigs and frequently bestowed Mum with a supply of fresh eggs and milk and for which she was forever grateful.

Up until 1954 there were five of us children living with our parents in that cosy but tiny house at 2 Phillip Street. The exception being Mehael, who spent almost all of his life living with Granny and Grandad and various aunts and uncles in the more spacious environment of Soldiers Cottage. He received a steady supply of comics such as TV Comic, Beano, Eagle and Dandy. His favourite characters were from the westerns such as Kit Carson, Hopalong Cassidy and the Durango Kid. We may have been slightly jealous but we looked forward to our regular granny visits so that we could read them as well. Mehael shared a room until Granny decided to make a new room for a growing Ado with whom he had previously shared. In many respects he regarded his twin uncles Oliver and Liam more as older brothers.

Granny possessed a number of small statues of saints which Mehael used to play with whilst imagining himself in their saintly roles. A number of surviving photos depict the angelic looking Mehael in his altar boy attire dutifully serving the priests at mass and on special occasions such as May-Day celebrations in honour of the Virgin Mary. It has to be said his adult life, mercifully some would say, was to be one full of life and a vitality that the saintly might not have fully approved.

Nevertheless, the fact that he had reached adulthood at all could be construed as the saints looking after him. At a young age he was assisting Uncle Anthony, then the gardener at the convent, when he entered the massive glasshouse full of tomatoes. Next to the convent was a water mill and fast flowing stream. He was so overcome by the overwhelming smell and the heat from the tomatoes that seemed to attach itself to him that he felt compelled to remove his shirt which then fell into the stream. In a frantic attempt to retrieve the situation he jumped into the water, was unable to reach the disappearing shirt and found himself in difficulties. Fortunately, a living saint, in the guise of Dad's post office colleague, happened to be passing and, at some risk to himself, jumped headlong into the swirl and dragged him to safety. He survived to live another day which was more than could be said for the shirt which had disappeared into a watery grave.

On another occasion he was walking with Uncle Liam to visit Mum. This entailed crossing the railway bridge and they both stopped to wait for and wave at an oncoming steam train. Mehael, wearing short trousers and perhaps becoming somewhat excited, lost his grip on the bridge and fell into a hedge of prickly briers next to the track and was perilously in danger of being struck by the oncoming train. Liam, with a rapid superman reaction, jumped over the bridge and managed to pull him clear by grabbing his trouser belt and hauling him clear of danger. On returning home, Mehael had to be covered in blue Iodine, an inky substance applied by Gran to any ailment known to man, reputed to ease the pain of bites, scratches and stings to avoid infection.

Monday morning at Phillip Street was traditionally clothes wash day. Buckets of water were collected in frequent visits from the black handled pump across the road and emptied into a large tin bath which contained a washboard against which the offending clothes were hand-bashed before being hung up to dry at the convenience of the prevailing weather. The same bath also served to wash us children in age related relays, though mercifully without the washboard.

From this home we would attend the church each Sunday and on holy days. One abiding memory is of a day when I would have been about five. On this occasion the compact front room was awash with wet clothes hanging around like a line of dead crows on a double bent wooden clothes horse. The house seemed unusually cluttered with dark closed curtains hiding the minimal light available on a dreary cloudy day that matched the solemn events of Good Friday. Mum and Dad seemed anxious to get us dressed and we were being unusually rushed to get prepared for the service. Having hurried to the church, I recall the seemingly unending service itself in all its dismal detail: stopping, kneeling and praying at each of fourteen station pictures spread around the inner walls and noticing the aching and pained faces of those depicted on the road to final crucifixion. I don't know why but that particular day has stuck in my memory to the extent that over sixty years on I am loathe to close curtains when there is still a chink of light to be seen outside.

In May 1954 our parents were allocated a more spacious home on the new Parc Muire estate. Number 12 was the second home in one of a large number of blocks of six terraced houses at the top end of the estate facing onto open playing fields. The pretty glazed door was placed mid-point so that on entry there was a large lounge on the left and a similarly sized dining room on the right. Ascending the stairs behind the lounge led up to two family sized bedrooms with considerable storage room and a comfortably sized bathroom. It was a real treat to have such a large bathroom and this is the room where Mum would often burst into little song ditties whilst bathing us children and I am forever reminded of one of her favourites; The Doris day song "Que Sera, Sera" that she would sing whilst bathing us. Other favourites included tracks from musical films of the time that she would have seen in the cinema and included *"Oh What a beautiful morning"*, sung by Gordon McRea, from the film Oklahoma and *"Bless yore beautiful hide, wherever you may be"* sung by her treasured Howard Keel in "Seven Brides for Seven Brothers". Collectively, the lyrics resonated with Mum forever. Retreating back downstairs and heading left presented a fully equipped kitchen, with more modern appliances, where a wood-framed back door opened into a wire-fenced garden. A walk down the 50-foot garden led to a strong metalled gate reaching out in turn to join a junction of tarmac paths forming a rear link with all the other gardens and neighbours as well as serving as an alternative route into the town centre, a simple five-minute walk. Compared to Phillip Street this was like a palace and Mum in particular must have been delighted.

Betty, as the oldest daughter, regularly assisted in the daily care of the rest of us, helping with washing and feeding and taking us to and from school. The first port of call in our school life at the age of six was the Presentation Convent situated close to the river Barrow and run by black habited nuns of the Sisters of Clare with large protruding white starched pointy hats. Mum herself took me to school on my first day but was unable to leave me there as I refused to let her go. This continued for a few days with me playing with wooden play bricks at the back of the room before the sisters decided that firm action was required and Mum was told simply to leave, me bawling or not. In a few days I was in the routine of going to school with Betty and Nicky.

The journey entailed a short walk to the town, turning right by the dominating church and then veering left along the riverside before reaching the convent. Lessons were taken by the Nuns and it is here that most of us first learned to read, write, spell and count. Our parents had to purchase exercise and reading books from Dad's earnings as a postman and assorted other jobs with the school providing only basic equipment such as pencils and paper. We each had our own tin mugs which the sisters filled with cocoa or hot chocolate from a very large urn that sat on a bench in a corner of the austere playground. Each morning they would also appear in the playground sporting large squared-shaped wicker baskets suspended from their necks by strong ribbons and heavily laden with fresh baked bread cut into large sizes accompanied with a supply of dripping for those who were so inclined. This is how we received our daily bread. Betty, alas, was so overcome by the constant daily supply of hot chocolate that on leaving the convent she and hot chocolate went their separate ways, never again to be reconciled.

*

Sunday generally followed a regular pattern. The morning would be taken up eating a breakfast of porridge followed with marmalade-coated toast washed down with tea and milk or juice. We would then be dressed in our Sunday best and trotted off to Mass where we would normally be found in the upstairs gallery. This afforded our hardworking mother the opportunity to obtain much needed rest. Whether it was due to exhaustion or the sermon, and much to our amusement, she was well known for falling asleep during the overlong service.

Afternoons followed a mixed pattern depending on the mood of the weather. Fine weather would see mum lead us around a nature spot known as Bolger's Rocks, within easy reach of our home. Here we would meander slowly along grassy tracks to encounter an abundance of bird life, including larks, nightingales and dashing swallows that hovered above scattering grey coated rabbits fleeting in and out of an uneven spread of mixed sized granite blocks, and skirting gorse covered mounds of grass. In early spring we would delight in spotting wild yellow primroses illuminating our way whilst in summer a screen of wildflowers shared the landscape.

I spent many an hour in solo playing the hero cowboy riding the range on my imagined horse, rounding up and jailing the baddies in my created cave. On other days, white fluffy clouds would descend, seemingly within inches of my trembling and prostrate body, as I lay on the grass between polished rocks whilst overhead claps of thunder and flashes of lightning would see me scurry for the safety of home, leaving my arrested quarry to fend for themselves.

Intermittently, we would visit the McGrath sports field to watch local Hurling or Gaelic Football or go swimming in the outdoor pool set by the side of the river Barrow. Major highlights of the year were eagerly awaited and featured the annual barrow race along the river and the swimming gala which culminated with a one-mile race that finished parallel to the swimming pool.

Distinctly recalled from our walks is the oft repeated refrain from Mum not to touch sticks or Elder Trees as to do so would almost certainly invoke a visit from the man-in-the-moon. I envisaged the moon-man opening his moon-door and descending in a shaft of silvery light to admonish us or worse. In Irish folklore there are many references to the Elder Tree as a symbol of a visiting evil spirit so that may have been responsible for her warnings.

More frequently, Sunday afternoon involved a visit to Granny's house. The downside was the head-first dip in the outside water butt for the weekly hair wash. Having survived what could pass as an attempted drowning we were allowed to play and spend time reading Mehael's comics. I would pedal madly around the gravelled garden paths on an old tricycle to my heart's content. In the summertime the whole family would gather for the harvest gathering with a huge threshing machine appearing amongst the golden spikes of hay in the fields at the rear of the cottage. By the end of a long day, interspersed with drinks, sandwiches and cake, a large collection of triangular haystacks would stand proudly reaching for the drying sun.

Wexford girl, Mum, was a great fan and supporter of the Hurling team, who had been dominant in the 1950s, led by the extraordinary Rackard brothers, of whom Nicky was her favourite. Many a Sunday afternoon we would listen to the commentary on a radio which held pride of place high up on a shelf set on the living room wall. Sometimes it would be rugby union, in the days when another of Ireland's, and Mum's sporting heroes, Tony O' Reilly, would be their leading player.

Hurling though was the number one sport with a goal in the net equating to three points as opposed to a single point when the ball was catapulted over the bar but still between the two high supporting posts. May 6th 1956 was a most memorable day and featured the League Hurling Final at Croke Park, Dublin between Wexford and arch rivals Tipperary, who had won the final the previous year. We gathered around the radio, on stools or chairs, and fully expectant of another win, ears perked like puppies in anticipation of a real treat. This match, became known as *"the great comeback"* and was indeed memorable.

Sean Moran, GAA correspondent of the Irish Times, in a timely and updated (April 2017) renewal of an earlier match report by his colleague PD Mehigan, described the action and provided a reminder to myself of the game I had listened to all those years ago. For 30 minutes Tipperary were said to have played probably their best half-hour ever in hurling and deservedly led by a massive 15 points at half time. Our excitement and anticipation had now turned to despondency as we could scarcely comprehend what was unfolding. Famous commentator, Michael O'Hehir, decreed that only a miracle would rescue the game for Wexford. Not easily defeated, these mighty hurling men epitomised the determination and grit of Wexford folk and we listened in ever increasing amazement as the gold and purple warriors, with the wind behind them, warmed to their task. Early second half goals from Nicky Rackard and Tom Ryan set the tone for an onslaught. With barely three minutes left, and only three points between the sides, Wexford responded again to reduce the deficit to two points. Another goal would win the game. Excitement was at fever pitch and the shouting and screaming in granny's room could have been heard in Dublin itself. Full cups of hot tea remained forlornly untouched on the large wooden table beneath the radio. Suddenly, and well into injury time, a mighty Vesuvius type roar erupted, almost bringing the house down, the breathless voice of O'Hehir echoed around the room. Unbelievably, he thundered, Rackard and Dixon, had scored again and yet again. The room was now fully alive with beaming faces and dancing feet replacing the earlier gloom. Mum was naturally delighted and we all celebrated as Granny laid on a sumptuous tea fortified with home-made scones followed by apple pie. As a bonus, I caught sight of the Wexford boys as they later sped through our station on their way home. A day not easily forgotten.

Hurling, it has to be said was not my forte. The Christian Brothers, who taught at the De La Salle School on Station Road where I was a pupil for a couple of years after leaving the convent, enjoyed the sport and one summer evening Brother Mark organised a hurling game for those on the estate presumably to identify great talent. My parents had helped me purchase a new steel capped hurley and this was to be its first outing. The teams were chosen and I threw myself into the fray with tremendous gusto replicating, in my mind, the heroics of the Wexford lads. Brother Mark, unfortunately, failed to appreciate my skill and enthusiasm and within a few minutes I received a first warning for reckless hurl spinning at the opponents' legs. Undeterred, I continued to display my unique talents for a few minutes more before he decided he had seen quite enough and promptly sent me off for dangerous play. So it was that my hurling career was brought to a shuddering halt, thus depriving my school, the Carlow County and Ireland of ever witnessing my true talent.

My schooling by the Christian Brothers was not the most memorable. Wooden desks with an ink pot in the top right-hand corner were arranged in formulaic rows, two by two. There were almost daily spelling and writing tests and we had to endlessly recite and remember our times tables. On top of this we were required to memorise the Apostolic (Catholic) creed word for word, usually at the end of the day. Failure to recall correctly meant you were dispatched to the back of the room and made to repeat the process time and again until you succeeded and were allowed home or you faced some punishment. To be honest, the fear of failure only made it more difficult to remember anything and I dreaded these tests. Being small for my age and of a rather shy disposition I was somewhat fearful and lacking in confidence.

This came to a head one day, in my first year, when I was in urgent need of the toilet but was afraid to ask for permission to leave or ask for the key. To my severe embarrassment, I soiled myself sat at my desk and in front of the whole class. My eldest brother Mehael was asked to attend and he comforted and escorted me back home to Mum where I received a consoling greeting before being immersed in a warm bath. On return to class the following day nothing was said of the incident and I was grateful my young fellow pupils who never ever raised the matter.

My brothers, Mehael and Nicky would both testify to the treatment they received at the hands of some, though by no means all, of the brothers, including the Head, Brother Dermott. Whilst Mehael took it in his stride Nicky was not so fortunate. He recalls an occasion when Mum noticed that he had huge blood blisters on each hand. He told her he had received six painful belts of a strong leather strap on each hand. Mum was so angry that she instructed Dad to go to the school and demand an explanation. Next day he accompanied Nicky and confronted the class teacher, who responded by accusing Nicky of hoarding secret notes under his desk in order to answer questions and was in effect cheating. Despite Nicky's protestations Dad accepted the reason given for inflicting the punishment and to add insult to injury he jabbed Nicky on the side of the head and told him to take his place in class. The effect of this sorry saga was that Nicky thereafter recalls self-harming and feigning stomach aches to avoid school whenever possible. Dad must have reflected on these events and it is fair to say that he never again reacted in the same way and certainly never with me. I would like to think that the eventual decision to leave Ireland was at least partly, informed by these events. It is instructive to note that in July 1958 £100 in damages was awarded to a nine-year old boy who had been beaten by a teacher in a national school.

The Christian Brothers would say that they were preparing pupils for the harshness and reality of life and were well intentioned. I could read well and write precisely enough, using real ink pens without incurring blots, no mean feat given the pressure from teachers who seemed to believe that punishment was a real motivator for learning. The harsh, stocky, sport loving Brother Mark was also a good story teller and would often break up lessons to regale us with stories of Irish heroes of the distant past, such as Bryan Boru, as well as reciting old fables and poetry. My own favoured teacher was Brother Killeen who set hangman type games on the blackboard to encourage us to think quickly on our feet and I found it good fun, especially as I was rather good at filling in the blanks in the spelling of names.

Learning to read was greatly assisted by Mum and Dad providing simple books to read. I constantly repeated favourite poems and books and soon mastered reading. Similarly, learning my times table followed the same pattern and was motivated by having to repeat them on demand at school. Our books were self-wrapped in brown paper to retain their crispness as did our lined exercise books all of which had to be paid for by our parents so it was drummed into us to look after them. It may not have been Shakespeare but repetition was an effective method of learning to read as far as I am concerned.

Growing up in our little town was a mostly pleasant experience. In addition to the Sunday outings to granny we were always excited when the annual circus arrived and set up stall and rings in a field more grandly known as The Fairground. A great fanfare of drums and blowing trumpets announced their arrival on a parade through the town. Allied to the noise of numerous animals, caged lions and elephants and silver horses ridden by a galaxy of floral dressed performers. The excitement of their arrival was palpable with half the town turning out to welcome them. Astonishingly, as children, we were allowed to wander into the fairground at will. I recall wandering around and finding myself standing beside a massive elephant with only a single rope separating me from this wonderful beast, a thought which now makes me shudder. We would attend as a family to enjoy the spectacle of trapeze artists swinging freely through the air and watch in awe as the massive elephants paraded around the outskirts of the ring corralled only by a few ropes and confident trainers. Cheerful laughing Clowns entertained us with a great deal of slapstick fun and the whole evening would be topped off with the lions, as we watched in terror as they obediently performed tricks behind what seemed a flimsy cage.

Directly across the road stood the Astor Cinema, which opened in April 1940 to replace the Palace Cinema. It commenced with a showing of *"Come on George"* starring George Formby. This is where I would discover the joy of film-ems (in Ireland) with parents and various aunts and uncles. Nothing had prepared me for the first visit when there was a sudden silence and darkness as the lights went down and a great hush descended. Initial fear gave way to open-eyed wonder and fascination. Western fil-ems were the staple diet where we would revel at the heroics of The Lone Ranger and Gene Autry and good old Hopalong Cassidy and would roar in delight at the moment when John Wayne appeared on the horizon, with bugles sounding. He led the blue uniformed heroes over the hill to the rescue, as the Apache Indians were about to slaughter the encircled men, women and children. It didn't then occur to me to consider how our hero survived despite having at least twenty arrows going directly through his hat and out the other side whilst every cavalry shot at the enemy proved deadly. Those were such innocent times and the history I would learn later of battles between the indigenous native tribes and the US army provided a more accurate reflection. Nevertheless, "going to the pictures" was a wonderfully anticipated treat and I became an enthusiastic fan. I was initially concerned as to where the horses and riders were going when they raced towards us, before disappearing into the wings. On departure, I half expected them to be outside the cinema. Daft but true.

In addition to granny visits, the circus and the pictures, our weekends would be eagerly anticipated for the arrival of the weekly comics. There would be a race to the paper shop to get in the first read. One of my favourites was TV Fun Comic and I fell in love with reporter Petula Clarke who featured in one such comic. I looked forward to her stories so much that it inspired the belief in me a that I too would become a reporter.

Daily, there would be the newspaper which featured a spectacled, pipe smoking ex-marine come private detective called "Rip Kirby". One day for example we would see an illustration of "Rip" hiding in a haystack with six pursuing German soldiers poised to prod the stack with fixed bayonets. How could he possibly survive? So, comics and newspapers were fairly prevalent in my early life.

In addition to reading these comics and watching fil-ems we would be taken swimming by one of our uncles. Sadly, one evening I was invited by Oliver and Liam to accompany them when they went swimming in the river Barrow which required a short cycle ride from Granny's house. I was invited along and set off perched on the crossbar of Liam's bike. We were crossing the road when a car suddenly appeared over the railway bridge speeding directly for us in the centre of the road. From out of nowhere, Granny's lovely old white-haired retriever Trixie appeared and raced into the centre of the road colliding fatally with the car but preventing us from taking a direct hit. I was thrown off the bike and hit the road sharply. The pain in my arm and shoulder and the sight of Oliver collecting up Trixie and forlornly carrying the dead weight in his arms back to the cottage, where he had enjoyed a full life, stands out in my memory as tears flowed that day for both these reasons.

The following day, the pain in my shoulder had worsened considerably. Dad decided that I should see a doctor or more specifically to see Dan O Neill, a man well known for bone setting, a quite distinct Irish practice, and I was taken into the corner pub where he practiced his art. I was lifted onto a very high stool and examined by the gentle and assuring Dan. He pulled and pushed and declared that I had dislocated my shoulder which he reset and would be as right as rain in a couple of weeks and dressed me in various bandages and a sling. As a bonus to me he decreed that I should not go to school for fear of inflicting further damage so I happily obliged to see a silver lining in the darkness of the events that led me here.

It transpired that Dan O Neill would one day become even better known as the owner of the racehorse Danoli, named after the man himself and his wife Olive and who became possibly the most famous and best loved horse in Ireland. I have to say that the treatment from the bone setting, horse mad Dan worked so well that even to this day I have never had any shoulder trouble.

Dad often resembled Batman instead of Postman Pat with his cape-like rain cover billowing wildly behind him as he rode furiously across the county, carrying out the job that ensured a steady income. My sister Betty remembers a number of occasions when she was tasked with meeting Dad upon receipt of his wages and hot footing back home with the spoils to enable Mum to pay outstanding bills and purchase weekly groceries. Money was always tight and Dad supplemented his income by working for Corrigan's Garage. Here he would help with the firm's accounts as well as serving a form of apprenticeship by undertaking a range of other electrical, plumbing and maintenance jobs, all learnt under the watchful eye of Mr Corrigan senior. The Corrigan's' were also instrumental in assisting Dad to purchase a diesel powered BSA motor bike to help him on his post round, which took him on a daily route of some 30 miles, serving series of lovely towns and villages such as Corries, Ballinkillen, Clowater, Ballyellen and Sliguffe linked by roads, laneways and undulating landscapes that skirted the Blackstairs Hills, and along the lower slopes of Mount Leinster. Dad was not only a postman but would deliver other goods and messages from place to place. Social stops for tea were of course obligatory and happily accepted regular offerings of tea accompanied by fruit cake, the ensuing intake of calories more than matching the energy and toil extended.

Delivering our own post was left to a man called Mr Lee. Short and portly, he would appear daily around mid-morning. Slowly unclasping himself from his trusty old bike he would waddle into our front room, drop his postbag on the wooden floor and grab a chair. He proceeded to turn it around so that he sat with his highly visible tummy held firmly in place against its back with his chin resting on the upper back rest. Mum would ask him if he would like a cuppa as she had done so many times and he would reply, to fits of laughter from any children present, "I don't mind if I do". On receipt of his cuppa, he would immediately empty the tea into the saucer and slowly slurp all the treacle-like liquid before once again extracting himself from the chair, whereupon he would bid my mother a fond farewell and depart.

Chapter Five

Aunts and Uncles

Emigration is a familiar scenario throughout Irish history in periods when work is difficult to find and times are hard. The 1950s were no different with many emigrating to England, uprooting themselves to travel in search of work.

In the early 1950s work was scarce especially after the closure of the flour mill that had provided such a welcome living for so many men. In the absence of any means to work and pay bills it was no wonder that many of Dad's siblings sought work outside Ireland itself.

Uncle Anthony was an exception. He lived in Bagenalstown throughout his life. Leaving school aged 14, he worked as a farm and general labourer for a few years before obtaining full time employment, as a gardener and handyman, at the Presentation Convent from 1947 to 1996. Following in his father's footsteps he signed up as an Irish Army Reservist in 1951. Based at Dublin Barracks he rose to the distinguished rank of Commandant. A surviving photo displays his pride in leading the army contingent that escorted the fourth Irish President Erskine

Childers at a service to commemorate the start of restoration work on Duiske Abbey, in 1974, not many months before the president died of a sudden heart attack.

Anthony married local girl Eileen Boyle. Initially they lived in a bungalow on Parc Muire estate before purchasing Soldiers Cottage, subsequently renamed Kilree Cottage in 1959, with the help of his family, after the death of his father. They lovingly tended and improved the family home for sixty years, always providing a warm welcome for any visiting relatives. Both Eileen and Anthony passed away in 2019/20, survived by their children Marie, Gerard, Sheila, James and Eleanor.

Michael left school and worked as a farm labourer at nearby Dunleckeny Manor until he was made redundant, then lived mid-week with May and Jimmy Murphy who lived in Clowater, helping out on their smallholding. In his mid -twenties the scarcity of work emboldened him to follow his sister Mae and he emigrated to England, where he worked on various building sites in Birmingham, Stafford and King's Lynn before he settled in Oxford. It was here that he met and married Margaret McEvoy, taking part in a double wedding with her brother Tom and his wife Adelaide to save money. Michael rented a home in Vicarage Road which he would later share with Dad before moving to Cowley. The rest of his life would involve working hard for six long days each week to raise three children Andrew, John and Ann before his retirement aged 63. Sundays would be his only day of rest and he would attend Our Lady Help of Christians Catholic church where he devoted his spare time to raise money for church funds. A popular member of the local area and particularly in the Irish community linked to St. Dominic's Catholic club, he organised dances particularly for those who had fallen on hard times, played cards and darts and generally socialised with all and sundry. He was an easy going, sociable and respected family man who enjoyed the company of many good friends and was always willing to help anyone in need.

When Uncle Peter left school, his father wanted him to follow in his own and our dad's postie footsteps but the mere thought of riding a bike around country lanes in snow and rain did not appeal one iota and neither was another option to join the army. Instead, he found work helping Anthony at the convent and tending the front and back gardens at St Andrew's Church. Their elder sister Peggy was married to Tom Carroll, a point-to-point rider, and he and Peter were both offered apprenticeships to Curragh racing trainer John Oxx, a proposition which was emphatically ruled out by their mother. Tom Carroll later accepted a post as stallion man at Ballylinch Stud in Mount Juliet in neighbouring Kilkenny leading Peter to join them as his assistant and general farm labourer.

Peter left for England when aged 21 and went initially to join Michael in Oxford and worked as a bus conductor before moving to Birmingham. His description of life at that time revealed blatant hostility to foreigners with some landlords openly displaying signs stating "no blacks and no Irish welcome here". The few establishments that were willing to accept them offered Dickensian conditions, with upwards of nineteen men sharing three bedrooms on a shift basis. Peter remembered days when any food prepared, and left on the table, was instantly captured and disgorged by the landlord's own kids. Nevertheless, they found work and got on with their lives.

Peter was a bit of a character and regarded as a ladies' man so it was no surprise that he once found himself engaged to two of them, at the same time, and fled back to Ireland and Mount Juliet to allow matters to cool before returning again after his father's death. He befriended, courted and then married Agnes, on 13th August 1960, and settled in Birmingham. Somewhat bizarrely he led his darling wife to believe that he was an orphan so their wedding was a rather quiet affair. Quite what she thought when she found out he had a football team sized family with hundreds of cousins has never been revealed.

He was a staunch trade unionist and once when working as a convenor for a Birmingham engineering company, in the chaotic 1970s, he recalled how he was instructed by his employers that that under no circumstances was he to permit a certain Derek "Red Robbo" Robinson, then a controversial and radical trade unionist, to be allowed onto their premises for fear of inciting strikes that would devastate their business. Robinson is said to have led hundreds of walkouts at British Leyland at a cost of some £200m in lost production and would address workers in mass meetings at Crofton Park. He was sacked in 1979 and was overwhelmingly defeated in a vote for strike action to support him by 14000 to just 600 in support. That was the watershed moment in industrial relations in the motor industry. Prof. Carl Chinn, a local historian, would later offer a more balanced opinion suggesting that both sides were equally to blame for the poor state of industrial relations. Certainly, many of his opponents regard him as a man of principle who had the interests of the workers at heart. It led to much improved cooperation in later years to the success of the company and workers.

Peggy and Tommy, by contrast, had now left Ballylinch stud at Mount Juliet and emigrated to upwardly social Newmarket where he was employed as a groom at Snailwell Stud.

Younger brothers and twins, Oliver and Liam, enjoyed contrasting fortunes in their early lives. Leaving school at 14 Liam, completed his Journeyman training at Mount Juliet in 1954/5 before becoming Head Gardener at the award-winning Eastwood Nurseries in Bagenalstown. They received a Chelsea RHS First Award for their Dahlia, Eastwood Glory, in 1950 and, whilst Liam was working there, celebrated success with the plant Gallardia Asteraceae, comprising soft lemon flowers surrounded by a brown centre, as well as cultivating a new Dahlia, named Richenda.

In the summer of 1956, Liam's girlfriend Anna (Hannah) was very unhappy at home due to imposed restrictions in their movements and she decided to leave home. Liam eloped with her to stay with his sister Lizzie and her husband Bill Monahan who had settled in Dublin. Unfortunately, Anna contracted measles and Lizzie advised that she should return home. Consequently, Granny hot footed onto the next train and escorted the love-struck duo back home to Bagenalstown. Shortly before Christmas Anna was taken to Liverpool by her brother Mick. Liam followed six months later, obtained a job as a bus conductor before escorting Anna back to Watford where they both worked for London Transport. They married a year later and settled in Redbourn where they lived until emigrating to sunny Perth in Western Australia in 1963.

Oliver was a quiet, gentle and sensitive individual. Departing for England in 1953 he found work in a Tarmac factory in the North Eastern town of Jarrow. This was not a happy venture, suffering consistent stomach ulcers forcing him to return home to be nursed back to health. Three years on he joined his sister Peggy and her husband Tommy in Newmarket, working on the stud farm before moving to a biscuit factory. At heart Oliver always wanted to be a Psychiatric Nurse but in Ireland he was deemed to be too short for such a profession.

Fortunately, in England he answered an advert and obtained training in London and at the same time met and married a dazzling young beauty named Helga, a petite Austrian with a strong accent and an eternal fireball of energy, bearing three children John, Linde and Trish before moving to a new post in Gloucester. Alas, this proved to be soul destroying when he soon realised that profit was deemed more important than helping the patients. This was the catalyst for a more successful and rewarding career move to Littlemore, Oxford where he worked his way up to being a Senior Rehabilitation Officer. Three more children were added to the family- Carolyn, Oliver the younger and Helga.

Oliver was also associated with mislaying at least one child on a trip to the seaside at Weston, only discovering that one had been left behind after travelling some 50 miles! Nevertheless, this was a happy time with lots of fun and activity before he and his wife Helga, who worked as a very successful seamstress and dresser, made the decision to emigrate to Perth in Australia, following a recruitment drive and a job offer. The job opportunity to savour some warm weather to help with Helga's arthritis, and to be reunited with his twin brother Liam, proved all too alluring so in 1979 they set sail for the land of OZ.

Ado, officially Anne Dolores, was the youngest of Dad's siblings. In company with my oldest brother Mehael, she left home for Newmarket to join up with Peggy and Tommy before moving to Oxford, initially at weekends where she stayed with Michael and Margaret and then permanently with the McEvoy family in Iffley Road. It was actually during one of her weekend Oxford visits that she met her future husband, Tommy Spearman. The story goes that Tommy, an Irishman from Longford Town, had spent years soaking up the nightlife in Oxford and London but had grown weary of fighting off the hordes of admiring women and desired to meet a nice Irish girl.

The rumour was that the best place to achieve his purpose was to attend a Temperance Hall Saturday night dance. To this end, he and his friend, appropriately named Johnny Rabbit, persuaded work colleagues to lend them their personal Pioneer Pins, a symbol of membership of the Pioneer Total Abstinence Association (PTAA), that would gain them entry to the dancehall and a bevy of ladies. Tommy soon spotted the lovely Ado and immediately fell in love with her. However, she was already in the company of another handsome chap. Biding his time, Tommy waited for his opponent to step away to buy a cup of tea and boom, he was in, asking her to dance and inviting her to lose the other fella. She told him in no uncertain terms that she was not getting rid of him as he was her nephew and Chaperone, our very own brother Mehael. At the same time, she was pleased as she was not then courting anybody else and agreed to meet with Tommy on other dates. Indeed, he would drive the considerable distance to Newmarket at the weekends just to see her. It was some time before he admitted that he was not actually teetotal and that the pin was borrowed but by then they were smitten with each other and, as Ado explained, it was all too late.

Ado moved to Oxford where she married Tommy in October 1962. Her older brother, Michael, performed father of the bride duties by walking her down the aisle before ceremoniously giving her away. Duly hitched, they lived in a smart top floor flat overlooking Abingdon Road, owned by Mrs Weatherby and where Tommy had lived as a lodger, it was just a few minutes' walk from our own house. Their big day was one I, at the ripe old age of fourteen, remember well. I was the eldest of the remaining children not at the wedding. Mum and Betty had prepared a veritable feast of pop, sandwiches, cake and jellies and such like. I was appointed Chief Childminder and Trifle Monitor for the day whilst the adults dressed to the nines went off to celebrate with the happy couple.

Tommy would often take me to watch Oxford United in his shiny new white Morris Minor and we went to a great many games together until they moved to Worksop. He and Ado would also invite me to go with them on Sunday afternoon outings to Weston-super-Mare. I happily accepted and, prophetically, years later that resort would become a significant factor in my own life.

Ado gave birth to daughter Fiona a few years later and, when Peggy and Tommy moved north to Worksop Manor Stud Farm, Ado and Tommy later joined them. Ado worked at Bachelors pea factory, apparently displaying her Irish fierceness and proving her socialist credentials when she spoke up in support of staff during a number of disputes with management. Fiona learned a great deal about Irish history, and standing up for her beliefs, from her mother. She took her growing daughter along to CND peace marches and progressed on to a number of public demonstrations, particularly against Margaret Thatcher and her policies. Fiona vividly recalls, as a teenager, her first anti-Thatcher rally which she described as a real classic. Somehow both of them got called forward to the front of the demonstration and the well-schooled young activist found herself walking and chatting away to the then deputy leader, and former cabinet minister, Michael Foot, an ardent supporter of CND and equally vociferous in his opposition to British membership of the EEC. Nicknamed, unkindly, as "Wurzel Gummidge", on account of his duffle coat and swirling grey hair, her new found walking companion subsequently led the party to one of its worst election defeats and duly resigned his leadership to be succeeded by Neil Kinnock, who proved no more successful. Still, it was an instructive experience for our young cousin. Ado was actually a gentle soul and as the years progressed, she stopped marching as it was evident that confrontations with the police were becoming more strident, with the deployment of batons, horses and the process of kettling being applied. Fiona, on the other hand was merely hitting her stride and the young idealist continued to battle on for a better future with her Che Guevara tee-shirts, books and diaries to guide her. To this day, and now married to Robert Cummins, she thanks her Mum and Dad for instilling her with strong principles and a fearless attitude.

Given her zestful desire to educate her daughter to meet the rigours of life, teachers, at the local Worksop school, took on more than they bargained for when they expressed the view that Ado's home teaching of the younger Fiona should cease as it afforded her daughter an advantage compared to other children. A robust exchange of opinion ensured such a request was never again repeated!

Ado and Tommy generously accommodated me when my work required visits to the law courts at Bradford, Leeds and Worksop. They even introduced me to the forgotten delights of bingo evenings at the local Railway Club. Being a southern softie, Tommy would often have to rescue me when I tried to place orders for drinks at the bar only to repeatedly come up against the locals, whose loud and tough no nonsense appearance, borne from years of hard graft and struggles, that belied a generous nature which became apparent when they knew you. Tommy duly instructed me in the art of obtaining service in such circumstances that basically amounted to following the advice of The Beatles song "twist and shout".

Tommy himself, supportive of his wife and daughter, did not participate in the great political diversions and became a bus driver when they moved to Worksop. The doting pair would work, rest and play in the mining town for the remainder of their lives.

These numerous aunts and uncles formed a community of support for each other, including Mum and Dad, over many years. At various times each of them visited our us at our home in Vicarage Road and our lives have been intermingled over many years. They played an important part in the lives of us children even as we grew into adulthood. Happily, despite the inevitable passing of most of the aunts and uncles, close family ties have been sustained through close bonds with our very numerous cousins.

Chapter Six

All change, the move to England

Saturday 16th **November 1957.** I well remember the day. Cold and damp and misty. Before going off to work Dad asked me to hurry along to Granny's to ask how Grandad was feeling as there had been some concern about him the previous evening. Running all the way and dressed in my school raincoat shielding a woollen jumper and a pair of short grey trousers, I met Gran at her back door and spurted out that Dad -wanted- to know-how-Grandad- was. She told me tell him that he was ok so I raced back home as fast as my skinny eight-year-old legs would carry me to breathlessly repeat the good news.

Later that day it transpired that dear old Grandad had relapsed and died. Within days there were aunts and uncles and an assortment of other people, some familiar and others we barely knew, appearing at our house and at Soldiers Cottage apparently from all over the country and from England in a frenzy of activity. To an eight-year-old boy, not aware of the long-term repercussions, it was rather exciting.

Grandad died aged 65, at home in the bed he had rarely left

for many years and surrounded by family. I remember the visit to his room on the day of my First Holy Communion, a major event in catholic life. The morning had been taken up with the communion service in the packed church, where having received my first holy wafer and been blessed by the Bishop I was presented with my own personal prayer book. Photographs were taken of me at my shiny best, red hair cropped and combed. I was dressed in a smart new grey blazer with matching short trousers, a white shirt and Irish green tie and attired in white socks that sat warmly inside my spanking new laced up black shoes. A hearty celebration breakfast ensued after which we departed for home and I made visits to the homes of neighbours, as did all other celebrants, receiving a small money gift at each stop. In the afternoon we visited Granny and Grandad. Ushered into his bedroom he bade me to pass him his trousers that were lying crumpled and forlorn across the sheets at the end of his bed. I recall the pipe tobacco smell when I neared him and that of pee arising from his chamber pot. Deftly turning his trousers upside-down he magically extracted a two-bob bit (two-shillings) that he placed in my surprised and grateful hands and wished me a happy life. That gift alone was enough to buy me several bars of Fry's chocolate creams, one of my favourites, plus a couple of comics. What had been a delightful day of good memories for me must in turn and, not for the first time, have been, an expensive one for my parents.

As the days wore on and the funeral neared the number of visitors seemed to grow even more all waiting to pay their respects, We seemed to be at the cottage every day and they would arrive, sombre in mood and mostly in dark or black clothes , express their sorrow, hug everybody in sight , sup a strong cuppa and slowly and deliberately select a piece of cake and biscuits laid out on the dining room table before moving next door and dropping on their knees on the right hand side of Grandad's bed, crossing themselves with the sign of the cross and, opening their handbags or reaching into pockets, would unfurl their Rosary Beads and engage in an oft repeated refrain of Our Fathers and Hail Mary's, some softly and others in a loud crescendo, together with a host of other prayers designed to ensure dear old Grandad received a right good send-off and with it the security of an eternal place in paradise. Then the unexpected happened. Horror of horrors some of us older children were ushered into the bedroom and instructed to say goodbye to Grandad, who appeared to my innocent mind to be more relaxed and happier than I had ever seen before with a gentle smile on his face. Reflecting back, I suppose it was the bodily expression of relief from the constant pain emanating from his war wound, of which I knew little detail at that time. Kneeling next to me was a tearful sounding nun in full habit who led us to join in a ritual of prayer and, it seemed to my young mind to be forever, before we were ushered out to come face to face with a richly laden refreshments table for which I, for one, was immensely relieved.

Betty, however, recalls with some terror the night before the funeral. Tradition it may have been but forcing an eleven-year-old to be reluctantly lifted up and held over the prostate body of Grandad to kiss him goodbye for one last time, whilst he was in the coffin awaiting departure for the church, made a lasting impression on her. Suffice to say, she has not forgotten the experience and even to this day has a horror of being asked to attend an open coffin visitation, so common in parts of Ireland.

Uncle Peter would regale us with tales of past wakes in Irish homes. On one occasion he was with a number of friends attending the funeral of a man with a humpback that required him to be tied down to secure him in place on the bed. A couple of nuns were reverently leading prayers when one of the lads received a nod from an accomplice and reached into his pocket, silently extracted a very small but sharp-bladed knife which he used to cut the holding rope surrounding the white shrouded soul who instantly sat up as if he had sprung back to life. The watching nuns, momentarily numbed with shock, then shrieked loudly and ran around the room in ever increasing circles of terror and disbelief. The culprit equally rapidly exited the scene.

The day of Grandad's funeral was a very long one. Following a formal Requiem Mass, the extended cortege set off, in typically poor rainy conditions, for the slow and dismal walk to the cemetery, about two long miles away. Following the burial service Grandad was finally laid to rest and we made our pedestrian way back to town. All I recall from thenceforth is the announcement by Uncle Oliver that we children should have an extra couple of days off school following these events, to which many thanks were offered to Grandad.

The passing of Grandad presaged a huge change of life for us as a family. Dad had been very reluctant hitherto to leave Ireland as most of his siblings had done. But there was the growing realisation that the expanded family would have to be schooled, fed and clothed and would themselves need employment in the future. Whatever discussions took place between our parents and wider family we were not aware of them.

Having served 23 years as a boy messenger and then postman, Dad resigned on 24th September 1958. He received a commendable recommendation from the senior postmaster, packed his bags, lifted each of us children in his arms and, face to face, told us to look after our mother and be good whilst he was away. Then he was gone.

On leaving Ireland, Dad initially went to live with his sister Peggy in Newmarket. Our eldest brother Mehael, who had hitherto spent virtually all his life at Soldiers Cottage with Granny, accompanied him. Dad soon decided that he would be better off joining his brother Michael who was working at the car factory in Oxford, where he believed there would be more potential job opportunities, leaving Mehael to live with Peggy and Tommy, where he succeeded in passing an entrance examination and was offered a place at Bury St Edmunds Grammar School. Dad subsequently obtained work at Lucy's Foundry in Oxford where he would also be sharing a home with his brother Michael and his wife Margaret and then informed Mehael that he wanted him to join the family in Oxford.

A new chapter in our lives was about to unfold.

Part Two

New Beginnings In England

Chapter Seven

Goodbye Bagenalstown, hello Oxford

My best friend was next- door neighbour Billy Hughes. It soon dawned on us that we would shortly be separated. We had enjoyed a few adventures together over the years and spent many a day dressed as cowboy sheriffs in the Badlands of Bolger's Rocks; playing on the slippery grass slopes behind the estate; crossing small streams and making our way over wire and wooden fences, some barbed and trudging across muddy cow pastures to take a short cut to reach the McGrath Park where we would watch Gaelic football, play conkers in season and generally wander about at will. Our parents were content to let us wander at will as long as we told them where we were going and to make sure we were back in time for tea and Bagenalstown was regarded as a safe haven for such a carefree existence

We had frequently fished in a stream located across muddy fields accessed from Parc Muire and on route to the McGrath Park. With old twine wrapped around the lip we dipped our jam jars into the stream, seeking out our prey of tiny fish or "pinkeens" as Mum always referred to them. This provided much fun for us but not of course for the poor old fish as they thrashed around in the shallows, eager not to become our supper. Given their size it would have taken a whole shoal simply to provide a mouthful.

One afternoon has stuck in my memory bank, a bit like a nagging cough that simply will not go away. We were wandering the town and came across the church of St Mary's on the Royal Oak Road. We had been warned of devilish consequences on ever entering this Protestant church. Being curious, our nosiness got the better of us when we saw the large front door had been left open and we decided to enter the forbidden citadel. Imagine our surprise when discovered that it was very much like our own church with stained glass windows and pictures of saints adorning the walls. The stark hard wood pews were set out in a familiar pattern and to all intents and purposes we could not see any noticeable difference. This was confirmed in our young minds when we came across a stand where candles were placed ready for people to light as a mark of respect to remember those who were either ill or dead and placed in a combined holder. Unfortunately, I forgot my manners and common sense. I proceeded to light virtually every candle before being accosted by a very angry looking man in priestly Cassock. There followed a ferocious telling off and the taking of names before we were unceremoniously removed from the sacred place. The telling off received from the man was nothing compared to the anger and disappointment expressed by my parents when they discovered what we had been up to. The candle burning was indeed shameful but I, for one, could not get away from the fact that both churches appeared to have more in common than I had expected, a fact that would reimpose itself on my mind in later years.

*

Famous actors and rich people boast of having one child and eight suitcases when travelling the world. In our case it was more a case of seven children and one suitcase. On a typically cold and damp Irish November day we gathered ourselves at the front door of 12 Parc Muire for one last time. Our friends and neighbours, including Billy, were out in the road to bid us farewell. Warm words were exchanged interlaced with some tears especially as Mum embraced Mrs Hughes and Mrs Furlong, who had become close friends and confidants.

Just weeks earlier, Mum had informed us that Dad, who had been away for two months, had found work in Oxford in England and we would be joining him in late November, twelve months after Grandad had died. Suddenly, everything seemed to be happening very fast compared to our previously unhurried existence. One day a pile of wooden tea chests arrived and we were asked to decide what we would like to take with us so long as there was room available after the essential items had been selected by Mum and Betty. In truth I have little memory of most of this and it largely passed me by as I had few precious personal belongings. I did select my First Communion prayer-book, a Christmas toy or two, a few photographs and comics. During the hectic two weeks both Mum and Betty were busily separating "must haves" from "likes" and wrapping the chosen items in small newspaper parcels for placing in the appropriate chest category, like household items required for cooking and feeding and cleaning; bedclothes and linen; and clothes that would be needed thereafter. These were to be transported ahead of us. Clothes for the journey were retained to one side and our few personal items packed into a suitcase and comprised family photographs, a well-used radio and bronze ornaments of two rearing horses which Uncle Oliver had presented to Mum after winning them at the Fairground. Soon we were packed and excitedly ready to go.

The reliable cream coloured and well-travelled VW camper van was owned by Mr Nolan, a friend of Dad, who had kindly agreed to drive us the sixty odd miles to Dublin to meet up with him at Aunty Lizzies house before catching the boat to Holyhead, England. Engine running, it stood expectantly at the front of our house whilst we gazed at each other and at the home we had lived in for the past four years and we became all too aware that the time had arrived. This was it. We were leaving and this was to be our last goodbye to friends, neighbours and life as we knew it. We were off to face the unknown, a whole new world. Sadness tinged with excitement as I joined a tearful Mum and siblings, climbed snugly into the plastic seats and exchanged final waves as our friends and neighbours slowly disappeared from view and indeed from our life. Forever.

Betty's recollection of arriving at Aunt Lizzies in Ballyfermot Parade was of Dad running down the steps and embracing Mum and herself and all of us children. We were equally excited as we had not seen him since he left home. We were ushered up the large concrete steps that led to our aunt's home. Aunt Lizzie was a lovely warm natured lady with red hair and a ready smile. She was married to her only true love, Bill. One thing Lizzy was renowned for was her magic teapot, which was always on the stove and ready to share its near treacle like contents with all those who entered her welcoming home. Her generosity extended to cake as well but I have never ever tasted tea like this and it was a pot that never seemed to empty regardless of how many cups spurted from its grizzly slender neck. She often joked that when the pot appeared to be almost-empty she merely placed it under her arm, squeezed hard and lo and behold it was soon ready to pour forth again. I assumed that the colourful heavy woollen cosy that surrounded it somehow prevented her getting as burnt as the tea leaves within. Given the continuous input of leaves into an already stewed pot it was a surprise to discover that any liquid ever found its way out. For me personally, her unique brand of tea left such a lasting impression that I now drink what my family refer to as "flea's wee" strength though I am not sure how that has been tested. It is true enough that my tea contains more dairy than tea leaf.

Our arrival at Dublin stirred memories of a fun filled holiday week I had spent with Lizzie and Bill a year or so earlier. Allowed out to play with her own children, and a trillion others who seemed to be attracted by a sort of magnetism to her presence, we had fun and games together in a nearby park or play area. She had dressed me in a cowboy outfit, complete with hat, holster and even a scarf around my neck and I felt that I was once again riding the range, chasing and arresting all the baddies. I recall going to the cinema just around the corner and enjoying a rare trip to the seaside at Sandymount, a long stretch of beach that seemed to disappear far into the distance when the tide bade farewell and what glee it brought forth when we clambered on board for a speedy pony trap ride across the ever-changing beach patterns, the wind blowing waywardly and spitting showers of mist into our joyful faces. This was a week that created long-lasting and happy memories.

Aunt Lizzie had as many children as our own family. She herself said that she and Bill could not meet on the stairs without them ending up with another child. They were quite delightful to be with. Uncle Bill had a false leg as a result of an injury sustained in a motor bike accident, the exact details of which are sketchy. Bill often recounted a story about his first replacement leg, created from the finest wood in all Ireland. One evening he noticed an increasing smell of burning whilst toasting bread over the open fire. Forgetting an old Irish saying, "A little fire that warms is better than a big fire that burns" he realised, too late, he had put his own false leg into the fire and had set *it* alight rather more successfully than the bread. His next replacement was made of metal which was fine until he decided to take a walk in the sea and the leg corroded. His final leg proved better able to match his creativity in the "how to lose a leg competition", years before he would sadly succumb to cancer later in life, very much as his beloved Lizzie would do.

So it was that we had arrived in Dublin, had tea and recounted past memories with Lizzie and Bill before it was time for our departure to Dun Laoghaire (Dun Leary) Port and the next stage of our journey.

*

Arriving at the Port proved to be an awesome experience for us children. From the moment we stepped from our taxi onto the dock we were surrounded by an avalanche of bustling activity. There seemed to be more people in this one place than had ever been seen in the whole of Bagenalstown, scurrying backwards and forwards, some over laden with bags with others mulling around in small groups, hugging, chin wagging and drinking. There was an air of great excitement as a very large boat, the like of which I had never seen before, came into view. Dad informed us that this was our boat. To the best of my recollection, it was named Hibernia which, with its sister ship Cambria, was owned and operated by British Transport Commission between 1948 and 1962, to sail daily between Dublin and Holyhead. It was no wonder I was excited at the prospect of boarding her. My only previous boating experience was as captain of a yellow plastic boat. I would swing it around in front and behind me whilst taking my weekly bath and trying as best I could to sink three different enemy vessels disguised as coloured ducks that insisted on invading my water.

Hibernia was awesome, with a massive white upper body and colour matching horizontal rails all around the viewing deck. Centre front was the magnificent Bridge, the boat's beating heart overseen by her Captain and beyond that the leant-back and rounded Funnel, emblazoned with the linked red arrows of the parent company and responsible for inhaling the engine and boiler smoke before spitting its toxic contents into the open skies. The main hull from the deck downward was a dark navy blue and comprised the bulk of the ship including the cabin accommodation. This ship may not have had the history or gravitas to match the SS Princess Maud, upon whom some earlier departing relatives had seemingly sailed, with her historic trips to assist in the evacuation at Dunkirk or its presence at Omaha Beach on D-Day. Nevertheless, to me Hibernia was a sight to behold.

My gloved hands clutched a small case and we followed Dad as he led us up a steep stairway that took us onto a vast wooden deck. We are all dressed in warm clothing for the long sea journey. I was wearing my woollen hat and a heavy overcoat worn as protection from the biting winds swirling across the deck on this damp and foggy Dublin night. The weather was not to Mum's liking and the mere thought of us being on deck in these conditions was clearly not a happy one. So, much to my disappointment, I would have been quite happy at that point to stay on top, she asked Dad to obtain us a cabin below deck. Nicky has memories of our parents and Mum in particular being misty eyed and fighting back a few tears as she looked at the Dublin skyline when waving goodbye to her beloved Ireland. After an all too brief time we were whisked down a narrow staircase to our cabin. The room was fairly small with a few hard chairs idling centrally around a table whilst a short hop or climb led to a set of bunk beds where we children would be able to gain some sleep.

Shortly after, the ship sounded a series of loud horn that heralded our imminent departure. Suddenly we were on the move and within ten minutes, much to my delight at least, Dad ushered us in twos or threes upstairs again to gaze at the retreating Dublin shoreline. We were on our way but this time I felt rather more unsteady, battling against the wind and trying my best to get my legs to move in tandem with each other let alone the deck. Sighing with a bit of frustration, we were escorted back to the protection and relative comfort of our cabin. The next couple of hours or so would see us rocking, rolling and riding the waves towards an unknown future. So it was, with our lives in tea chests, we sailed across the Irish Sea on a magic wave of hope.

At some point Mum dipped into her hay-coloured shopping bag and magically produced an array of goodies. In the food lottery my younger brother Pat was gifted a ham sandwich, took one bite and decided it was not to his taste but rather than offend Mum he silently entombed the offending sandwich down the side of his bunk. Years later, after regularly relating this episode to friends he was nicknamed "ham sandwich". For my part, I was offered a chocolate bar but feeling a bit unwell and unable to sleep much and fearing sea sickness Mum beckoned me down to sit with her and Dad at the table. The next thing any of us can remember was the hooter again blasting out across the boat forewarning us that we were close to Holyhead, the sign for us to gather our belongings and make our wobbly way upstairs to join the chattering and shivering mass of passengers now exposed to the cold night air. It was dead of night so little was seen of our new land apart from an array of twinkling lights that appeared all around us and seemed to be waving a cheery welcome as we slowly made our way into the harbour. An eerie silence ensued as the engines were lulled to sleep and an orderly departure ensued. Patiently, we made our way off the boat and let our feet take their first unsteady steps onto English soil. Dad, in his fancy trilby styled hat and heavy coat zipped off to organise the next stage whilst we huddled together for warmth, rather like penguins in an ice storm. On his return we were hurriedly walked the short distance from the dock to the adjacent train platform and the magnificent sight of a massive train engine, billowing huge streams of steam into our path as we made our way down the platform as fast as we could. The reason for speed soon became apparent as there was a stampede of fellow travellers all in search of a compartment and a seat for the long journey to London, though for us we would be changing trains at a place called Crewe.

Dad explained to us we would be travelling overnight on the "Irish Mail" train as far as I can gather. This, it turned out, was a hugely popular express service that linked Holyhead and London Euston from its inception in 1848 until 2002 and connected with ferry services to Dublin. It was a magnificent specimen, a huge billowing steam monster with a tender coal wagon that pulled up to 16 coaches. Dad, as a former postie and with great enthusiasm, explained about the mail carriage. In addition to numerous bag-loads loaded at our departure point it also collected post from sacks hanging on long poles at the side of stations as we sped along and then sorted by posties. He also provided a bit of history from eight years earlier when a mail train had been involved in a very rare collision resulting in six fatalities and some 35 injured. However, the enginemen became the heroes of the night. The fireman, who had suffered severe injuries himself that required later hospitalisation, was made aware by the driver of an oncoming large freight train that would have careered into the stricken wreckage and the fireman set off warning detonators down the line that ensured the second train stopped just short of the accident site. Such were the men of character who operated the trains that we were privileged to be part of on our own journey.

Our own "Irish Mail" venture ended at Crewe where we had to alight and change. The long wait on a cold and windy platform still lingers in the memory and it was a great relief when we later skipped onto the warmth of a fresh steam train which would take us to Oxford. We had a whole compartment to ourselves and I managed to find a place by the window where I excitedly anticipated being able to look out and watch the lights as we flew past farmhouses and factories flashing furiously through the night in our fiery warhorse. Sadly, it was not to be as Mum and at least one of my siblings was affected by the lights so we were instructed to pull all the blinds down. Even so, I couldn't resist the temptation to occasionally dare to lift the blind slightly and snatch a quick peep only to be interrupted by a stern reminder from Dad. Eventually, with daylight returning the blinds were raised and a pack of biscuits and few bars of chocolate were handed around and eagerly devoured. After what had been a very, very long day the train started to lose speed and the engine-driver marked the passage under Hinksey Bridge and its bustling sidings with a cloud burst of steam. Dad leaned over to the window and, as the train slowly stuttered to a signal stop, he pointed out a large lake to our right and to an area of houses beyond where we would soon be living. Shortly, we were on the move again, travelling cautiously past what seemed to be hundreds of train wagons filled with an array of goods but mostly coal, we gradually picked up the tempo before once again slithering ever-so -ever so-slowly and gently to a crawl that it was possible to see the smiles and frowns etched on peoples' faces along the approaching platform. We had finally arrived at Oxford station.

Taxis were ordered and filled and quick as a flash we were driving through the city. Even at the station I was wide-eyed and agog at the sight of so many bicycles all lined up against a set of railings outside the station. Everywhere you looked there were there were crowds of people, many riding bikes, some hurried, others stopping for a chatter in ones or twos or larger groups.

Many wore strange looking clothes with black capes and hats and I knew this was an altogether different place. And oh my, what a difference to dear sleepy old Bagenalstown.

I may have been excited at the first view of our new home town but nothing prepared me for the shock of arriving at our new home, 14 Vicarage Road. Because a shock it most certainly was.

Chapter Eight

Vicarage Road, first impressions

Standing next to Mum in the back garden, I distinctly recall expressing my disappointment with our new home, blurting out my immortal first impression to her – "It's not very nice, is it?". To which she immediately responded by telling me to "Whish you, be quiet".

Squashed between my sisters, Betty and May, I fought to see what I could of our new surroundings as our taxi took us over a bridge and a river below which looked so very different to that of the River Barrow with a large number of boats, big and small, seemingly bobbing up and down whilst moored to the spot. People were walking along a broad path and it appeared at odds for the time of year, with Christmas just around the corner.

All at once the taxi stopped and we managed to disentangle our stiff legs and exited onto the pavement outside 14 Vicarage Road. The first thing that struck me was that there was no front garden, just a plain old wooden door with number 14 centred on its top and about halfway down and next to a letter box, a brown knob stood ready to be to clasped and squeezed for probably the millionth time. More confusing, stood side by side was another unremarkable numberless door.

Taxi duly paid, and cases and children all accounted for, we waited for Dad to lead us through one of the doors in front of us. Suddenly, the numbered door slowly opened to reveal two faces, who came out to greet Mum and Dad with a machine gun rattle of welcome- "hello Mary, hello Paddy, you made it then, glad to see ye, did yous have a nice journey? awful weather it's been here, what was the crossing like? Jesus, you must be worn out be now, I expect yous would like a nice cup of tea" and a string of other welcomes and greetings were exchanged as us children lined up to be introduced to our Uncle Michael and his wife, Aunty Margaret.

We were gently ushered along a grey painted bricked hallway that reeked a faint air of dampness. Ahead of us stood a door that split the hallway and hid a dark coalhouse and a direct entry to the garden Instead we were guided sharp right into a compact lobby with a staircase to its left leading upstairs. An opening to the right introduced a fair-sized lounge where the unnumbered door in the far-right corner revealed itself from the inside. Ignoring all turns we entered the dining / living room, heartened by the sight of a warm open fire directly opposite, with orange spiked flames that erupted to highlight floral papered walls.

A large wooden table protected with a blue and white squared plastic tablecloth stood beneath a window that afforded a view of the rear garden. In the far-left corner was an entry to the kitchen area where yet another door led into the garden.

I was now in a state of near panic as I was in dire need of bladder relief, I absented myself and, not for the first or last time, found relief in the garden in full view of any neighbours. What a glorious welcome that must have been. My mother's intervention prevented Dad from chastising me as she, supportively, pointed out that we had not been told the location of the bathroom. Then it was revealed in all its horror. *There was no bathroom.* The small hut I had noticed at the end of the garden but had assumed, from its it distant position and shabby appearance, to be a shed actually turned out to be the lantern-lit toilet. Dad informed us that any washing, personal or otherwise had to be done in the kitchen area where on the left side was a bench that opened up and doubled as a bath to be filled by using a pipe leading from the cold tap on the small white sink whilst hot water had to be heated via kettle or saucepan before being emptied into the bath.

A few minutes later with just myself standing next to Mum I distinctly recall expressing my disappointment with our new home, blurting out my immortal first impression to her – "It's not very nice, is it?". To which she immediately responded by telling me to "Whish you, be quiet".

Retreating indoors we were then taken on a tour of the upstairs after climbing a large number of uncarpeted steps and swinging left at its top onto a landing. Walking slowly left we encountered bedroom one, large and green with a big window that overlooked the rear garden and was reserved for Uncle and Aunty. Ahead was a dormitory sized room where two cast-iron double beds with rounded silver knobs occupied the left wall, separated by a small wicker basket bedside table. Beyond them two wardrobes were embedded into the far wall and separated from each other by an open but rarely used fireplace. Scanning around the room revealed two large windows that afforded a view of the street and the shop opposite. A third but single bed rested in the corner just beyond the second window. This was to be the boys' room. Retracing our steps back to the top of the stairs we stepped down into what would be the girls' quarters, a bed to the right where you could overview the neighbour's house and garden. A few steps beyond the bed a flimsy doorway provided access to a small additional windowless room.

Curiously, during the bedroom tour no mention had been made about our parents themselves. Downstairs, it became apparent that they would be sleeping on a red sofa-bed in the room doubling as a lounge, with the unnumbered door in the right-hand corner. The tour of the house completed, we made our way into the living room to be greeted by the joyous sight of tea, assorted sandwiches and cake, prepared by Aunty Margaret.

*

I could not help but reflect on the contrast with our old home. Newly built and spacious it had possessed a modern kitchen and a bathroom with a matching bath and toilet suite; three family sized front and rear bedrooms and front and rear gardens. Having moved upwardly, from the tiny house in Phillip Street to Parc Muire, we were now about to share and live in a large but old house, somewhat in need of repair and decoration. Brother Nicky initially described it as a mansion. Certainly, it was very big but, in the books that I had read, all mansions invariably made reference to several bathrooms and toilets, where all manner of games would be played out that would inevitably result in grisly murder being committed in either one or the other. So, if our "mansion" was a shock to me then I can only guess at what our gentle and kindly mother must have been thinking. She retained her thoughts to herself and after my initial hasty remarks I duly followed her example. She and Dad had made their decision to uproot themselves and forsake their family and friends. Future actions would reinforce their determination, commitment and support to each of us children and to each other.

Margaret and Michael having welcomed us to share their home must also have wondered what was in store for them. One minute they had the house to themselves and the next they were surrounded by a clutch of eight boisterous children.

Chapter Nine

Exploring Hinksey

The first few days and weeks after our arrival was exciting albeit hectic for our parents. Suitcases and tea chests were often opened and re-opened as a home was found for hitherto imprisoned items. Arrangements were made regarding Catholic schooling, bus routes checked and six school uniforms obtained, some second hand, and equally divided between St Joseph's, for the under 11s, and Edmund Campion for the elders. Medical registration was completed and no doubt a host of other official documents had to be requested, signed, witnessed and dispatched to the appropriate council or authority. Dad, of course, was also busy working and Mum, helped by Betty, was busier than ever cooking, washing, sewing, ironing, bedmaking and cleaning and a host of other work that must have seemed like 30 of the 24 hours available, before she was afforded a few hours of sleep. When not called upon to help with shopping or cleaning chores, us older children were free to explore the neighbourhood.

On the weekend of our arrival our parents had taken us on a brief tour of the local area known as Hinksey, from where we had easy access to a range of shops and, even better, a play area. Leaving home, we turned left, past a small bakery and delicatessen shop run by a delightful mature lady named Amy Wigmore. Opposite stood the grocery and hardware store owned by Harry Purvey, a tall, thin man with a small moustache and trade pencil stapled behind his right ear. He nearly always sported a white overall that hid a smart white shirt and black tie with matching black shiny shoes. Betty well remembers the bewildered look on the poor man's face when, on her first visit to the shop and speaking in a sweet Irish brogue, she asked for a stone of potatoes as well as a sliced pan, nothing to do with either stones or pans of course. This led to some amusing and good-natured exchanges for few weeks as shop-keeper and customer got to grips with each other's odd ways of speech. Looking back, it must at times have resembled an episode of a later TV comedy show *The Two Ronnies,* when a request for four candles was interpreted as fork handles. Mr Purvey took it all in his stride. I think he quietly relished those early visits as he certainly greeted each of us with a knowing grin. He was helped by Phil Bonner, a short, stocky and genial assistant who wore a brown overall, to denote his status, his head topped with sticky-up fair hair earning him the affectionate nickname Barney on account of his remarkable likeness to the character from the Flintstones, in the television comedy series.

At the end of our road, by the Morrells Pub, Dad escorted us left along the main Abingdon Road which led to the city centre, about a mile away. Soon passing the entrance to Lake Street and opposite Alden's Butchers, we came to Hinksey Park. Fronted by public toilets it was guarded by a black iron railed fence that was locked at night and patrolled by a uniformed resident "parkie" with whom we would become well acquainted over the next few years. Dennis, our menace, would put the fear of God into anybody who entered his fiefdom and dared to infringe the park rules, official or his own making, and who may have been ill advised enough to disobey his most frequently shouted and stern instructions to "get off that bike", as riding within the confines of the park was strictly frowned upon thus rendering it a "must do" to earn some street cred.

Entering the park itself we were agog at the heavenly sight. A row of swings, of sizes to suit all ages and with straps and chains tied to wooden seats, attracted immediate attention and, with turn of foot that would have graced our great Irish Olympic Gold medal winner Ronnie Delaney, brought us into contact and so began our first English playtime. Alongside stood a metal monkey frame that required the dexterity of its namesake to avoid injury but we had already spied a short distance away the attraction that would provide endless hours of fun for so many years ahead. A huge slide stood glinting in the faint winter sunshine with steps that required the stamina of an Everest climber to reach its steely peak. Next came the supersonic take-off with us scooting, butterflies-in-the- stomach, down the steep runway which, when well waxed, had the potential to project the slide-skier a mile away at Carfax thus saving the inconvenience of having to catch a bus, a fitting reward for an exhilarating experience.

Our parents, aware of the looming onset of early darkness, called an end to the playtime and Dad resumed his role as head guide. Trudging a couple of hundred yards over a terrain of muddy playing fields brought us within sight of another surprise. Lurking behind a row of uniformly lined trees, as azure blue swimming pools revealed themselves, surrounded by gravel paths and box edged flower beds similar to those at Soldiers Cottage. We slowly followed the line of the pools as they curved to reveal a large boating lake which separated us from a tennis court off in the distance. Dad took this opportunity to point out that next to the tennis courts was the HQ of the Park-Keeper Dennis who, in an hour or so, would be on his bike and herding out visitors prior to locking all the gates for the night. Distancing ourselves from the pools on our left we rounded the top end of the smaller boating lake on our right where Dad pointed out the reservoir-like Hinksey lake that we had seen from the train. Over the years, we would all discover the absolute beauty and wonder of the huge ball of the bright red sun setting over its calm water. Shortly, we arrived at an exit gate, at the top end of Lake Street we marched sharp left, past the Community Centre and the Seven Stars pub where Dad would become a firm local and card game winner. A right turn took us into Gordon Street and, before reaching Vicarage Road at its end, we stopped to gaze at the entrance to the Local Defence Social Club which, in a previous life, had been Wesleyan Chapel built in the 1882, with a wonderful stained-glass window at its front. Subsequently purchased and used by the local defence force in the 1940s it morphed into a Social Club before its closure in 2010 and reversion into flats in 2012. Family wise, it would become one of Mums great pleasures over many years, with her enjoying her relaxing Monday night bingo evenings where sandwiches supplemented with a cup of tea were on offer during the interval. She was even more thrilled when the charming voice of the former RAF veteran and bingo-master, known as "Ted", pronounced "five and nine -the Brighton Line", signalling her full card and she could softly call "house" to walk home with the star prize of tea, sugar and butter, lovingly packed inside a crepe papered cardboard box. Aside from the bingo it was a family club and over many years we would attend numerous dances and seasonal events.

*

The time lapse between our arrival at Vicarage Road and commencing school in January allowed further time to acquaint ourselves with the neighbourhood, building on the tour with our parents.

Nicky and I passed a few days exploring on our own, beginning with the first Monday. Leaving the house, we turned right along Vicarage Road, swept past Gordon Street and advanced beyond Hinksey School, standing opposite the King Edward pub, before entering St John's churchyard and rectory. Exiting through a small side-gate we entered Wytham Street. Nicky chose to route us along a hedge lined path that meandered around back-to-back steel barriers. In short time we found ourselves alongside some poorly fenced, bricked up buildings which we later discovered was a former air-aid shelter and most definitely out of bounds but would in future years provide a convenient refuge for a number of us including Betty and friends to gather as teenagers to play the latest hit records. Armed then with a portable record player and pop drinks such as Tizer we would play LPs and the latest records of singing stars like Lonnie Donegan (My Old Man's a Dustman and Cumberland Gap) together with Mario Lanza and others. The height of sophistication indeed. I suspect I was later allowed along on sufferance as the annoying younger brother but I was grateful just to be able to partake.

The unmistakable sound of an oncoming steam train hastened us onwards and we raced about 100 yards before taking the path that crossed Hinksey Lake before vaulting up a scores of steps onto the plateau of the railway bridge. Our arrival was greeted by hooting and hollering as were momentarily sucked inside white clouds as we greedily soaked ourselves in the coal induced fragrance of the rising steam as the train passed beneath our feet. For me, this would be the first of my many visits to see these giant locomotives thunder majestically under the vibrating bridge. Scores of wagons were shunted daily up and down the six plus lines in the sidings, loading and unloading, coupling and uncoupling thus providing many hours of pleasure. On the other side of the bridge open pasture fields appeared on either side of the tree lined path that we followed as we wove our way to Hinksey village itself. Having spent a few pence on a drink and a bar of chocolate at the local shop we headed back over the bridge but, instead of retracing our steps by the air raid shelter, we headed to lake Street and another look around the park before returning home in time for tea. We then related to Mum what we had been up to and our exciting discoveries.

Suddenly, the thought surfaced in my spinning mind that maybe, just maybe, Vicarage Road might not be such a bad place to live after all

*

Reflecting back on those early days and the connection with Hinksey lake and bridge, a couple of events feature prominently. During school holidays I would frequently absent myself and disappear across the bridge and imagine all sorts of goings on as I perched somewhat perilously near the tree tops, hidden within branches as walkers of all ages ferried themselves below me towards the village. Two occasions stand out in my memory as they both induced different phobias that would be with me for life.

The first occasion led to a fear of cattle. I built myself a den under a small dry bridge in a dip between two fields and with great skill curtained the front and rear entrances with a range of branches plucked from overhanging trees and reeds from the nearby river before settling down to enjoy a comic with a bottle of pop. In the throes of reading, my peace was shattered as a rotund and smelly cow poked its large and inquisitive head into my face. Trembling with concern, having never encountered such a huge beast at close range, I decided that I would hastily exit to my left. Shaking was replaced with fear as my great escape plan was blocked by two more such beasts moving down the bank as I poked my head through my branch window. I was surrounded and my mind cast back to the "pictures" and the occupants of wagon trains who were under siege and in danger of being arrowed to death. Where was the sound of bugles and the advancing cavalry? Indeed, where was the Lone Ranger, the hero subject about whom I had just been reading. Nobody knew I was here and in my own mind I was in danger of being gored and possessed thoughts of being trampled and eaten alive by cows. Suddenly, with nothing but sheer bloody mindedness, I raised myself up, stooping to gather my comic and leftover pop, and made a frantic dash from under the bridge, came face to face with the enemy but somehow managed to clamber under its scrambling legs. I dragged myself onto the top of the bridge in one mud splattered piece, all much to the amusement of the cattle who carried on chewing and seemed serenely unconcerned that their slimline dinner had escaped. Fear, or at least caution, in front of cattle has remained with me and has indeed served me well when out rambling. Needless to say, any thoughts of ever being a matador were quickly dismissed from my list of potential careers.

In the very same field just a few weeks later I had indulged in another once in a lifetime experiment. My brothers, Nicky and Mehael, and a lad named "Butch" were sampling the delights of the great outdoors by camping overnight. "Butch" was a charming lad who had struck up a friendship with Mehael whilst playing football. Blessed with an infectious smile and boundless enthusiasm he was a joy to be around. Mum absolutely adored him and he was welcomed into our home like a son. I was walking down the path having been train spotting when they called to me to join them. I happily did so and had a cuppa something and was fed biscuits. Everybody seemed to be smoking a cigarette and I was invited to sample one. I received instructions on how I should hold the "fag" between my fingers and inhale the juicy delight. Sadly, or with great relief in retrospect, I fluffed my lines. I placed the burnt offering in my mouth in eager anticipation and inhaled ...or not as the case may be. Next thing, I was bent over coughing and spluttering for about ten hours whilst those around me were also doubled up but with laughter, broken only by intermittent advice on where I had gone wrong. Needless to say, the horrible taste of eating tobacco offended my taste buds for so long afterwards that I concluded I would stick to Mum's apple pie and custard. The experience actually ensured me a healthier life as well as saving me a substantial sum of money.

"Butch" lived not far away in a large rented house along the Abingdon Road. One day his parents decided to return home to America and held a leaving party to say good bye to all their friends, inviting Mehael along for an overnight stay. After the guests had departed, Mehael and "Butch" helped in the clearing up, collecting and washing glasses, plates and dishes. Unable to resist temptation, both took sips of remnant beer as they gathered up the abundance of glasses, unaware of the accumulative effects until hit by a wave of never experienced sickness that still held them captive the morning after. Such was the effect that Mehael could never again stomach the taste or smell of beer. Even today, he drinks wine and avoids standing anywhere near a bar, as it releases a form of nausea reminiscent of his beer experience. To be sure, he has not forgotten his last night out with his young mate.

Writing this book, it is somewhat awesome and un-nerving, to reflect on the amazing capacity of the mind to store such a wealth of school and social memories, often hidden away in the darkest recesses of our being. Its power to resurface and catch us unaware, releasing forgotten experiences and rekindling the same emotional response experienced at its very inception. This is reflected in the long-term impact of a mixed range of poor school or social experiences that has affected so many of us in different ways, be it beer, hot chocolate, cheese pie, near fatal accidents, medical issues or over-strict teaching methods.

Chapter Ten

Church and Christmas in Oxford

A firm Catholic upbringing demanded that one of our parents first tasks was to find a church and a school. The nearest Catholic parish church at the time was on the northern side of the city and we soon discovered there cannot ever be a Sunday church walk to match that from our home to St. Aloysius, appropriately the patron saint of students. Not because of its length and the demand for an early rise from our slumbers, to dress in the cold morning air and queue to wash in equally cold or tepid water before awaiting a turn to use the toilet at the far end of the garden which was tiresome enough. It turned out to be an historical route that introduced us to the splendour, mystery and history of the city. Heading along Abingdon Road, beyond Hinksey Park, past the White House Ground, where Oxford City played something called soccer, we then hot footed over the free-flowing River Thames, courtesy of Folly Bridge, and onto St Aldates Street. Here we chanced upon an amazing little stone-built 15th century house selling gifts associated with Lewis Carroll's *Alice Through-the Looking Glass* where the shop is featured as part of her adventures in Wonderland. The seventh of July is known as Alice's day in Oxford and celebrated by the shop with walks and talks centred around her adventures.

Almost unnoticed, in a narrow turning beyond the shop, was Rose Place, the home of Oxford University Catholic Chaplaincy, where very occasionally we would attend Sunday mass in Rose Palace, a tiny chapel with a congregation to match. I once attended here with Mum when my brother Mehael stepped in to perform altar-boy duties, a role he had performed with distinction back home in Ireland. At the time I do not think any of us that day fully appreciated the enormity of doing so in such an historic venue. On the opposite side of the road stood the magnificent Christ Church Cathedral and Meadows where over many years we would wander and gaze incredulously at the sumptuous surroundings.

Moving quickly on would bring us to possibly the most magnificent sight in the whole of Oxford, Tom Tower, so named after its bell, the Great Tom, and said to be the loudest in all Oxford, standing proudly within Christ Church University. Another hundred yards along and we found ourselves at another famous landmark, Carfax, with its own 74-foot-high belltower offering great views over the city as a reward for those willing and able enough to clamber up its 99 twisting and punishing steps. Formerly part of a 12th century church this remains the central hub and there is seemingly a ruling that prevents any other central building from exceeding its height. A well renowned meeting point, with a concealed drinking fountain tucked away on its left corner, it stood as the link between St Aldates, Queen Street, High Street and Cornmarket.

We would stride out at a brisk gallop along Cornmarket as Mum hated being late, even if her famed church shut-eye caused her to miss most of the soon to be forgotten sermon, when we reached the wide boulevard of St Giles, well known for its church and martyrs' memorial and the annual crowd pulling two-day fair held at the beginning of September. Here the wide road obligingly splits between Woodstock Road to the left and Banbury Road to the right. Our destination took us left, sweeping past the Grandiose Randolph Hotel and Ashmolean Museum to sidle alongside the ancient, bicycle-festooned wall of the Dominican-founded Blackfriars, we finally arrived at the Catholic Parish Church for the centre of Oxford, the Jesuit founded St Aloysius. Here we would be frequent attenders until the opening of the Holy Rood church in 1961, next to Folly Bridge, and its home as our new parish church and importantly within a ten-minute walk of home. Nevertheless, our early Sunday outings to mass served to instil a sense of wonder at our surroundings and the occasional purchase of a comic and bar of chocolate at the bridge shop on the return home provided another incentive.

Uncle Michael and Aunt Margaret had accepted an invitation to spend Christmas with her brother Tom and his wife Adelaide, who lived along the Iffley Road before moving to London. Tom's stature was that of a typical McEvoy, short and slim with a mophead that was in recess and would never need to trouble itself with Brylcream. He is believed to have been an aircraft engineer who had spent a number of years living in the Bahamas with his wife, Adelaide. By way of contrast, she was tall, slim and well-spoken with the air and grace of an actress. On their return home for a short holiday, they stayed with another sister, Kathleen, in London and from there would visit us in Oxford and they were always a joy to see as they had much merriment to convey.

The surprise and welcome arrival of our eldest brother Mehael meant the family was reunited for our first English Christmas, much to our parents' delight. Mum had been busy baking as ever and we were treated to home-made mince pies, sufficient in number to feed her small army over a few days; her own marzipan coated Christmas cake, adorned with iced holly trees and a dancing Santa; and, of course, her Christmas trifle and her especially delicious brac (Dundee) cake that was reserved for its St. Stephens day (Boxing Day) tasting. The Christmas pudding, served with custard, had to be eaten with care lest an embedded silver sixpence would be lost into an aching stomach awaiting its release at nature's call. Mostly, us children were engaged in preparing the homemade decorations, inter-looping a mix of small green, yellow, red and blue paperchains, that festooned the ceilings and windows supplemented by sprigs of red berried holly and a sea of balloons that had to be individually breathed into life and tied with knitting wool before we collapsed exhausted into a heap, glad not to have sucked one of the expanding balloons into our oxygen starved mouths. On Christmas eve Dad arrived home with a surprise Christmas tree tucked under his arm ready for decoration by Mum and Betty. Fairy tree lights, test-checked by Dad, and strands of mostly silver tinsel, were extracted from an old festive scene biscuit-tin, before being artistically caressed around the tree and topped with a silver star before finding its temporary home within sight of the glowing coal fire.

Attending Midnight Mass has always been a huge feature of Christmas for many Catholics across the world, including Mum and many of my siblings, although I suspect Dad was less enthusiastic in his conviction. There is something difficult to define but intrinsically spiritual about its appeal and for many it may be their only church visit in the year. Perhaps it is a feeling of brotherhood, of recalling a childhood of long ago now lost in the passing of time, or remembering old friends and family members, of the simplicity of the Christmas story itself and its message that "love came down at Christmas". Whatever the reason, it has always possessed a unique capacity to unite people in a common family theme, the celebration of a birthday. Many of us children would join Mum who loved to attend this service particularly after the 1960s opening of the new Holy Rood church on our doorstep. Exuding calm and, with her soft toned voice, she eagerly joined in the singing of the carols, especially her favourite- Silent Night.

The enthusiastic and heartfelt singing, in the form of Hosannas' and ding-dong- merrily-on-high, echoing around the church always seemed to draw such joyous feelings, was not a regular feature of the Catholic Mass. The enlightened mood that broke the chains of the normally restrained congregation and set hearts free to release a crescendo of hitherto restrained emotions was always a treat to behold. The response possibly reaped the benefit of an abundance of a boozy pre-mass warm-up. Regardless, it demonstrated to me anyway the renewal power of both music and spontaneity. Leaving church feeling uplifted and free following such a midnight service was such an unalloyed joy compared to the stricter adherence to conformity and ritual that would be the normal pattern of Catholic life at home and school for us as a family, a theme I would warm to later in life. Mass over, we would retreat into the dark night and, happily, make our way home served with a bedtime drink and accompanying biscuit to await the excitement of Santa's visit!

Christmas Day itself would see us rise early for the opening of presents from Santa or our parents. These barely affordable gifts included a comic book annual for some, a toy car or doll, a game of Ludo or Snakes and Ladders, a jigsaw or pair of socks and a small chocolate treat for each. Casting aside the numerous overcoats, serving as additional blankets to offset frostbite in the cold unheated rooms, we wasted little time getting dressed before dashing downstairs where the traditional Christmas breakfast of sausage, rasher, black or white pudding, fried egg and well-fried bread awaited. Mum, donned now in her Christmas apron with holly and Santa embossed, had unselfishly been up early so the living room fire was already well ablaze as we sat down to our tasty feast. Christmas Dinner normally commenced mid-afternoon, to coincide with Dad, fully enjoying his temporary escape from work, returning from the pub in time to plunge the carving knife into the turkey and perform his singular Christmas duty before retiring for a snooze. Thus began the eating fest that seemed to last forever. What Mum really looked forward to was relaxing with a cup of tea, and a cold turkey sandwich, later in the evening whilst listening to the radio or watching television on our rented set.

It has to be said that TV in the late fifties was fairly mediocre compared to today's offerings and multitude of choice. Our first Christmas Eve TV included old favourites such as Watch with Mother and the Flower Pot Men, a film named Tall in the Saddle starring John Wayne followed by the Eamonn Andrews show. Christmas day offered The Queens Speech, Billy Smarts Family Party, Music and song with Harry Belafonte and the Fred Astaire and Ginger Rogers Film, Top Hat. Radio was limited to the BBC Light Programme, featuring Family Favourites with Pete Murray, Life with the Lyons and the Tony Hancock half-hour. Mostly, we entertained ourselves, listening to and singing and dancing along to familiar Irish tunes.

The sixties brought in a whole new genre of music and entertainment and Mum's joy knew no bounds when confronted with the sight of her new lover boy. Not Dad, although he was much in the running. He could not compete with Mum's newest crush and so would take himself off to the pub for a well-earned pint of Guinness, leaving Mum in the company of her beloved, a man who gazed adoringly at her from behind a small screen, wearing a great smile that was destined for her eyes only whilst sitting in his rocking chair. This heartbreaker turned out to be none other than the man in a cardie, the gentle Irish charmer

Val Doonican. He touched her heart with a rendition of old Irish songs that reminded her of home. Singing either "Paddy McGinty's Goat" or "O Rafferty's Motor car" had her swirling in tears of laughter, always a lovely sight for one who worked so hard.

By contrast, new year was not the huge event it is today and not greatly celebrated as most people had to work on New-Years Day. It was more common for the family to sit around in the evening, afront of the fire watching kilt wearing Andy Stewart parade his talents at the White Heather Club during the Hogmanay celebrations from Scotland, first broadcast in the year of our arrival, and entertaining Scots and Irish alike for some ten years, much to Mum's delight. In addition to singing along to the music we would spring up and make our way to the uncarpeted space behind the old red sofa with Betty, ever one for dancing, coaxing one and all to join her in reels and jigs, so we received the bonus of dancing lessons as well.

*

Dad, on his initial Oxford visit had found work at the prestigious Lucy's Iron and Brass works, initially opened in 1825 and a long-standing Oxford manufacturing icon. Located in Jericho, about one mile from the city centre and set alongside the Oxford to Birmingham canal for ease of early transport links, it became known as Eagle Works and still remains the HQ of the Lucy Group. He was employed in the offices in some form of accountancy work. We eagerly looked forward to Friday nights when he would arrive home with a bulging paper bag of wafer biscuits that would be shared amongst us as a weekly treat. Better still, the company provided a Christmas party for children of the employees up to 12 years of age. These were great occasions and Dad would take us by bus to the giant works. Entering via the hardwood mahogany doors into a long hallway, we would plonk our coats on hooks, lined up in rows like ducks at a fair, before being escorted up wide iron stairs to the huge canteen, illuminated and decorated for the Christmas fare. We were entertained by watching cartoons and a magician; spoilt beyond delight with a huge mix of jelly and ice cream, sandwiches, sweets and cake and oceans of lemonade. Close to the end Santa, and his sledge, appeared on the balcony to distribute presents to everybody and there would be music for us all to join in and sing along. Quite unforgettable. Dad would re-appear at the end and listen to our excited stories about what had been going on as we happily chattered our way home. I was personally sorry to reach my 12th birthday in the month before one Christmas so missing out on a third party but my younger siblings carried on until Dad sought a better paid job. He had made many friends at Lucy's. One of these, a kind foreman named Nobby Clarke visited Vicarage Road in an effort to try to persuade him to stay. Alas, increasing expenses to run the home and educate us children resulted in him moving to a better paid job at the Cowley car plant, where he would remain until retirement.

Chapter Eleven

An English Schooling

In our first year, Christmas and New Year at Vicarage Road soon passed and the arrival of January witnessed our introduction to our English schools. Mehael had briefly returned to live with Peggy and Tommy at Newmarket but made it clear that he wanted to come back home to live with the family, which he would do within two months. In the meantime, Betty and Nicky were enrolled at Blessed Edmund Campion Secondary Modern whilst myself, Pat and May were set fair for St Joseph's junior, a split that required the purchase of mixed uniforms for two sets of children at two separate schools.

In preparation for the big day, Dad had taken us younger ones along the soon to be familiar bus route to St Clements, taking us along the Abingdon Road then, via Carfax, down the High Street with its many ancient colleges and shops, over the Magdalen Bridge where May Day was always celebrated with enthusiasm by half naked students jumping blindly into the icy Cherwell River below. Having crossed the bridge we arrived at a floral draped roundabout called The Plain, with a trio of roads leading to Cowley, Iffley and our venue Marston which took us into St. Clements where we decanted at a stop opposite the school gate and conveniently close to Souches sweet shop, a haven where we could buy, if we were lucky enough to have a few pennies in our pocket, sumptuous delights such as Lemon Sherbet.

The inaugural morning trip posed no problems and we arrived safely at the railed school gates to be met by the school head Mother Scholastica, dressed in her familiar black nun's habit with a pointy white shield round her neck and a rosary bead that dangled menacingly alongside a squadron of keys from her hipster belt. A short introduction completed in her office, situated upstairs and accessed by a narrow and steep iron stairway, she escorted us briefly around the pitifully tiny play area, pointed out the shabby, and often smelly, outdoor toilet block before introducing each of us in turn to our respective form teachers and fellow pupils. Most of the details of the day remain lost in a haze of fog save for the recollection of laughter and jibes about my accent and most particularly my pronouncement of three as *tree* and film as *Fill-em*, which would continue until they became bored and the novelty had worn off.

What happened on our way home has been locked in my memory, like a limpet clutching to a rock, aided by recollections from both Pat and May. The bell sounded the end of the day and, like a good shepherd, I gathered my flock to see us home, having ensured we had our own satchels, with tin cocoa mugs safely tucked inside. My eyes lit upon the approach of our number-eight bus destined for New Hinksey. It pulled up directly outside the school gates and in a fit of panic and over excitement, I decided that we would have to jump straight on as if fearing there would not be another bus for a hundred years. Aping *lassie*, a comic hero collie rounding up his sheep, and clutching both siblings, I attempted to usher them into a pen

that was now a moving bus platform with legs flailing, half of
them in the bus and the rest dancing on the car-filled road with
satchels rotating around our necks. In the melee I heard the
shouts and screams of onrushing teachers as the slow-motion
drama unfolded. The bus conductor was sweating profusely on
such a cold day and, not expecting three outriders to try and
hijack his moving bus, was frantically shouting something in
my sticky out ears. I am pretty sure it was not "welcome to my
bus". Mercifully, with the driver realising that the sea of hands
waving madly in his direction were not wishing him a happy
new year and, observing the potential carnage from his wing
mirror, he screeched his willing bus to a shuddering halt. This
allowed the teachers and other adults present to manhandle us
from our straddling position, half on and half off the bus, onto
the pavement, no doubt with a huge sigh of relief. A few words
of "advice" were offered into my ears before we were escorted to
the appointed stopping place to be reunited with the jelly legged
conductor as we climbed safely aboard the same bus. And, so
it was we had all *tree of us* survived our first day in an English
school, just.

Mother Scholastica could occasionally be free with her
use of a ruler across the fingers and wrists as could Mr Lunt if
provoked though most regarded him as an excellent teacher.
Miss Enright was quiet and pleasant. My time at St Joseph's
was mostly enjoyable and like a breath of fresh air compared
to school in Ireland. Friends were readily made and many of
us would transfer to Edmund Campion together, including
brothers Paul and Pat Curley, who eventually married my sister
May. Among pleasantly treasured days were regular visits to
nearby Angel Meadow, a vast green space of open fields used
as our sports field for running, football and cricket. Winter
swimming lessons took place at Temple Cowley baths whilst
the Summer saw the occasional visit to the nearby "Duck

Pond". Playground games included flick cards, obtained when purchasing a box of sweet white cigarettes with a red tip. The game involved "flicking" a card gripped between two inner fingers at a row of your opponent's cards lined up against a wall. A direct hit resulted in winning all of his cards to add to your own. During breaks there would be games like "tig", rounders, hopscotch and football, all contained within a very compact concrete playground.

A pleasing period towards the end of my stay at "Holy Joe's" was a friendship I developed with a lovely girl named Jennifer Cann. We would spend time on the playground steps just talking about goodness knows what. Now Jennie Adby and living in Australia, she recalled that she had once been caned and sent home by Mother Scholastica simply because her mum had sent her to school in warm trousers, not unnaturally, on what was a bitterly cold day. By contrast she found another nun, Sister Francis, was very kind. We went to the pictures together on a few occasions and visited her grandmother who lived down the Abingdon Road. It all came to an end when summer holidays started and I went off to big school to join with Betty and Nicky at Edmund Campion.

On a less fortunate personal note, a lasting distaste for cheese was prompted by Mother Scholastica. Eating school dinner at the nearby rectory road canteen I was presented with the no-option dish of cheese pie. One mouthful informed me that this was so horrible I could stomach no more and duly downed my knife and fork. The Eagle-eyed Mother Superior flew across the room and landed next to me, seemingly without ever moving her feet. Stern faced and with fire exiting from her hidden ears she looked at me and demanded I eat the dinner placed in front of me, pointing out to me, and half the school, that my mother had paid for the meal, although I was sure we were on free meals, and she was jolly well not going to see it wasted. My protestations that I could not eat the pie as it made me feel sick was met with further fury. She instantly planted her ample bottom next to my lean model, picked up the fork, pitched it into the remains of the dead pie and forced me to swallow its wretched contents. My complaints ignored, she fed me several distasteful unwanted spoons of the grunge before her come-uppance was re-delivered in spadefuls, across the table. In fairness, she suddenly displayed a more sorrowful look, produced some towels, issued instructions for someone to clean me and the table up and departed. That, sadly, was the end of my love affair with cheese. Since then, I have never knowingly eaten cheese except in a Lasagne, a quirk which seems to amuse my wife and children. One evening, during a bingo night out I had to explain what had happened when I turned down Mum's offer of my hitherto favourite tomato and cheese sandwich at the social club and her simple response said it all "she didn't need to do that".

*

Whist I was in full adventure mode on my first day at St Joseph's, Betty and Nicky were experiencing a different welcome at Blessed Edmund Campion, catching the same bus before changing onto the Iffley Road bus at the end of the High Street by Queens College. On arrival, with no nuns in sight, they were greeted by a senior pupil and led through a reception area, escorted down a few steps and led into the office of the headmaster Mr Taylor. A smart suited, stocky, be-spectacled and otherwise decent man, his friendly demeanour was spoilt somewhat when he drew close to you and confirmed his love for cigarettes by the emission of a horrible fag induced breath. Following introductions and other formalities, my elder siblings were taken to separate rooms and introduced to their respective teachers and pupils.

The building itself, unlike the run-down state of St Joseph's, was a new purpose- built school on two floors with indoor toilets and modern facilities including a domestic science room for cooking lessons as well as a fully equipped science laboratory. To the left of the school entrance, on its own site, stood a woodwork room. Each day a morning assembly would be held in the large concert-style hall that also served as a canteen. Alongside was an extensive fully equipped indoor gymnasium with showers and changing rooms. The school playground was large and beyond that, as far as the eye could see, were green fields used for sports and recreation.

Betty, somewhat shy and diffident, recalls being introduced to her teacher and classmates but has no real recollection of the day or indeed much of her school life. She found the move from a girls' only class in Ireland to the mixed classes of Edmund Campion a difficult transition. Joining a new school in mid-stream simply made it hard to integrate, as all the other pupils had already formed well established friendships or cliques, and was often referred to as "skinny Lizzie". She did establish a rapport with an Italian girl named Claudia, a girl with who a tough, worldly and devil may care attitude who kindly took her under her wing and protected her.

Nicky, on the other hand, was tasked by his teacher to inform his new classmates about his family. He duly told them about his five *brudders* and *tree* sisters in a broad Irish accent that wrought tears of laughter at his pronouncements. Nicky, however, had an easy-going nature, was good at football and sport generally and soon found friends and settled in well. Compared to Ireland he found English school life to be an altogether agreeable and enjoyable experience and he never needed to repeat the ploys he had used in Ireland in order to escape lessons. Both did have to overcome an embarrassing first day experience when they joined the other pupils for lunch in the canteen. Asked to produce a shilling each for their lunch neither were aware of the requirement or indeed had any money. The cook, although unable to provide them with a full meal, fortunately took pity on them and provided a meal of Semolina! With the assistance of the school secretary and our parents the matter was soon resolved and meals duly provided thereafter.

Meanwhile, Mehael returned home again around February to be enrolled at Edmund Campion to join Betty and Nicky. On his first day he was subjected to the usual nonsense regarding his accent but in this case the teacher stepped in and appointed the tall and tough looking Patrick Reidy to look after him and the two by all accounts got on well. Assigned to Mrs Bedlington's class, he soon became one of her favourites. Aware that he had passed up the chance to join a grammar school she recognised that he was a very bright boy who should be encouraged and in his own words, "I think she saw me as a future great Irish poet or artist" and that she would be lauded for discovering such a talent. He did by all accounts produce some novel poetry for which he received a number of school commendations and rewards. Now it has to be said that being a Poet and linked to the likes of Dylan Thomas and Oscar Wilde and even more so, following in the footsteps of Irish Literary giants such as W.B Yeates, Heaney, Joyce and Behan would have been an exacting task, especially given that many who have possessed unique or outrageous talents had contrary traits bordering on being dangerous to their own health. This was accepted as the price to be paid for bestowed genius perhaps. So, maybe he had a lucky escape and his subsequent career choices actually saved him from a life of infamy, misery and penury. Mehael was a dab hand in his use of charcoal as an artistic tool and produced one beautiful sketch of four modern houses opposite our home which earned him a school award for his skill but again this did not feature in his future career.

Mehael's literary and academic ability earned him praise and he was always in the top two in the annual examinations. His abilities resulted in his promotion to Prefect and ensured he had a gilded life at Edmund campion. He actually got on well with PE teacher Mr Powley, who considered he had some potential for the school football team. He had played as goalkeeper in a Junior Hurling team for the Christian Brothers in Ireland. Granny Carton was happy that he was selected in this position because it was considered far safer than being involved in the mad headlong lunacy that often resembled a sword battle that took place up field where injury was so common. A fine footballer he may have been, playing at Inside-Right, or a Number 10 in today's world. However, he possessed a major flaw in his game, namely the frequent tendency to pick the ball up when it came within sight, having been so used to Gaelic football. It seemingly took ages to eradicate but once he had finally been re-trained to keep his hands to himself, whilst on the soccer pitch at least, he played for the school team where he amply rewarded the teacher's patience through his goalscoring prowess using either foot in a very Roy of the Rovers style. His football ability was also noticed by talent scouts of the Boys Brigade watching boys playing in Hinksey Park. He happily agreed to play for them for a few months before Mum realised that they were not Catholic and requested him to leave.

No doubt rubbing salt into the wounded ego of other pupils he was soon chosen to sing in the choir and at concerts, having inherited a fine voice from Mum. To our parents' excitement he decided that he would like to play the guitar and they forked out the then princely sum of 12/6d (63p) to purchase one from HQ General and Supply with the condition that he learned to play it properly. He performed, singing and playing at the end of term concerts. On one occasion he was up against the school girls' favourite, Martin Doyle, who sang some Marty Wilde songs such as "Teenager in Love". He responded creditably with a Lonnie Donegan hit, "Pub with No Beer" and, to Mum's delight, a rendition of the Irish song, "The Boys from The County Armagh", with the favourite only narrowly securing first prize. Dad, however, was less impressed when Mehael endlessly practiced and learned to play, with some degree of success, a complex arrangement of the tune "Apache", a number one hit for the group named The Shadows, causing him to complain "can't you fecking play anything else?". The dreamed of route to stardom and riches was somewhat halted when, within a few months he finished his schooling at fifteen and with a clutch of SLCs (School Leaving Certificates) went off to work as an Articled Clerk with solicitors Darby & Son in the fussy and staid legal profession.

Mehael's departure meant that Nicky, one of the few still in short trousers, grabbed the chance to inherit his elder brother's long pair only to discover they were a poor and baggy fit that made him look as though he was auditioning for the part of a circus clown. At this point, and to his evident relief, Mum and Dad decided he should have a new pair of his own.

Chapter Twelve

Teachers and life at Edmund Campion

Succeeding in the Eleven-Plus examination guaranteed a Grammar School place, intended, to separate the sheep from the goats and identify and educate the best academic brains destined to become movers and shakers in the brave new world. The rest of us, comprising the vast majority and including myself, were destined for the Secondary Modern school, supposedly with the emphasis on the three Rs; Reading, wRiting and aRithmatic (maths) as well as practical subjects such as cooking (Domestic Science) for the girls and woodwork for the boys. This was long before the days when boys would don funny white hats and dress themselves in pinny's standing by ovens and wrench-clutching girls would work happily in oil covered pits for the joy of dismantling engine parts. Another R, for Religion was a significant subject throughout school life.

In any event, September 1960 saw teenage Mehael join the world of work and me off to Edmund Campion, in the company of Betty and Nicky, exchanging the green and grey uniform of St Joseph's for the badged navy-blue blazer and short grey trousers of Edmund campion. Dad had by now moved to Cowley works but our hard-working parents were by no means wealthy and in common with many other pupils we were initially entitled to free school meals. Uniforms for us boys included hand me downs from siblings and neighbours as well as second hand purchases. We were not alone as the majority of people were in the same boat so we were not in the least embarrassed.

Accompanying Betty and Nicky to school by bus took us past the famous Iffley Road running track where athlete Roger Bannister broke the four-minute mile barrier on 6th May 1954. The alternative, cost free and most frequently taken journey, was the forty-minute trip down Abingdon Road, walking in the opposite direction to the bus, before forking left to reach and climb to the peak of Donnington Bridge, a very old and at its highest point scary narrow pedestrian bridge that strung across the Thames near Weirs Lane. The opening of the new modern bridge in October 1962, offered a huge improvement encompassing a wide pedestrian walkway on either side of the two-lane carriageways and encouraged me to use a bicycle thereafter. I well recall an episode that occurred years later, on my first cycle venture, as it nearly landed me face down in hospital or worse. Having crossed the apex of the bridge I decided to take up position ready to veer right at the road next to the old confectionery shop situated about 100 yards ahead. Enjoying the ride, my unhurried demeanour changed in a flash brought on by the screeching noise of brakes that forced me to a dead stop, though not literally, I turned to see a car door flung wide open and observed a decanting, fist waving man with hair standing up as though magnetised from above, shouting furiously, "you bloody young fool, what the hell did you think you were doing"? Not being quite as dim as the weather, I immediately gathered he appeared none too pleased so I opened my defence by mouthing "sorry", though not quite sure why, before shaking like a jelly as I remounted my bike and proceeded on my wobbly way. I was relieved to discover he was not a teacher on way to school and that I was not on my way to a hospital.

Arriving at Edmund Campion on day one I immediately met up with some old classmates from St Josephs, we chatted excitedly about our summer break, before breaking off into teams for what would become the usual early morning kick about in the wide playground. We were formed into groups, directed into the morning assembly for the usual outline of social events and school matters, the religious ritual of prayer and the singing of hymns, which to me always seemed rather jolly. My favourite hymn was the traditional, "O Mother Blest, whom God Bestows" with a chorus that still resonates with me even today.

"Thou art clement, thou art chaste, Mary, thou art fair;
Of all mothers sweetest, best, none with thee compare".

The jolly uplifting singing in praise of Mary, after whom Mum was named, was in direct contrast to life of Edmund Campion himself, after whom the school was named and the naming of three of the four "Houses" into which every pupil was allocated for the duration of their school life.

J K Rowling invoked the four-house system in her Harry Potter books. The four "Houses", in my old school, included three named after Catholic martyrs who suffered a cruel death, which perhaps was not quite so jolly but demonstrated the values of principle, belief, conviction and bravery to very high standards. I was allocated to the House named after Thomas More, Chancellor to Henry 8th, beheaded because he refused to accept the supremacy of the King over the Pope. Another House was named after John Fisher, chaplain to Henry and said to be held in high esteem, but not sufficiently to save his head, for the same reasons. Margaret, giving her name to Clithero House, was horribly crushed to death for refusing to enter a plea to a charge of harbouring Catholic priests. The remaining house bore the name of John Henry Newman, who was the only one to have died naturally following a long life as a theologian and a poet. He was heavily involved in the famed Oxford Movement, ahead his conversion to Catholicism. His frequently quoted statements highlighted ways of living.

"To live is to change and to be perfect is to change often".

He spent many years around the poorer people of Littlemore in Oxford, where a church stands proudly in his name.

The three grisly deaths and subsequent martyrdom may be considered mild compared to the excruciating death of Edmund Campion himself. An English Jesuit, he was arrested by priest hunters, imprisoned at the Tower of London, tortured on a rack for days and subsequently convicted by a jury of High Treason. then hung, drawn and quartered at Tyburn. Whatever religious belief one now has, there can be little doubt that these Catholic leaders possessed enormous courage in standing by their convictions in the face of the most extreme pressure to conform.

The school had its own motto, "Ad Majorem dei Gloriam, meaning "For the greater glory of God", from Latin Motto of the Society of Jesuits, attributed to Saint Ignatius of Loyola and incorporated within the school song. The song itself, which all pupils would have sung a thousand times concluded with these words:

"In paths of learning show the way, with standards high on field of play, like you, Our Patron, true we'll stand, To God, our Queen and native land".

We could have attended the school in the same road where we lived, sparing us a lot of travelling and expense and avoiding my own near fatal experiences with bus and cycle. Mum and Dad had themselves been brought up within the strict confines of the Catholic faith and were determined that we would also follow in the same tradition, believing in its capacity to educate and develop us children to face the future ahead, academically and morally. Travelling in all weathers either walking or by bus or bicycle we sensed how to cope; mended bike tyres and wheels; learned how to save money by keeping feet on the ground and bums off bus ensuring there was enough money to buy "jammy dodgers" at school play time or purchase a paper bag of bashed up custard cream biscuits from a local shop, where the owner quickly realised that it was more profitable than selling them intact.

Nicky recalled the evening that Dad had given a once only pep talk, asking us to do our best at school so that we would have a good future and reminding us of what he and Mum had given up to come to England.

My first year at Edmund Campion stands out because I had somehow managed to be Top of the Form in the annual examinations, much to my surprise and my parents delight, especially Dad who waxed lyrical about me going to university. I was soon to discover the raising of expectations can be a millstone around a slender neck. One year on and my examination results saw a spectacular fall from grace. The worst day of my school life began when the results from the different subjects filtered through to the form teacher, Mr Powley, tasked with aggregating them and calculate overall scores to decide class placings. First up was Woodwork where Mr Westlake the carpenter had judged my efforts worthy of 9/100. A gasp rang out around the classroom from my fellow pupils and Mr Powley decided that it should surely be 90 so asked for a re-check. Now,

I was all too well aware that in the previous year ninety per cent of marks were based on the theory of identifying wood types and tools and how to design, measure and cut angles etc. and relied more on a half decent memory than any skill, whereas this time we were required to produce an actual piece of practical woodwork.

All too soon, the checker re-appeared and confirmed the original mark and, as I gradually sank beneath my desk, howls of laughter erupted at the sight of my exhibited craftsmanship, unhelpfully supplied by Mr Woodwork to justify his score. I have to admit that no self-respecting coat would ever wish to hang itself upon my unique work of art for fear of slipping under the throes of passing muddy feet as for all the world it resembled an upside-down duck rather than an intended coat hanger. My wife and children would fall over laughing if I were to suggest doing anything remotely complicated in the house. In the longer term my practical skills did have the added bonus that my children do not feel any urgency to call upon me to undertake any serious DIY work, unless they wanted a shelf that resembled the leaning Tower of Pisa, which today would probably qualify as the design of a genius, Perhaps, I was merely just ahead of my time.

Mr Whitehouse, the Music teacher, was a pleasant chipper fellow with a huge amount of enthusiasm for his subject. He introduced us to the folk singer Joan Baez and often played her music as well as encouraging us to pay attention to classical music in the form of the Planet Suite by Gustav Holst and, more daringly in my later years, to Ravel's Bolero which had the class swaying along in dream like trance. Sadly, from my perspective, his second-year exam was again more practical and required me to compose a short tune with quavers, demi-quavers etc on a sheet of paper. Unlike Mehael, who could play and sing, I was content to untunefully sing *doe ray me, I'd like a cup of tea* and enjoy the music but my understanding of, and ability to compose, was only marginally superior to my woodwork skills. My music mark slumped from the dizzy upper seventies of the first year to a mere forty-five, further adding to my abseiling down the class rankings. I never did get to hear what my piece of composed music actually sounded like and thankfully neither did anyone else but I fear that it was more rhubarb and custard than Rogers and Hammerstein. Consequently, within twelve months, my first in the class ranking had slumped to a humiliating twenty ninth in year two.

By some miracle, and to the astonishment of my family, who mostly consider me tone deaf and unable to even clap in time, I was chosen to sing in the school choir at a major event at Oxford Town Hall. Still dressed in short trousers, sporting a new smart white shirt and school tie we performed reasonably well enough for Mum to say she had really enjoyed it, thus doubling the miracle.

This was the year, as I recall, when I had been referred to a specialist at the Radcliffe Infirmary as the school nurse had raised concerns about my low weight for age. Consequently, I spent a couple of weeks at the Churchill Hospital where they undertook a lot of tests and fed me with the best food available. My brother Nicky and a neighbourhood friend, Charlie Collins, used to come and visit me and we idled away many days by playing football on the large green outside the ward as I was not confined to a bed. The attempt to improve my weight failed but, unfortunately, doctors identified that I had a heart murmur. Dad informed me solemnly that I would not be allowed to take part in any sport, including swimming in the local pool, for the next rather miserable six months. The only consolation was that I was excused PE lessons and cross-country running, spending the time moping around or reading. Perhaps that is why my parents generously accepted my reasoning regarding woodwork and music for the year's poor exam results. There were no recriminations or arguments and I was left to reflect on the level of expectation and the need to revise more carefully and the remaining years would see me always in the top six to the satisfaction of my parents, courtesy of higher marks in my favoured subjects that offset my still moderate scores in the practical skills department.

In any event, after the six months, I was released back into the sporting arena but advised against strenuous activity, whatever that meant, presumably to avoid a sudden collapse whilst excitingly scoring a winning goal. It was explained that I could still suffer bouts of tiredness and resulting irritability at times which provided me with a ready excuse for any odd behaviour. The teachers were advised about my "illness" so I rarely came into any contact with many of their chosen disciplinary weapons.

Newcomers to the school after me, including my siblings May, Pat, Paul, Ann and David encountered these and various other teachers. Sisters Betty, May and Ann received Domestic Science lessons in classes with either Miss Clarey or Miss Anderson and any boys in the vicinity tended to gather outside to scrounge a few fresh baked cakes.

White gloved Mr Stevens usually took charge of the newcomers in year one. He compensated for his lack of mobility by firing, with uncanny accuracy, a flurry of Exocet-like missiles, disguised as coloured chalks or rubbers, towards his chosen target. Enigmatic Mr Powley sporadically lived up to his strong man reputation in a poem dedicated to him. Fortunately, he attributed the limits of my athletic talents, my inability to vault a gymnasium horse or even reach the sandpit in the long jump, together with my foresight in limbo dancing to the other side of the high jump, were associated with my physical issues rather than lack of effort so I was rarely troubled by him.

Ferocious looking and Deputy Head, Mrs Bedlington, notwithstanding her doting upon our eldest brother, was another who could be free with the use of a ruler across the fingers or a strap, mostly left me alone because of my love of History as I possessed a good memory for events and could write with some fluency about them. Mr. Craine, was the well-liked, Renault owning, French teacher who considered it highly amusing for me to speak French in my Irish accent, though I cannot recall ever being asked to translate the word *begorrah*. Mrs Edwards was an enthusiastic in Art and Craft lessons. She did her best to encourage pupils to be creative tried to persuade me to take up teaching as a profession but I was well aware that my small under-weight stature would be no match for coping with unruly pupils. Mr Makin, the English teacher, was a kind and gentle soul, who encouraged interest in English Literature and the very tall Mr Astle proved to be a very able maths teacher for me.

My own artistic vent came to the fore through Mr Hughes, the slightly eccentric science teacher who maintained pupil interest through a fierce growl on his face and by using a range of practical demonstrations involving Bunsen Burners and exploding kettles, all in the goggle-free days before Health and Safety strictures. He was also responsible for writing and producing the play that always finished off the annual school concert, in more ways than one. He chose me to act the role of Boo-Boo, the companion of Yogi Bear, who appeared in a popular TV series named The Yogi Bear Show. I had to be dressed as a bear so Mum had her work cut out to ensure I looked the part for my thespian debut but she liked the idea that Boo-Boo always sported a purple bow-tie set against his brown/golden bearskin colour as this reminded her of Wexford. Designing, cutting and stitching together with Betty, they ensured I was fully kitted out for my potential Oscar winning role, where I would utter the words that would be remembered through history as the day a new giant of the stage made his debut and so nearing the end, with some of the audience still actually awake, I uttered the well-rehearsed and immortal words *"The ranger sure ain't gonna like it Yogi"*. And that was it, except it wasn't.

The most exciting part followed after the play and I realised then that standing on a stage or speaking in front of people held no fears for me at all. Whilst we were backstage the headmaster was addressing the audience and I grabbed one of the props, a CND (Campaign for Nuclear Disarmament) banner which had been used in the play although the context escaped me. On the spur of the moment and taking care not to reveal myself, I pushed the sign through a parting in the stage curtain and waved it around. The audience suddenly woke up and started screaming and shouting much to the bafflement of the Head, Mr Taylor, who was facing the audience and thus oblivious to what was happening behind. I quickly withdrew the sign and he proceeded with his talk. Adrenalin soon got the better of me and I once more pushed the sign through the curtain to the renewed delight of the audience and the utter dismay of the Head. He frantically tore at the curtain seeking the culprit but I quickly withdrew and disappeared from his sight. Order was soon restored but I had been bitten by the bug, drinking in the nectar of hearing an audience in response. I knew standing up in public would hold no fears for me and demonstrated the appealing power of spontaneous action and this unscripted episode was a confidence boosting catalyst that would form a big part of my future career and life.

I am not certain whether our parents were ever fully aware of the character, and sometimes eccentric nature, of some the teachers they had entrusted with the education of their precious offspring, the basic foundation stone for all of our future prospects and a crucial part of their decision to leave

Ireland. These, then, were some of the professionals who had an influence upon each of our lives.

In the late sixties I would eventually join my older brothers and sister Betty in the strange and wonderful world of work but not necessarily in the profession for which I had for so long dreamt.

Chapter Thirteen

Life in early sixties

The beginning of my teenage years in the early sixties are regarded by many as the infancy of popular music. Hitherto music was comprised of sentimental ballads and dance bands. All of a sudden there was an explosion of colour and light as revolution thronged the air. Popular crooner and television host Max Bygrave's, with his song *"fings ain't what they used to be"* probably didn't realise just what a momentous change was about to arrive for the next decade, with the period from 1963 being especially vibrant. The ensuing years saw rapid changes in culture and style, mini-skirts and the propensity for teenage boys to lather and control their hairstyles with Brylcream was curtailed with the advent of Beatle mania and the fashion for much longer hair. Elvis, after army service, returned to the pop scene. Cliff Richard who had previously caused panic within the UK Establishment as he was seen as a malign influence on the youngsters, with his rapid gyrating hips and pouting suggestive actions, now remodelled himself. The UK Establishment feared that their own post war view of tradition and certainty was about to end. They may have been right but not in the way they believed.

My parent's generation, my father more so than my mother, would watch on in amazement as musical tastes resounded across the country and the airwaves. The Beatles released their first hits *"please please me"* and the record breaking head-shaker *"She loves you"* and evolved into a worldwide phenomenon with audiences dominated by screeching mini-skirted girls. I shall never forget the look on Dad's face as he sat in his armchair and watched on TV as action man Freddie Garrity, from Freddie and the Dreamers, pranced around the stage to their hit, *I'm telling you now* prompting him to comment "what is that effing eejit doing!" He astounded us all when, on listening to Gary Puckett sing *young girl*, he commented *"That boy can certainly sing, he has a great voice"*.

I was still at school at the beginning of the decade. With the old wireless playing passively in the background, schooldays followed a familiar pattern. Breakfast consisted mainly of tea, with maybe a slice of toast and jam, followed by a bowl of porridge, cooked in a huge saucepan, salted for taste and sweetened with sugar. Fortified with this flaky intake we were then dispatched into the day with an aura of hot steam invisibly surrounding our frames as we trundled out to greet the school day ahead. Our daily diet at school included free milk, delivered to the playground for the morning break in one-third of a pint bottles that rested tightly in steel crates where we helped ourselves, and more than once if there were leftovers. I was one of the playground sellers of tin captured wafers and jammy dodgers available in exchange for a penny and would spend as much time swatting away hand dippers attempting to Robin Hood my goodies as I would collecting the pennies. I am sure that we had free school meals at the beginning of our school life but Mum and Dad were very proud and determined that they would pay their own way so it was not long before we were shilling out with our classmates to purchase our dinners, alternatively comprising over-cooked sausages, shepherd's or mince pie, something loosely described as a stew or a portion of liver and to my horror, the cheese flan. All were served with a helping of mostly watery mashed or boiled spuds and a portion of veg, most notably peas that were best described as bullets. Being Catholic, fish was always served on Friday, regarded as a fasting day from meat to reflect that Jesus was said to have died on that day. A second course commonly included apple pie, rice pudding or semolina, jam roly-poly or my favourite, cornflakes atop a treacle tart, all accompanied by custard that was more often as runny as a waterfall. Nevertheless, in common with most pupils during this period the dinners provided a decent meal especially for hard up parents.

Mum was a dab hand at baking and the enticing aroma of her warm freshly baked bread stimulating our nostrils, like the scent of sweet peas on a summer's day, as we entered the front door on arriving home, was an absolute treat. Hastily dropping bags and suspending our coats onto poking out hooks at the end of the long hall, we would crush into the living room, where laid before us on the dining table would be a circular baked white or brown loaf, separated by a cross into four distinct sections or, on other days, a platter full of warm scones, accompanied by creamy butter and homemade jam. One very appealing treat was when the fresh bread was matched with a large dish of stewed apple. The fun of spreading the mashed apple onto the naked slice of bread before eagerly devouring it is still fresh in my mind even to this day. Now the French are quite rightly renowned for their fresh baked baguettes, that do indeed reach taste buds that other loaves can never equal, they could not hold a candle to that baked by Mum.

Her apple pie, often laced with cloves for enhanced flavour, may have been legendry but her sponge cakes were an especial favourite of Uncle Oliver, who years later teased Betty that her cake was "almost as good as your mum's" whilst Dad's favourite was baked apple with sultanas.

It could not have been easy for Mum or aunty Margaret in the early days at Vicarage Road, sharing the kitchen and cooking facilities. Although all the children, excepting twins Paul and Ann were at school all day, it would still have been an exacting role combining cooking, washing and cleaning with looking after two young children and tensions were bound to increase. There is an old saying that two women sharing an oven often leads to strife. In any event, Mehael once found himself in the middle of one such domestic storm. Arriving home from school one afternoon he met Mum crying and in a distressed state, apparently having had a heated exchange with Aunt Margaret. Not one to hang about, he jumped in with both feet firmly in the fire and shot a broadside at aunty, causing her also to fall into a tearful state.

Returning home after a hard day's work, Dad was upset for Mum and he and Michael were annoyed by Mehael's fanning of the flames. Calming emotions, they sensibly negotiated a peace accord which resulted in a fresh set of rules being applied. Washing facilities for our family were hereafter to be undertaken in the front room and not at the kitchen sink. A wooden table was stationed behind the unused front door, to store all the appropriate washing and cooking equipment. Access to the kitchen or outside toilet was to be via the garden and coal store entrance and not through the living room as previously. This required us all, and more frequently Mum, to have to go into the hall, down the long dark passage past the coal storage, out into the garden regardless of the prevailing weather conditions and walk round the side of the house, not especially easy or convenient, in order to obtain water for washing and cleaning and then return to dispose of the same. In fairness to

Aunty Margaret, she had lived in the house before we had all descended upon her and that alone must have been a shock to the system. It transpired that at the time of the incident she was also expecting her first child Andrew, born eight months later. Given the combination of her pregnancy and the pressure on Mum of having to cope with so much recent change it was hardly surprising that there were some tense moments and the odd flare up.

The few months of the new accord, although not ideal and initially difficult, soon passed in a spirit of co-operation and goodwill before another major and lasting change took place. Michael and Margaret purchased their own house in Temple Road, Cowley, in anticipation of a growing family and near to where he worked. Dad decided to buy Vicarage Road, hitherto a shared rental home, from the owner, Charlie "porridge man" Gardener, so named due to the fixed breakfast he served in his nearby guest house. So it was that aunty and uncle left, on good terms, in the summer. Mum and Dad were able to move upstairs to the privacy of their own bedroom and the front room resumed its rightful place as the lounge. Vicarage Road now belonged to us and over the next couple of decades would earn a well justified reputation as a warm and welcoming home to all and sundry, embracing the excitement of the sixties and the turbulence of the seventies.

Mehael was the first to leave education for the world of work. His first job as an Articled Clerk earned him the sum of £3 a week of which mom deducted £2 for his keep. The staid and stuffy legal profession was not really suited to his questioning and active mind. He interpreted the expression- "tis better to give than to receive"- to mean he was pre-destined to give orders rather than follow them so he moved on to work at Pressed Steel as a better paid stock controller followed by a spell at Aldens' Butchers, located in the covered market. He recalls with relish his first musical purchase, for Mum, a Frank Ifield yodelling number called *"I Remember You"* which she loved and would often sing it for family and visitors. It was whilst working in the covered market he met (yet another) Margaret. Fuelled by testosterone he desired to take her to Bournemouth and decided to sell his guitar to pay for the trip, much to the displeasure of our parents. Margaret later fell pregnant and, with no home of their own, they lived with us for some months, re-occupying the front room and making use of the famed red sofa before their son Noel, and our parents first grandchild, was born in December 1963.

Around this time, Uncle Liam paid a visit from a place called Hemel Hempstead, some 25 miles north of London. He counselled Mehael he could earn good money working for Brooke Bond and invited him to join him for a fresh start. What Liam failed to mention was that he had already applied to go to Western Australia, on a one-way ticket to the Perth sunshine, leaving Mehael to quickly find alternative accommodation in nearby Redbourn. Subsequent to Liam's departure, he continued to work very successfully for the tea company. Dad was pleased he was getting on so well and Mum was very proud to hear he was sporting a Wexford purple strip denoting his promotion. Sadly, his marriage broke up and Margaret left, causing Mehael to leave the company to look after the children Noel, Margaret, Marie and Elizabeth, only for Margaret to return to obtain custody. He subsequently worked for a number of companies including Everest Windows, and T & H Tyres, from where was made redundant when the business was sold, shortly after re-mortgaging and moving house. Working for a firm called Abbeyfoam brought him into contact with his future wife, Barbara. His job was to evaluate and sell the product which involved keeping homes warm by the injection of foam insulation into the cavity wall. When he attended her at home it appears that her own daughter Becky instantly connected with him and followed him around the house, impressing Barbara. To Mum's joy, a friendship was struck and they later married. Mehael decided he needed to get back into mainstream business for more security. He was recruited for a job at Golden West Foods who supplied buns and soft drinks to the McDonalds chain, he being employed as a Purchase and Materials Controller. Combined with Barbara's own employment at Hoover, it has enabled them both to support their respective children and grandchildren over many years. He still chuckles as he recalls Mum asking him on numerous occasions whether he would be wearing a white coat, a potent symbol to her that he was improving his life. He remained in this lucrative job until his retirement. Our parents would indeed have been proud of such an achievement given the trials and tribulations that had to be overcome.

*

In the summer of 1961, Betty bade farewell to Edmund Campion and began the search for work. Shortly before, the school headmaster announced at morning assembly that he was trying to identify the girl who had greeted an important visitor and looked after him before ensuring he was comfortably seated by the headmaster's office. The visitor congratulated the school on the manners and attitude of the school and this is why the headmaster was anxious to discover this pupil's identity. It transpired this well-mannered young lady was none other than our lovely sister.

On leaving school, a friend suggested she try making enquiries at Kemp Hall Bindery, a factory originally located close to the old police station near Folly Bridge. She knocked on the door, eloquently stated her interest and was immediately interviewed by Mr Lee the manager. Normally seen as a fiery and impatient man, he took a distinct liking to this friendly, poised and classy Irish lady and sensibly hired her on the spot. This was before the avalanche of rules and regulations that smother such initiative by employers today and any reference to a CV in those days would more likely have led to a discussion of the merits or otherwise of the 2CV, a French car often referred to as "four wheels with an umbrella". It was at Kemp Hall that she met her future husband Michael Murphy, albeit not an Irish Mick. Fate had dictated that he would join the company a couple of years earlier. He really wanted to work at University Press in Walton Street but to his dismay, he discovered he was colour blind which precluded him from his preferred career choice. Instead, he was advised to *get on his bike* to Kemp Hall to enquire about work as a bookbinder, which he duly did and was offered a job. Their recollections of working at the factory, which later moved to bigger premises in Osney, reveal that workers even had to ask permission to go to the toilet and some of the supervisors would act as mini tyrants. Nevertheless, they both remained, made long-lasting friendships with colleagues and were married. At this point, they were poised to leave as they required somewhere to live and had sought jobs at bookbinders at Exeter. According to Mick, Manager Lee was distraught at the thought of losing Betty, his long serving and reliable worker who had a rare knack of smoothing feathers during occasional fractious working incidents. He offered them both the use of a rented flat by the river, next door to the factory, and thus persuaded them to stay, pleasing the manager and delighting our mother.

Nicky joined Dad and uncle Michael at the Cowley car plant a year after Betty started work at Kemp Hall, and there he would remain for many years. It was common for generations of the same family, from grandfather to father and siblings, to work at

Cowley, which then directly employed around 30,000 people. In Nicky's case he worked in the Trim shop where he met his future wife-the short haired petite brunette Margaret, whose own sister Wendy and brother John also worked at the factory. The Trim shop women were largely employed in sewing covers for the car seats. The Cowley connection continues today, with Nicky's own son Darren and grandson Adam continuing to carry the flag for the Cartons.

Nicky initially worked on a boy's job in the Trim shop as rules prevented under 21s taking a man's job and being paid accordingly. When he worked in the Body shop his job was to receive car body parts from nearby Pressed Steel and to drop the steel carcass into waiting engines, hopefully making a successful connection as any mis-judgment would halt the line and disrupt production.

Girlfriend Margaret became a warmly welcomed and regular visitor to Vicarage Road. Their decision to marry in 1967, caused a bit of a stir as Granny Carton would be also attending. Dad, although not especially religious himself, asked if he would consider having a Catholic wedding. Nicky had to enter negotiations with Margaret and her generously minded parents, Doris and Bill, who were content to go along with what the couple decided. In the event they were happily married in the Parish Church of St Andrews in Headington with myself as the inappropriately named Best Man. The reception was held at The Civil Defence Club in Gordon Street, just around the corner from our house.

Nicky was a keen footballer and played in the Trim Shop team in the year they won the inter departmental trophy. This was a fiercely contested major event in the Cowley workers social calendar, with all divisions represented. However, his day of glory was thwarted due to appendicitis and was unable to play in the final but he nevertheless received his prized trophy. The

Trim shop foreman and team manager was Ron Bateman. Ron kindly donated the wedding flowers and a Vase to Nicky and Margaret as a present thus saving them a considerable outlay which they greatly appreciated.

He worked at Cowley until the year 2000 when he accepted a pension and redundancy package. Daughter Lisa prepared a CV for him when he was looking for other work. He had always wanted to be a postman, just like our dad, and had previously been accepted as a postie when he applied for a job during one of the numerous absences from Cowley due to strike action. He became a Messenger and served as postman for eight colleges whilst based at Wadham College for seven years, describing the post as "my dream job".

The additional working wages of Betty and Nicky contributed significantly to the family finances during the sixties period. Mum obtained an evening job at Lyons corner shop where she worked in the kitchen and I vividly remember the delight when she arrived home, often to be armed with a bag of unsold cakes, shared amongst the staff and laid out before us on the table. My personal favourite was the delicious cream and jam sandwich roll.

In the meantime, slow Improvements were being made to Vicarage Road. Although we still had an outside toilet and the old tin bath in the kitchen, we frequently had to await our turn in the steadily cooling and murkier water, until it was replaced by one installed alongside the coal store in the passage. In a scene reminiscent of a Dickens novel, tired grey woollen blankets were framed around the enamel bath with an old curtain draped across the tiny window that overlooked the garden. An ancient lead pipe supplying water fed from the gas geyser poked its way through a hole in the kitchen wall but it did at least provide an improved degree of privacy for a quiet, warm soak whilst freeing up the kitchen for anyone wanting a drink, a personal wash or waiting to wash dishes or clothes.

Around the same time Slipper Baths were opened around the corner in Lake Street, so called because they resembled a slipper that was deeper at one end with a sloping back designed for comfort. It was estimated that at least a third of all homes in Oxford were without bathrooms. To meet a growing need, the council developed municipal baths at a cost of six old-pence per bath or a bargain four pence for a shower. They were a blessing for us all and I certainly appreciated the warm cosy Saturday night half-hour soak whilst reading the Green Un, published on Saturday nights and delivered to the local off licence around 6pm, it contained all the football results and featured Oxford City or United on the front pages. So engrossed did I become, on one occasion, that all the lights went out and I found myself still in the bath in complete darkness, with only a distant muffle of keys to alert me that the warden was closing up. I shouted very loudly that I was still on the premises. Suddenly, the lights reignited and a shocked head banged on my door demanding to know why I was still on the premises, presumably I was well past my allotted time. The look on his face as I departed, after the quickest spin dry ever, suggested that my antics had robbed him of an extra pint of beer at the local Seven Stars. However, the baths were underused and it was decided they would be closed down a year later. That was the catalyst for Dad to decide that we should have our own bathroom at home, extending out through the kitchen into the coal store.

Thinking back on those early days the very mention of coal brings to mind the suffocating smog that once floated over Oxford and our street when prevailing conditions combined. Our coal shed relied on deliveries from the dust splattered coalman who would hump hessian type bag loads of the black rock down our long passage before heaving the contents into the wood surrounded concreted store. From there Mum, or one of us children if we were within ear shot, would collect enough of the black stone, in a cone shaped metal carrier, to be placed by the fire. It was sometimes necessary to use an axe or hammer to break up the large anthracitic lumps. Although providing fuel for the lovely cosy fire inside during the coldest nights it helped create a fog of immense density. Taking a step outside the front door you would occasionally be very fortunate if you could see much beyond the end of your nose, which in the case of the "Carton Conk" was a fair stretch. The Clean Air Act of 1956 was the government response to the Great London Smog that had an impact on the whole country. It sparked a significant increase in the use of lighter smokeless fuels and, even from my own perspective, I noticed there were far less smoggy days in just a few years. Builders were chosen to turn half our coal shed into a modern bathroom and were extremely fortunate to work for my parents. Our ever kind and generous Mum looked after them as if they were her own family, supplying them with cups of tea and cake as well as cooking a warm dinner to boot. I have often wondered whether the endless excuses for the bathroom taking longer to build, much to the annoyance of Dad, was their desire to enjoy the freebies provided

I have no idea how much the bathroom cost, as our parents always kept such things from us, but a suitable deduction for Mum's catering would probably have resulted in them paying us money! One evening, after the builders had departed for the day, I noticed that a water pipe outside the back door was slightly dripping. Applying my natural plumbing craft, hastening to tighten the nut, I succeeded in making matters even worse with the tap itself coming off in my slender hand. I watched as Niagara Falls appeared in front of my eyes as I danced around, the gushing pipe in one hand and the forlorn tap in the other with neither destined to connect. Desperate efforts to stem the flow resulted in my drenched screams for help being answered by Mum, Betty and Nicky, no doubt less than well delighted to be dragged away from watching the latest episode of "Rawhide". Once the fits of laughter had subsided, a water engineer was summoned, the tap reunited with its pipe and an order for Noah's Ark 2 cancelled. And another potential career path sunk.

Waterworks was not my only minor calamity. One Christmas, whilst putting up the decorations in our lounge, I managed to pierce a gas pipe that surrounded the ceiling above the lounge door. We recognised the slow hissing sound of escaping gas and duly turned off the supply. The Gas Board was informed via the red, penny guzzling telephone box a couple of hundred yards down the road and urgent arrangements made for a fitter to arrive the next morning.

Fitter (engineer in today's language) was not a word Dad would ascribe to the hapless fellow he met and led into the lounge. Describing to us the situation that followed would have graced a comedy show. Having led him into the room, the aged man with huge rimmed spectacles that made him look more like a frogman wandered around the room, climbed his stepladder shouted to Dad in the next room *"I have found the root of the problem"*. Dad, somewhat startled, found he was staring at what "frogman" had identified as the pipe was actually a curtain rail above the doorway. Pointing out this fact, he then ushered the would-be candidate for *Specsavers* to where his son (me) had pierced the pipe with a drawing pin. The embarrassed man promptly welded the pin pricked pipe and departed with his tail between his legs and Dad in a fit of giggles as he repeated the story to us.

The bathroom was eventually finished and thankfully ended the long walk down the back garden, sometimes by the light of the silvery moon but more often in the darkest and dismal of nights where spent sunflower heads and tree branches were imagined as eerie assassins waiting in the night, ready to pounce on and devour a lone beer filled ginger haired reveller.

This improvement afforded much needed relief to Mum and us older children tasked with transporting the heavy-laden contents of our very own portaloo, disguised as a couple of aluminium buckets, as we negotiated the daily wobble downstairs before depositing our mush into the outside toilet, some fifty yards down the garden.

We were still without a washing machine or a dryer for Mum, who continued to boil clothes in a very large old tin basin before bashing any grime into submission against a wooden washboard, scrubbing brush in hand. The surviving garments then had to be force fed between a pair of rollers, contained within a wooden structure, by use of a hand turned contraption known as a mangle to coax the remaining water out. No wonder then that Mum's twisted fingers became very arthritic and quite often she asked one of us to do the mangling. Mangling completed, the clothes were then placed in a basket and one by one were hung out to dry on a line set alongside the garden path, with Mum holding one peg in her mouth whilst reaching into her apron pocket for another. To save space and maximise the use of the pegs, she would pin two adjoining items with a single peg all along the line. Finally, the line would be raised skywards on a pole and left dangling until dryness was satisfactorily achieved. One amusing sight was when jack frost made an appearance and the stiffened clothes could easily have walked themselves into the house. This was all very much akin to hard labour for Mum, given the number of children, but I never heard her complain about her lot.

Butter, bread and milk were an integral part of our diet but the absence of a fridge, especially in the summer months, posed another challenge as the larder sat next to the kitchen and attracted heat from the cooking. To keep produce cool, or at least to stop the butter from running away under its own meltdown, we utilised a makeshift cooler in the form of a green square-shaped tin cage with numerous perforations, that hung on a shady wall outside the back door with varying degrees of success. It makes me and my siblings wonder how on earth our parents managed to remain sane and uncomplaining for so many years without any of the mod cons that are now taken for granted.

One reason, perhaps, was Mum's long commitment and reliance on her Catholic faith and her complete devotion to family above all else. She continued to attend church, mostly on Sundays and feast days, as she had always done and often accompanied by several siblings. Fortunately, a new Catholic church was built on a site of a former orchard near Folly Bridge under the direction of the Polish priest, Father Crozier who had travelled widely across Europe to study and learn from church designs that would best reflect liturgical revival and desire to better involve the congregation. He was said to have been much impressed with the design of the British Pavilion at the World's Fair in Brussels in 1958 which he considered "would make an admirable church on a riverside site". The church, built by Bartlett Brothers based in Witney, cost £35,000 with funds provided by Fr. Reginald Schomberg, a priest, soldier and diplomat. The design was inspired by the Second Vatican Council with its unique tent shape, incorporating an octagonal base and topped by a pyramid roof, said to reflect the tent of the Tabernacle in the Old Testament. The church, named Holy Rood was barely a ten-minute walk from home and became renowned for the quality of its furnishings. It was certainly different to any church we had ever encountered with its unusual shape and interior settings. It was dedicated in December 1961.

The likeable Fr. Crozier was certainly a character with his strong Polish accent and fervent enthusiasm for change and involvement. He soon became a regular visitor, encouraged to no small extent by Mum's baking. On his initial visit he noticed the absence of a picture of the Sacred Heart of Jesus. This symbol of "God's boundless and passionate love for all mankind" is a feature of almost all Catholic homes, so its acquisition and blessing became an immediate subject for his attention. The Jesus picture depicts an open bloodied heart surmounted with a cross and thorns and conveys one of the deepest meanings in Roman Catholic practice. Its origin is said to date back to Saint Margaret Mary Alacoque, a Visitation nun and a mystic, in the 17th century. Irish novelist James Joyce referred to her in a short story entitled *Eveline* contained in his book "*The Dubliners*" written in the early 20th century. His premise suggested that Irish traditions were barriers that prevented many people from following their own dreams and breaking free to start afresh. Not a charge that could be levelled against our own parents and certainly Mum managed to integrate freedom of opportunity for us children with her traditional Catholic faith.

The priest returned shortly with a Sacred Heart picture and a signed portrait of Pope John the Twenty Third. All of our names were incorporated into the picture to ensure we would be held in safety and the picture was duly blessed and took its place on a wall hanging over a cage occupied in turn by a couple of mum's budgies, snowy followed by Joey. The Sacred Heart picture reminded me of a story printed in Irish Catholic in 2018.

Joe was the eldest boy in a large family who emigrated to England. He had a poor relationship with his family and all contact was lost. He became an alcoholic who ended up in a hospice, all alone. He mentioned he had two siblings and had a family in Ireland. The hospice staff gained access to his flat to search for details that could identify them but no documents were found. However, there was on a wall the picture of the Sacred Heart with the names of siblings that enabled staff to trace and contact Joe's brother who caught a flight that same day and arrived at the hospice just hours before Joe's death. The Sacred

Heart picture was the only thing he had taken from his Irish home and that had enabled his estranged family to be present as he departed this world. His ashes were brought home to be buried with his parents.

This story bore a remarkable resemblance to the history of another of Dad's brother John, whom none of us children have ever seen. He was said to be a happy soul working contentedly for grocer Dan Kelly in his Bagenalstown shop. He was also fond of a drink or three so Grandad decided to send him to join his brother Michael in England. Unfortunately, when Michael left Birmingham, to move to Oxford, John stayed put and all communication with him ceased. I know Dad and Michael made trips to Birmingham in unsuccessful efforts to locate him. In the end it was Granny Carton who somehow discovered that he had become an alcoholic, had lived with a lady in Birmingham and traced him to Hereford where she found he had died and been buried in a local cemetery. Who knows, perhaps if John had followed the tradition of the Sacred Heart picture there may have been a different conclusion.

All of us Catholic educated children were infused with the faith, attended mass as required and observing feast days and Lenten traditions. The praying of the Rosary was undertaken at home on occasions when Dad took the mood but most definitely when granny would be on one of her annual visits but it was not overtly imposed on a regular basis. Granny was always a welcome sight for Mum as she would be a great help around the house, always active and assisting in the housework. One feature of her visits would be the row of thrupenny pieces which she lined up, like attendant soldiers, along the mantlepiece shortly prior to us setting off for the Sunday Mass. Betty tells a lovely tale of when she and Granny shared a bedroom. In response to Gran's question on what job she would do when leaving school, Betty confidently declared "*I would like to be a prostitute"*. Apparently, Gran's flushed look of absolute horror and her repeated utterance of the words *"Jesus, Mary and Joseph, what are you saying"*, as she clung to the protection of her faithful rosary, almost brought on a heart attack. Betty instantly realised that perhaps Gran did not appreciate her career choice. Gran asked the inevitable question, beloved of children and lawyers, *why?* Betty innocently replied *"I have seen a television programme where such a lady had earned an awful lot of money to support her family."* A relieved Granny duly explained in colourful terms precisely what that job entailed and Betty ended up working in the respectable Kemp Hall Bindery.

Gran may have been a church going lady but her behaviour on a Sunday was in marked contrast to her enthusiasm for male fighting. Saturday afternoon portrayed another, darker, side of her personality. She was transformed into wrestling fan. World of Sport on ITV in the sixties and seventies featured bouts for an hour or so before the evening football results. She would waltz into the lounge, cuppa in hand and plonk herself full square in front of her favourite wrestling stars, Mick McManus and Jackie Pallo, as seemingly walloped hell out of each other simply for the fun of it, and much to Gran's evident delight and encouragement, and very much to our amusement.

Mum and Dad, even with Gran's assistance, must have been utterly exhausted and this would have increased even more when, at the age of 43, Mum gave birth, much to our surprise it has to be said, to our youngest brother David, born just two days after the twins Paul and Ann had celebrated their fourth birthday. Giving birth at that age was in those days was considered extremely risky but thankfully all went well and there were no complications. In fact, she confided to Betty that, following an internal examination, a hospital doctor expressed the view that she was extremely healthy in the baby producing region for a woman of her age who had born so many children.

Notwithstanding the unstinting work involved in running Vicarage Road there was also much fun and relaxation.

Mum herself loved listening and singing along to the radio, usually on the BBC Light Programme during the day before switching to Radio Luxembourg 208 for the evening where there was a greater choice of more popular music. She happily had her head re-tuned to the pirate station Radio Caroline. The station had been fitted out in seclusion at Greenore in Ireland and anchored for action off the Essex coast at Felixstowe. It was launched amid a political storm and with great fanfare on Easter Saturday 1964.

I suspect that a big part of her interest was that it was headed by an enterprising clean-cut young Irishman, Ronan O Rahilly, whose grandfather Michael was killed during the Easter Rising of 1916 in spite his own efforts to prevent the assault in the first place. The story goes that Ronan decided to launch his own station after Radio Luxembourg wanted too much money to play a recording of his discovery, Georgie Fame, and the BBC refused to play it because he was unknown. So here was Ronan, almost 50 years later, in front of a packed house of sceptical old journalists whom he had gathered at "Ye olde Cheshire Cheese" pub in London to celebrate his opening night. However, it almost failed to take off as no signal could be found in the pub and the hardened cynical journalists muttered something about a load of Irish blarney. He saved the day by leading them out into Fleet Street where he picked up a signal and tuned into the appropriately chosen Rolling Stones number "not fade away". Radio Caroline had lift off and would go on to storm the airwaves and attract millions of new wave listeners, substantially young teenagers plus our mum, desperate to spend a whole day soaking up the latest pop music, including The Beatles and The Who. The great DJ Johnny Walker would become a regular on the station until the spoilsport Labour

Prime Minister Harold Wilson passed legislation that cut off advertising and the income collapsed. The BBC stepped in and established Radio 1, under DJ Tony Blackburn, and a new era of state supported music was born.

*We often listened to the music in our living room whilst at least one of us was on ironing duties. Growing up in a large household ensured we were well trained and capable of performing a full range of chores, from window cleaning with newspapers to removing coal ashes, lighting an open fire and cleaning floors. We washed clothes, made beds, polished shoes and even darned socks. In my case Betty once tried to teach me how to use knitting needles before giving me up as a lost cause after a few miscues.

Music would be played on our wooden encased radiogram with a turntable that catered for long playing (LP) and 45s (single) vinyl records, piled one of top of another, necessitating a frequent replacement of the stylus brought about via poor quality and constant use. Mum's chosen plays would invariably involve singers' Mario Lanza and Hank Williams, Bing Crosby, Perry Como or Slim Whitman. We naturally had a collection of Irish *hi diddle I diddle* music for dancing away the evenings accompanied by a collection of Irish singers including Ruby Murray of "*Softly, softly*" fame, who made chart history in the mid -fifties by having five singles in the top 20 in a single week, a feat later matched only by The Beatles. Sometimes, Uncle Oliver would bring along his accordion, which he had self-learnt to a high standard, and play us a merry medley of Irish reels whilst we hoorayed, yelped and wheeled around the room, arm in arm.

Halloween or All Saints Day, was well celebrated in our home. Colcannon dinner (potato and cabbage with lashings of lovely full-creamed butter) would be followed by a helping of Mum's home baked Brack cake, with the reward of a thrupenny bit hidden away for the lucky recipient of that slice and said to be a portent of future prosperity, assuming the recipient was not choking their way to Accident and Emergency. My uncles have said that in the even older days in Ireland there was a tradition that the cake would also include a piece of cloth, signalling future money problems (a not unknown feature of Irish rural life) as well as a ring, said to depict a future of romantic entanglements. I suspect Uncle Peter must have received a few ring-inclusive slices given his later exploits. Apple plucking was a favoured event. One game involved an apple or two being hung from the ceiling and I recall being blindfolded, with hands tied behind my back, primed for a harrier-like take off in an effort to grab a large enough mouthful to justify being declared the winner of the well-bitten apple. Other apples were sunk in a basin of water and had to be plucked from the water with eyes closed, hands again tied behind back, which all proved to be good practice for learning to swim. Board games, including Snakes and Ladders and good old Ludo, were very popular and were interspersed throughout the evening.

Outside the home, Hinksey Park was a delightful haven for all of us children. Three large swimming pools, a shallow for infants, another one deeper for adult swimming and training and a third adorned with a centrepiece fountain of white surf, attracted children and adults alike from across the city especially in the heaving summer months. Although initially free, it later had to be fenced off following a drowning and a small charge of a shilling (5p) made for entry. A small café on the rooftop served delicious ice cream and lollipops. Regardless of the weather or a water temperature that in winter could freeze a block of butter in minutes, I recall happily splashing away the hours until it was time to return home for supper and bed. One feature of the park that greatly appealed to me was the late evening view. Sitting in cross legged silence on the grassy lakeside bank, I was often bewitched by the sheer joy of watching a spectacular red and orange sunset, and its shimmering reflection on the lake, as this golden ball of power and life slowly slid off to sleep beyond the distant hill. On occasions, there would be the added bonus of seeing a mighty twin winged Beverley Aircraft from RAF Abingdon silhouetted against this fading light as it dipped from the skies. On reflection, I do not know how our parents always found the money to enable my siblings and I to have a such a rollicking good childhood over so many years.

1963 turned out to be a particularly eventful year of the early sixties, involving a deep freeze, a limp that almost led to a gelding and a shooting that shook the world.

Gran & Grandad's wedding, Dublin, Bloody Sunday

I

Mum in cadets, 1930s

II

Mum & friends, 1930s

Mum's sister Bridgie with husband Simon and Nick & Nellie.

An early picture of Dad

Dad working as a messenger boy, 1930s

Mary & Paddy on their Wedding Day, October 1944

Bagenalstown

Betty, Paul & David, early 1960s

Soldier's Cottage

Me, outside the Phillip Street house

Our 1950s home at Parc Muire

Betty & May, Oxford, 1960s

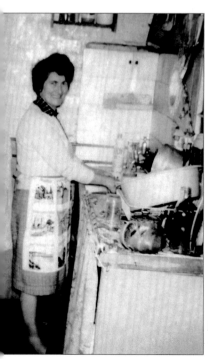

Mum in her home help uniform

Mum in the kitchen at
Vicarage Road, 1960s

Mehael, Me, Betty, Pat, May, David, Nicky, Paul

Michael, Peter, Ado, Peggy, Oliver, Paddy (Dad)
1991

Ann

VIII

Chapter Fourteen

A Freeze, a Limp and a Murder

By a curious set of circumstances and co-incidence the number 63 has featured a number of times in the lives of the Quirke family. Granny Quirke (Elizabeth) died aged 63; Thomas (Mum's brother) died 1963 -also aged 63; Mum herself would die in 1981, also aged 63. it is perhaps fitting to recall some notable events of the year 1963.

The beginning of the year saw the arrival of the worst snowfall in my life and the coldest temperatures for some 200 years. To be more precise, the snow started to fall overnight on Boxing Day 1962 and continued in blizzard fashion until the following morning and intermittently until well into March. I well remember the bitterly cold nights that preceded it around Christmas when the wind chill drilled its way into our bones as we walked home from midnight mass with Mum, assorted brothers and sisters and Aunty Ado. There was excited talk that it might even snow on Christmas day itself, thus bringing to life the words of carols we had been enthusiastically singing and reflecting the snowy scenes that adorned Christmas cards that were strung with knitting wool around our house. That day came and went without a flake of whiteness on display. However, nature was only biding its time and when least expected, a snowstorm of unequalled ferocity appeared from the Siberian East and dunked its magical carpet of cream right into our midst.

I spent much of the snowy night in question darting from my well shared bed, festooned as it was with a double layer of overcoats to keep out the cold, to peep in awe through around the edge of the curtains as hour by hour the snow layered itself in huge drifts down the street. Even with the curtains closed and cosily covered in the bed I could see the silhouette of the driving snow as it sped past the window like a light shining into the darkness. My teenage mind purred with pleasure at the unfolding spectacle.

The arrival of the new morning saw all of us open mouthed at the depth of the snow outside, front and back, here there and everywhere we looked. Roads and paths were long disappeared, troughs of snow had nestled themselves onto window panes and door frames. Roof tops resembled chalets from the snowy Alps. Only the cold howling wind broke the silence of the first moment of the day as we surveyed nature's incomparable handiwork in all its fearsome beauty. Our parents had lived through the previously coldest winter of 1947 but even they were shocked at the sight of so much snow and the biting cold. What we had not realised was that this was just the start of a freeze that would last for months. It was reported that the sea had frozen in places and that temperatures had dropped below minus 20 degrees.

In Oxford, The River Thames froze and I watched on as unsteady would-be ice-champions made their way across its widest stretch at numerous crossings all the way from Folly Bridge to Donnington Bridge. A famous story got around of an

Austin Seven motor car attempting a crossing near Donnington, presumably assisted by a driver or two. Our park was snowbound and crowds of mostly children and teens enlivened themselves through regular bouts of snowball fighting and snowmen building. Traipsing the park was like crossing a battlefield and required some heavy woollen head scarf protection as snowballs, some as big as a cricket ball and made of solid ice, would fly through the air from random sources. The Lake also froze over and on many occasions a scream could be heard. I observed rather brave or perhaps foolhardy elder children making their wary way from the bank attempting to dance on the icy but deceptively frail surface before watching as at least one leg sank, leaving them to resemble a drunken sailor walking the plank. Thankfully, hard as they tried nobody actually drowned and it was all taken as a bit of fun. We were constantly warned by our parents not to walk on it as it was extremely dangerous and very deep. Arriving home, freezing cold and drenched to the skin did not appeal to my sense of adventure and having to explain the cause to my father would not have been a pleasant experience.

Central Heating was non-existent so we had to make do as best we could with a coal -fires in both the dining room and lounge, relying on the coal merchants to somehow make their deliveries. Despite the long-lasting icy conditions people continued to go to work, including Dad. He walked considerable distances in slippery conditions to ensure that there was money coming in and food on the table. Busses did bravely run as snow ploughs made efforts to clear a lane along the road but the ice would re-form overnight and fuel would frequently freeze. I do not recall missing any school days and still remember walking across Donnington Bridge to get to school, where we would simply wrap up in hats, scarfed overcoats and gloves during lessons when the heating failed, as it often did. School meals were still provided although the milk had to be thawed before morning consumption. Games continued in the playground and often resulted in big snowball fights between various groups. I suppose there must have been a few broken ankles or legs but we coped and just got on with it. All a far cry from today's more safety conscious concerns. One thing that has not changed in my lifetime is the appearance of experts to predict the future based on current unusual events. We were warned to expect more of the 1963 weather in future as we were heading into a new ice age! Fast forward to 1976 and a gloriously sunny and warm summer brought predictions of a new warming and we would all be advised to install swimming pools for the predicted constant heatwaves. Nature seems to me to choose her own timing for events and I learned to take such predictions with a pinch of very low-fat salt.

Grand National day, 30th March 1963. A day that has left a lasting legacy in my life. On the morning of the race with my mind still actively concentrating on the big race the runners and riders, Mum noticed my hitherto disguised limp as my gait made a passable impression of a cowboy riding into the country minus his horse. I confessed to some serious discomfort in a sensitive area and, without a moment's hesitation, she dispatched me to the doctors and a confrontation with the stocky and perennially unsmiling Dr James. Not the most jovial character at the best of times his serious demeanour as he peered over his glasses at my discomforted region, suggested all was not what it should be and he arranged that I should I should immediately get myself off to the Radcliffe Infirmary for further investigation, despite my protestations that I had serious race-form study to undertake. He muttered something to himself as he wrote out a letter, whose contents were not disclosed as I was after all only the patient and a mere boy at that. He sealed his thoughts in an envelope before directing me to hand it in at the Infirmary and sent me on my way. Returning home, I informed Mum that I had to go to the Infirmary and set off on the bus. Fortunately, the big freeze had by now relented and transport was again fully on the move.

On arrival at the Radcliffe Infirmary, stopping only to pick up a copy of the Sporting Chronicle, I duly handed in the envelope and I was directed the waiting room. Soon I found myself de-trousered in a curtained cubicle, being stared at by a very important looking fellow, who turned out to be an eminent surgeon, dressed in a pristine white overall and surrounded it seemed by half the medical students on the planet. The object of their ogling was my left testicle which had now ballooned to the size and texture of a cannon ball, hence the cause of my limp. After much poking he stood back, stroked his chin, scratched his head, wiped his oversized glasses and told me I would have been admitted to hospital whilst requesting family details so that my parents could be contacted. I was mortified as it was now only a few hours before the Grand National and I had still not selected my bet.

Events moved swiftly on and, oblivious to the reasoning, I was instructed not to either eat or drink anything in the meantime. My chocolate coated and jam filled Wagon Wheel, my favourite Saturday treat, together with my paper-bagged supply of white bon-bon sweets were confiscated. I was soon wheeled off and deposited in the only available bed which happened to be in the children's ward. Finally, I got some time to plan how I would spend my Grand National winnings.

It was probably about an hour later when my suited and concerned looking Dad turned up at the end of the bed, accompanied by the doctor who by then had reached Professor status. Asked how such an injury might have been incurred I could only remember going out for a recent bike ride following the end of the big freeze and sliding down onto the crossbar whilst performing an emergency stop, a possibility that drew a knowing smile and a distinct "aha" from the learned medic. I earwigged their conversation as they contemplated what to do. I may not have been a medical student but the general tone of their discussions, combined with my knowledge of racehorse anatomy, left me in no doubt that I was about to be gelded. Suddenly the horror of my predicament struck home.

The professor departed, leaving Dad to convey their conclusions. He explained the possible causes and possibilities including surgery. A provisional diagnosis of pain and swelling meant that *"operation gelding"* was suspended. This would allow time for the cannonball to revert to a tennis ball and, with luck, a golf ball. So that was it. I would remain in hospital and would miss the Grand National. Fortunately, before Dad left, I decided that a gelding called Hawa's Song would be the horse to make me rich so my shilling each way was invested. I was able to listen to the race on the hospital radio and my gallant steed romped in third at odds of 28/1. The winner though was 66/1 chance Ayala whom I had of course considered as he was trained by Keith Piggott, father of my favourite jockey Lester. It is always so much easier to pick the winner after the race. So, the long day ended with me still intact and a few extra shillings in my pocket.

I remained hospitalised for a week whilst swelling reduced. Most nights I had the company of a young nurse as I was the only semi adult in the ward whom she could talk to. More seriously, a decision was finally taken not to operate but to leave my body to heal itself as best as it could. I was thus discharged into Dad's care and provided with some vague advice designed to enable a long-term recovery. Nearly sixty years on and now married with two children and two grandchildren the decision was clearly the right one, albeit with some minor complications along the way.

*

People often ask "where were you when such and such happened". 1963 saw the political scandal of the Profumo affair that dominated the news headlines and resulted in the resignation of the Prime Minister Harold McMillan and, of course, the continued dominance *The Beatles* and their music. But for me the outstanding event was the assassination of President John Fitzgerald Kennedy (JFK) in November. It stands out is because I had been out playing football in the park with Nicky and some friends until darkness had closed in. On arriving home, happily mud splattered and in need of a sink wash and a change of clothes, we were greeted by an eerie silence as we entered the house, which was in almost total darkness. We entered the lounge to find all the television programmes had been taken off the air. Mum, Dad and Betty were in a state of shocked sadness. Mum informed us in hushed tones that the President had been assassinated in Dallas, Texas. He was an enthusiastic and vibrant Irish American and a Catholic who had faced down Russia's Khrushchev over the Cuban Missile Crisis the previous year.

This was a standoff when world leaders held their collective breath as fears were voiced about a real threat of a nuclear war between the Russia and the USA. Russia had announced its intention to install missiles in Cuba capable of attacking the USA. In the end, Khrushchev ordered the removal of the missiles and the crisis was averted. From a personal perspective, apart from reading the newspaper and watching new flashes on television, I was not in any way fearful as our parents expressed their conviction that President Kennedy would solve the problem. Mum absolutely adored him and the fact that he had relatives in County Wexford enhanced his status in her eyes.

His Irish connections stemmed from the time his great grandfather had lived in Dungastown before emigrating to America. He had made visits to visit his cousin Mary Ryan, first time in 1947 but, more importantly for Ireland and Wexford, he visited in June 1963 as the American President. He was well loved in Ireland and his untimely death within a few months of his last visit cast a dark shadow over the whole country. A Museum and Visitor Centre now stands in the farm of his cousin and is known as the Kennedy Homestead. Ironically, it contains the very rosary beads that were in the President's pocket when he was shot though sadly did not save him from his fate.

It was also the year that Aunt Peggy and Uncle Tommy transferred to Worksop Manor where Tommy was appointed stud groom, a move that forty-five years later would lead me all the way to Melbourne, Australia to realise a dream conceived during my holidays.

Chapter Fifteen

The Cartons, Carrolls and Horses

I was fortunate to spend many summer holidays in the sixties with Dad's sister Peggy and her husband Uncle Tommy Carroll but it all began when they lived in Ireland in the fifties.

"And what the bloody hell do you think you are looking at?".

Uncle Tommy regularly teased me about my first holiday visit to their house at Mount Juliet in County Kilkenny, following his retirement as a jump jockey to Paddy Mullins, and his employment as stallion man at Ballylinch Stud. I was quite young and sitting on a potty in his front room, stared at by the stallion man, and this was my eloquent response to his gawking that apparently sent him into a fit of laughter.

I became a regular visitor to join them for a summer holiday over many years as it helped out Mum and Dad, with one less mouth to feed or worry about. I have fond but faint recollection of Mount Juliet but a highlight was the annual haymaking. Together with my cousins Sean, Maureen and Ann, we would be rope-tied against a giant haystack, onto the rear of the horse drawn bogey as it cantered its way from field to storage barn.

It seemed as if the sun always shone on these trips though this being Ireland that is probably more a reflection of my memories rather than reality.

My first English holiday with the Carroll's was after they moved to Wiltshire in 1960 when Tommy took up his post as Stud Groom at lovely Alvediston Stud, near Salisbury, after four years at Newmarket. The stud was a dozen meandering country miles from Salisbury and was a wonderful change from the confines of city life in Oxford. I suppose for my cousins it was a bit different as they had to be up early in term times to catch a bus to school in Wardour, near Tisbury. On my first holiday they lived in a modern bungalow with open views all around before later transferring to the Old School House and it was exciting to daily observe so many mares with their foals, destined for sale and hopefully a successful racing life.

Aunt Peggy was a lovely, graceful lady. Kind hearted and well-spoken, she mixed easily with the Lords and Ladies within the Sport of Kings horsey community. Sundays were of course reserved for morning Mass and the Catholic owners of the stud, Una and Leslie Beckingham who owned a large estate and lived in the historic 18th Century Manor House. In 1966 the manor farm estate was bought from the trustees of Una by Anthony Eden, a former prime minister and he retired to live in the Manor House. Leslie would transport us in his luxurious Rover P4 on the scenic twenty-minute journey over undulating twisty roads to the Sacred Heart Church, in the picturesque village of Tisbury, where the priestly sermons were matched by the splendidly dated ancient village churches as far as I recall. Returning home, it would be time for lunch and Peggy, like Mum, loved music and her radio. It was here that I first heard teenage singing star Helen Shapiro belt out her signature tune *"walking back to happiness"* as I listened to *Family Favourites* on the BBC. Little did I then realise that we would cross paths some 50 years later when, as Chairman of Redditch Ramblers, I contacted Helen who graciously permitted us to incorporate her song as the theme tune on our website, as well as agreeing to perform a Christian concert for our local church. For her midweek listening, woe betide anyone who interrupted my aunt's daily therapy of *The Archers*.

Peggy may have been well loved but, like my own parents who had experienced rough times, she was no soft touch. Steely and determined she did not stand for much nonsense and charged me and my cousins with a diet of chores including cleaning, brushing or hoovering as well as peeling and washing the deliciously tasting and freshly picked home grown vegetables. Alvediston was where I also learned to ride a bicycle at the same time as cousin Ann and I took advantage of the opportunity to practice my new skill up and down the quiet country roads. Close to The Crown, a 15th Century thatched inn, they moved to a new home that was larger, had more green space and was within a few yards of a huge hay filled barn where I would enjoy playing amongst the bales with my cousins. I think it was cousin Sean who first introduced rabbits into the family unit and before long one or two had morphed into a large number, all of whom were housed in a couple of large hutches set in the garden. Demanding feeding and daily cleaning of their homes I was only too happy to help out. Ann reminded me of the year we decided to build our very own grand national course adjacent to the barn, using a scythe and hand clippers we soon had a sizeable pile of grass cuttings and combined with some hay we built our masterpiece with our very own Beecher's Brook and how we enjoyed regular races against each other. Peggy was perhaps not so amused at our soaking state and muddy appearance when we concluded our races on our grand design and promptly dispatched us for an early bath. Not one to linger over misdeeds she would take us for days out on the less than luxurious red country bus to

Shaftesbury and to Salisbury Cathedral so it was all a very new and educational experience for me.

In 1963, that fateful year again, Tommy obtained a much bigger job, for Home Ales Brewery owner Mr. Brian Farr who owned Worksop Manor Stud farm in Nottinghamshire and I again joined them for many summers and much enjoyed my holidays. I vividly recall the evening I joined Tommy and Sean when they set out on their evening task to collect some yearlings (one-year old horses weaned from their mothers) from the paddock. They had to be caught, placed on a rein and led into the correct stable for feeding. Following the template of a young child, one of them decided he wasn't ready for bedtime and cantered off in a yearling strop. Tommy asked me to hold two others by the open gate whilst he went in pursuit of the miscreant. Sensing my nervousness and lack of muscle they decided they wanted their feed and wanted it now, pronto. And they just took off, with me sandwiched in between. My arms were being forced from their sockets and my mind cast back to the martyred saints being drawn and quartered. By the time they dragged me to the stables I was long past worrying who should go where and they were no help so I gratefully released them into the stable of their choice. Tommy, arriving soon after, asked where the horses were and seemed less than impressed when I explained that they had declared independence and made their own way home. Apparently, each horse had a feed mix specified to their individual needs. Nevertheless, he just muttered something under his breath and we all went back home for supper with me happy to have two stretched but still attached arms.

Tommy could be a hard taskmaster at times and he expected others to work themselves as hard as he did, something which was not always possible as he was a big, strong, muscular man who had wrestled with a ton of horse flesh in his time as a jockey.

He was ferociously active, with a large flower and vegetable garden to maintain which provided an ample supply of fresh food for all the family. The daily Stud routine, where cousin Sean (Irish version of christened name John) would work was long and arduous. Breakfast was taken after the horses had received their seven in the morning feed. Walking them to the paddocks was followed by mucking out the stables before wheelbarrowing the resulting rose fertiliser to a central depository before a luncheon relief was taken prior to an afternoon of field mucking and, sometimes, cutting hay or grass plus other chores ahead of exhaustedly heading home for a deserved dinner around 6pm. Evening rounds followed a couple of hours later when the neighing hoofs had to be corralled and led back to their Ritz style bedrooms for feeding before being lulled to sleep with a nice fairy story about how to win a Derby, to remind the expensive beasts that they had a purpose in life other than crushing bones and frightening skinny young visitors.

One summer night there was a tremendous rainstorm when the family were living at Menagerie Cottage, set in its own secluded woodland surrounded by paddocks and reached from the stables by a long and winding road through the woods. Tommy had gone to do the usual night feed for the mares and yearlings and had not returned when the heavens opened. Sean decided that it would be a good idea to drive to the stables and collect his dad to save him a drenching. He extracted his dad's pride and joy from the garage, a cream-coloured Ford Consul named *Connie* for some reason, with its gears mounted on the steering wheel. I joined him for this exciting rescue operation. We had barely travelled half way to the stables when we met a very well soaked Tommy, now resembling a fisherman in a gale. However, he was far from amused and refused to enter the lifeboat as the water was dripping from every part of his being with his sleeves operating as drainpipes and he did not wish to contaminate poor old *Connie*. We were instructed to not only take his rescue vehicle back to its cosy home but also tasked with making sure it was cleaned and dried into the bargain. It was a long hour or so before we finally put the finishing touches to the car and made our way into the warm cottage, where the old rogue was enjoying his hot cocoa and eyed us with a very impish grin on his well dried face.

I recall visits made to Skegness (skeggy) as well as country parks, saw Robin Hood's numerous oak trees and hideouts and historic houses

It was in Worksop that my interest in horse racing expanded to cover breeding and betting in addition to actual racing. Tommy hoped fervently that the Stud would produce a Derby winner, the goal of so many smaller breeders at that time and it so very nearly came true. The mare, Peterkin, produced a colt named Corifi, who won the Craven Stakes at Newmarket in 1965 on his first race as a three-year old by an easy five lengths raising hopes that Worksop Manor had bred a real champion. Trained close to Epsom by Staff Ingham, a setback forced him out of the first classic of the season, the 2,000 guineas. However, exercise gallops against some top horses convinced the trainer that he had a world beater on his hands whom he believed would beat the French trained hot Derby favourite Sea Bird which led to great excitement. The trainer, to his eternal regret, sent Corifi to Lingfield for a warm up in the Derby Trial, for which he was backed down to favourite. I backed and expected him to win easily and I raced home from school only to be told crushingly by Dad that he had finished down the field. It transpired he had suffered a cannon bone injury on the firm ground that put an end to his promising career and dashed all our high hopes.

Horses and racing had always been an interest in our family. Uncles Tommy and Peter had worked at stud farms In Ireland. Dad and his brothers' and sometimes with Nicky, perched, on

Dad's handlebars, would join uncle Anthony's children Gerard and Sheila, to attend nearby Gowran Park races.

I was an avid reader of the weekly *Handicap Book*, a trait that led me to study form so that I could convince myself that I knew what I was doing and would one day make a fortune in the process. Many tipsters used to advertise in the paper and would boast that they had *inside information from the stable* about horses that were guaranteed to win. One summer, Sean and I responded to a few of these experts, received their advices, usually a whole sheet of recommended good things including a couple that *"had been burning up the gallops with their speed"*. Needless to say, the only burning that took place was our own fingers as our savings dwindled whilst the enriched tipsters sat back and toasted us mugs for our benevolence. We learned our lesson that if something sounded too good to be true then it most certainly was but it was unfortunate that I had also informed Dad that we had received news of expected winners so he too could reap some deserved reward. Several losers later, he told me in no uncertain terms that he wanted no more tips from me.

Close to our home in Vicarage Road, two men named Mitch and Titch, operated as de-facto bookies. Titch, of small and stocky in stature, certainly looked the part with his permanent Trilby hat covering his lush grey mop. He sported a long white raincoat, with pockets sufficiently deep to hide the cash placed in envelopes or enclosed in folded strips of white paper that would be thrust into his hands, as he did the rounds of his manor to collect bets from neighbours. A mafioso style cigar would inevitably be seen protruding from his puffed face intended to announce himself as a big-time operator. Off course betting was not permitted until the 1960s and that led to the establishment of private bookies as a large number of working people liked their *"daily flutter on the gee-gees"*. Their "betting Office", mostly supervised by Mitch, contained a large room with copies of the racing pages of the daily papers and the sporting life spread-eagled across several long tables.

Dad would have a small daily bet after studying post breakfast his version of The Bible, better known as the Daily Mirror. Nicky would sometimes be tasked with dropping the sealed envelope containing our dad's couple of shillings and the names of his potential jackpot winners on route to school or work. I would subsequently do the same. Unfortunately, one day, I rushed for the bus and forgot to place the bet when I was on my way to work. Realising I still had the envelope in my pocket, on my way home, I confidently popped into the established bookies shop in St Clements to confirm all was well and I could return his few shillings ready for another day. To my horror, and with my eyes popping out of my head like Poppy's on a stem, the results board showed, for the first time in his betting life, my father had actually picked three good priced winners combined in doubles and trebles. Horses named Night of Gladness and Deadly Nightshade were two of the names that still remind me of the day. Rather than disappoint him and mindful of my part the earlier tipping disasters I informed him that I had placed the bet with a bookie in St Clements whilst on my way to work and I would pick up his winnings next day. I at least knew how to calculate the odds which I duly did that evening with still shaking hands. I suspect he may have guessed, as Mum asked me quietly if I had actually placed the bet. He deserved his bit of good fortune so I paid him up and said no more. Today, I rarely place any bets unless it is during a trip to the live races or for a major event like the Grand National, only too conscious of how easy it is to lose hard earned income.

I read many of the books stacked on the shelves in Worksop. One such book, a racing story entitled "The Old Mares Foal" had a very profound impact on me. It was a gripping tale about an old mare giving birth to a foal that went on to win the

Melbourne Cup in Australia. The story immediately caught my imagination and the description of Melbourne was such that I resolved that one day I would travel to Australia to watch the race myself and enjoy the spectacle.

I was at Worksop in 1966 for the final of the World Cup and this was to be my last holiday before I ventured into the world of work. The day of the final is memorable for England winning the cup of course but also for the impact it had on Tommy. He had been up most of the previous night nursing a new born foal but very sadly it had died in the morning. Tommy, displaying his tender side, took it very badly and was inconsolable. The day was saved when Geoff Hurst scored the winning goal bringing a big smile to Tommy's face and his emergence back into life.

Tommy left Worksop to take up a position of Stud manager at Sandley Stud in Gillingham, Dorset. I spent a weekend there to introduce them to my fiancée Shirley before he left to take up a non-racing position at Chateau Impney near Redditch in 1975. A few years later, he and Peggy hosted myself, Shirley and our two young children for a week whilst we were viewing property after my move from London to work at Birmingham Crown Court and for which we were very grateful.

Tommy subsequently became ill and decided to retire to Lincolnshire where he was looked after, with immense care and patience, by Peggy and daughter Maureen. In 2002, Peggy died unexpectedly but in a happy state after a good night out whilst on a visit to Ireland, and she was buried in Bagenalstown. Tommy returned to England, largely oblivious to what was happening around him, and over the next four years, was gently cared for in turn by his children Sean, Maureen and Ann, on the Isle of Wight, from where he was repatriated to be reunited with Peggy.

The family paid a fitting tribute to their father when they sponsored a race in his name, The Thomas Carroll Memorial

Handicap Hurdle at Market Rasen on 19th March 2007. Appropriately, the race was won by a horse named Shamrock Bay with Maureen presenting the trophy to the winning connections, watched over by the Carroll family, myself and Shirley representing the Cartons and Susan Clark, with her sons Alex and Tom. It was a very noble tribute to him and an appropriate conclusion to his life.

Sean continued to work at the Worksop stud for many years before finally retiring. I had visited them regularly when working in the northern courts and always received the same warm welcome, with a ready cup of tea and cake awaiting. Maria was still baking Christmas cakes for everybody until she was taken ill and unexpectedly died of complications during the pandemic. This considerably reduced the number of attenders permitted at her funeral leaving only close family to mourn the loss of their mother. Sean was himself receiving medical treatment over the past few years and never fully recovered from the shock; He also lost his own life in 2022 dealing a further major blow to the family, still reeling from the loss of Maria. Even up to the end, Sean and Nicky were exchanging betting tips most Saturdays before watching the action on television. There was a huge post pandemic gathering of family and friends that ensured him a memorable service, and send-off, as he was spirited away to be re-united with his beloved Maria

Chapter Sixteen

Life in the Later Sixties

Mehael, until his marriage and the birth of my parents first grandchild, Noel, in December 1963, together with Betty and Nicky were contributing to the running of the Vicarage Road household. For my part, I was at least able to assist by earning myself some basic income before I too joined the ranks of the full time employed. I tended to the garden and fencing and undertook interior decorating with the colours chosen or at least agreed by Mum.

Youngest brother David having now started school, Mum took on another job as a Home Help complete with a smart green uniform. She said she enjoyed the work because it enabled her to meet other people and help those in need though I suspect that our parents' secrecy about their finances might have been another reason.

Once Nicky had started work at the car factory at Cowley, I took over his paper round for a while so had a few shillings extra in my pocket. Furthermore, during the two years I was studying for my "O" levels, I was fortunate in obtaining an evening job at Hertford College, helped by my near neighbour Colm Sweeney who recommended me to the Bursar. Overall, the college is probably best known for its iconic Hertford Bridge, better known as The Bridge of Sighs due to its resemblance to the famous bridge in Venice. Despite his initial, albeit accurate, comment that I was rather on the small side he gave me a job, serving evening dinners to the gowned undergraduates, in the wood panelled and inspiring Old Hall adorned with portraits of alumni. There was a clearly established order with undergraduates, and us servants, standing firmly to attention whilst the scarlet robed chancellor and senior professors took their place at the high table.

The students sat opposite each other occupying at least three double sided rows of old oak tables, stretching from the top table to the common entrance and the kitchen, from where we would emerge to dispense the meals. This was performed under very strict supervision, obeying codes of dress and complying with regimented service standards. Carrying three bowls of hot soup followed by dinner and pudding proved a challenge initially but I was soon allowed to serve with only one bowl or plate in each hand as I could still serve the requisite number of students on my allotted table. Mum was always interested in hearing about the history, students and their ways. For me I was in awe of the fine and hallowed surroundings for some time as it provided a stark contrast with my earlier life in Ireland. In my final year I was placed on the table serving the Hertford Boat Crew in readiness for their battles during the summer eights where the college had a reputation to uphold as one of the stellar performers in this summer events.

I think as a part time server I would have received no more than £3 for my variable hours of work which at that time actually made me feel pretty well off. As an added bonus, we servers each shared the fine array of leftover deserts at the end of the evening. Money and desserts, Such bliss! One of the first things I did with my new found riches was to follow in Dad's footsteps and purchase a bag of wafer biscuits on my way home for us all to share.

My interest in the garden drew on the pleasant visits to Soldiers Cottage and had heightened during my holidays at the Carrolls' where colourful raised beds of petunias and geraniums caught my eye. Armed with my new found riches I decided that our own garden could do with a bit of oomph. Bagging a few old wooden boxes from Mr Purvey, I chose some seeds on the basis of their colour and longevity and planted them up, covered in polythene sheets, before placing them in full sun on the old toilet roof. To my surprise and delight most of them seeded well and by summer we had a garden full of love Lies Bleeding which appropriately is what my fingers were doing as I tended the roses that climbed above them together with a selection of orange Marigolds, mixed Pansy and Petunias by the score. I set about adding stone surrounds to the beds but was "advised" by Mum to be careful not to turn the garden into a "Babby House", by which she meant by being over-fussy about design. To this day my garden is more often a scattered oasis of mixed colour with annuals wrestling with the perennial herbaceous plants and intermingled with wildflowers, whose main purpose is to make it appear sunny even when it isn't, to save on weeding and nowadays to protect my knees.

Following the example set by cousin Sean, a fair proportion of my earned money would be deposited at the post office in exchange for savings stamps sealed into a savings book and hidden away from temptation of rogue tipsters but readily available to be exchanged for cash when required such as at Christmas. This enabled me to wander at will around Woolworths store bagging up a few pressies and once allowed me to buy some Pantomime tickets for the family at the New Theatre, at a cost I think of 2/6d each (13p).

On Sundays I used to help out by taking youngest brother David out for a spin in his pram. My route normally took me across the park but one day, being curious, I took a detour through the open gate of Brasenose College Sports Ground, almost opposite the park. On a third trip I met the genial groundsman, Mr Beasley, and got into conversation as I was so inclined. He asked me if I would be interested in collecting the boundary markers after the cricket matches that took place each Sunday and on some evenings in the summer. I graduated from just placing and collecting markers, for which I was rewarded with a sandwich lunch and an afternoon treat of delicious trifle in the pavilion, to be responsible for updating the large scoreboard under the direction of the book scorers.

One fateful evening, one of the two book scorers was unable to attend and I was asked if I would like to stand in. My immediate yes was premised on two erroneous assumptions. I thought that it would be like a training session and the senior scorer was under the impression that I knew what I was doing. All went swimmingly until the operator responsible for updating the public scoreboard, sensing he may have missed a few runs, asked me to confirm the current score. I confidently shouted out the score in my book. Suddenly a puzzled looking face appeared over my right shoulder, cast a glance or two at my sheet, coughed up the remnants of his latest smelly cigar and loudly informed me that were not at the same match. Leaning further across he spluttered out that our recorded scores differed by some degree and wondered how that could be. At that very moment, the on-field umpire raised his hands in the air well above his white capped head and I saw my colleague hurriedly repair to his own book and crossed a line out in a box which recorded a six hit. I noted there were a number of such markings in his fours box column as well whilst mine was virginal. It suddenly dawned on me that what I had believed to be a friendly mixture of hand-waves and hands-over-head drink-summoning were actually signalling either byes, fours or sixes. For my penance I was thereafter relegated back to my old boundary collection duties.

For some unfathomable reason I was never invited to be book scorer again even though I was now probably better equipped to do so. It did give credence to two unassailable beliefs -never assume anything and that we often learn more from our googlies than from doing things right. That was my take on it anyway and something I was able to impart with conviction when I became a management trainer many years later. So, unlike my scoring sheet, the evening was not a complete write off. Furthermore, I was able to dine out on the experience for many years.

My parents having given me their blessing to continue with my education I set about the task with some gusto, desperate to justify their faith, and by the time England had won the World Cup in 1966, I knew I had achieved the qualifications required.

I was all set for the world of work but what was I to do? I had long dreamed of being a journalist. Combined with an interest in Horse Racing I cheekily wrote to the *Sporting Life* and asked them if I could be a racing correspondent. Their polite response was that I should contact my local paper, the Oxford Mail, and learn the job as a journalist before considering a specialism. I followed their advice and accepted an invitation to meet The Editor. Dressed smartly for the occasion and accompanied by Mum, I have little recollection of what happened in the half hour or so that I was there but on leaving I was led to believe that a trainee position could be offered subject to satisfactory O level results, usually announced in July. On my return to school an appointment was made to see the forceful Careers Officer. He listened to my excited views on being a journalist, rolled his eyes in a despairing fashion and pronounced the words that I have never forgotten.

"Journalism is too hard a life, no- it's the Civil Service for you, young man".

He handed me a bundle of literature detailing the work of a range of government departments and invited me to consider the options. Somewhat disappointed with the turn of events, I went home to consider the material and spoke to my parents. I decided to apply for a job in The Lord Chancellor's Department of Her Majesty's Civil Service as the legal work appealed to me. Assisted by the Careers Officer, I completed the appropriate forms and attended an interview with the Civil Service Commission, succeeded in the interview and to my parents' delight I was about to join the ranks of the Civil Service.

My working life commenced on 1st September 1966, as a clerical officer in the Lord Chancellor's Department of the Civil Service, located in Castle Street, close to the Shire Hall, home of the Assize Courts and Oxford Castle and prison. It was a disappointingly shoddy old building and on entering the office I imagined I had been teleported from the pages of a Dickens novel. Black iron bars guarded windows while well stained curtains hung miserably over paint peeled radiators. Lined up along a long wooden reception desk where I nervously introduced myself as the new boy on the block was a sea of mainly well weathered faces, peering at me pityingly as if I was the last in a line of sacrificial lambs inducted into the house of misery. This was compounded when I tagged along behind a very tall and thin man who sat me on a hard seat in the very cluttered office of the head honcho, the Chief Clerk. I would soon learn that a cluttered office was seen as an indicator of importance. The man himself, a Mr Hodgkinson, when he arrived after supervising the post opening was actually jovial and welcoming in manner even if his red-faced appearance suggested otherwise. Having checked my qualifications and satisfied I was not an imposter he explained office basics and, more importantly to my mind, the availability of luncheon vouchers to be used at the Post Office canteen in the nearby telephone exchange building where a three- course meal could be purchased at a bargain rate.

Matters took a turn for the better when he summoned a very lovely lady called Liz who was deputised to look after my induction and who introduced me to the rest of the staff. Liz was a very personable lady with a ready smile who, not surprisingly, had been a recent winner of the Miss CCOA (County Court Officers Association) competition. She saw me to my prepared school-like desk where I was sat next to the rather stern looking lamp post who had earlier guided me to the chief. He was an avid smoker and, it turns out, a senior clerk of many years who would be my supervisor.

Briefly, he introduced me to something called a Default Summons which was issued by creditors to poor people who had failed to pay their bills. It contained a response form indicating their intentions as to whether they would admit the debt and make an offer to pay or whether they would dispute it and require a court hearing. He explained it would be my job for the foreseeable future to prepare these summonses to be sent out and deal with the replies or lack of one. Now, I have to say this is not what I thought I was signing up to. I had seen police detective series on TV like No Hiding Place with Lockhart of the Yard, Dixon of Dock Green, Z cars and courtroom dramas such as the film 12 Angry Men. I had observed robed judges and wax wigged men dressed in gowns arguing fine legal points and being ever so important and it hinted of a life of excitement and intrigue. Sitting in an overcrowded office was not in my plans. Even worse, as the clock struck five, and everybody continued to beaver away, it dawned on me I had miscalculated the length of a working day. Come half past five I was released from custody and sent home, there to explain to Mum and Dad all about the summoning of poor people for failure to pay their debts, little knowing that they must have sailed very close to that fate themselves.

At the end of the Month, I was summoned to see the chief and watch him, with his fully inked fountain pen, as he painstakingly wrote out a cheque for all my efforts. Detaching it with care from the cheque book and holding it aloft he slowly breathed the ink dry and, beaming gently, he handed it to me as if it was the most precious thing in the world, as if to say remember this, the first monthly pay day of your career. I looked at it with disbelief-£32, clearly and lovingly crafted in figures and letters and addressed personally to me. It may have seemed fuddy-duddy at the time but he was right, I have not forgotten the moment that he had created and which I so under estimated at the time. He was far more astute than I ever gave him the credit for so I belatedly do so now.

I had never ever had that much money before and it wasn't long before Mum relieved me of most of it to pay for my board and lodging. First though, I had no bank account to deposit the earnings. Our friendly grocer, Mr Purvey accepted the cheque being paid over to him in exchange for cash as he reasoned there was little chance of the government having a cheque bounce. Mum handed me back my pocket money and that was the way it was for some time but I had no reason to complain and was still better off than ever. I duly opened a bank account with Barclays and I was on my way. I was now able to earn my keep and had a good bit of money to spend.

*

The period between starting work and the end of the sixties oversaw many changes for me personally as well as our family and in the cultural and working life of the City of Oxford and the country itself.

Independently funded I was able to wander the city centre, regularly visiting Russell Acott's, a beautiful preserved old High Street music shop dating back to the 1890s where you could request a record at the counter, step into a wooden booth, don earphones and listen to the music with no obligation to buy. My late purchase of The Beatles double sided hit *Day Tripper and We can work it out* for my eighteenth birthday cost me about seven shillings(35p). One early lunchtime purchase was an LP entitled "Gutbucket", featuring Alexis Horner was illustrated by a pig's head on the cover and it provided much head shaking and the usual refrain from my office seniors about it being a sign of the times and the shallowness of youth. Mum simply looked at the offending cover, then at me and departed for the safety of the lounge and Radio Luxembourg.

An alternative to the original more expensive records could be found at the new Woolworths Store in Cornmarket, designed by Sir William Holford with a mission to create a store worthy of the city. "Woolies" as it became known opened in late 1957 and was billed as its most extravagant, and most modern, store of the thousand or so in the country, comprising a de -luxe café, upstairs offices, a roof garden and a multi storey car park. The store consisted of spaced-out rows of long narrow counters each served by its own assistants with cash registers. To me the real attraction was its sale of cover versions of these hit records, many performed by the highly regarded group *The Typhoons* and sold under Embassy Records for around half the original version price and included most of the top stars including The Beatles. One such hit, Connie Francis's official release song **Stupid Cupid**, by Maureen Evans, was so good that it outsold the original. One tall tale that did the rounds was that Tommy Steele recorded his own covers for the label only to have it criticised for not being the real thing!

The top selling LP albums were Irish and Scottish music recordings and top hits compilations, more especially around the Christmas period. So it was that we were readily able to satisfy Mum's desire for her chosen music. She loved "Woollies" and Betty recalled how they would happily wander around the store as she shifted slowly from counter to counter. She would select a white blouse say, pick it up, caress it and place it across herself inviting Betty to comment on its suitability against her hair, skin and lord only knows what, then humming and hawing before finally making her mind up, always commenting about how much it cost, regardless of the fact that Betty was treating her. Having spent all her life being conscious of money it was difficult to break the habit but all the more endearing for it. Finally, they would finish the trip by settling into the upstairs café for a cup of tea and a slice of fruit cake.

*

Stockport on a cold wet and windy night in April 1968 might not be considered everybody's cup of tea but it was significant for me in that it was the first away game I attended as an Oxford United fan, finishing work early in order to catch the supporters club coach. It was a game we won four nil in a season when we won the last four games to clinch promotion from Division Three. Memorable also was the protection afforded us visitors by a number of very large police heavies who suggested we remove our hats and scarves and tucked them inside our waterproof jackets. They surrounded and shielded us from the wrath of a gang of locally aggrieved and scary sounding ruffians during the game and then escorted us to our coach with advice not to stop for a celebratory drink until well out of Stockport. Arriving home in the early hours I then had to find my way from Headington back home in the early hours of the morning and being careful not to allow the elixir of probable promotion and drink to awaken the rest of the family. Fifty years on and I am still the same fan and a season ticket holder with my brother-in-law Mick, having followed the team's ups and downs now for over 50 years.

My interest in football had been aroused a few years earlier. Dad brought me along to watch Oxford City play in the Isthmian league, playing teams such as Tooting and Mitcham, Dulwich Hamlet, Kingstonian and Ilford. It cost about a shilling per game and a military brass band provided pre-match entertainment before a crowd often measured in thousands. I had the pleasure of watching top local players such as goalkeeper Mick Honey; Bustling – "thou shall not pass" defender- Big "Dougie" Buswell and great forwards such as Tony Bricknell and prolific striker Arthur Howlett who notched 100 goals for the club accompanied by tricky winger Bernie Harris and the mercurial John Woodley and a host of others. Sadly, in later years after I had transferred my allegiance to Oxford United, City began a steady decline that eventually resulted in the sale of the famous White House Ground. It appears that the ambitious and over optimistic signing of Bobby Moore and Harry Redknapp as managers proved to be the catalyst for change, with players being recruited from London at the expense of local lads. The ground was owned by Brasenose College and in 1988 they evicted the club and sold the ground for housing development, causing them to resign from the league before being reformed and beginning their slow climb back up the leagues and finding a new home near Marston where they still play today in the National League North.

Watching the "hoops" in their blue and whites resulted in my forming a life long association with wagon wheels, a circular chocolate coated biscuit that encased a layer of jam and mallow cream, each mouthful being slowly savoured from its outer edge to the final crumb to extract the maximum taste. I would always buy one with either a bottle of pop or an Oxo drink if it was cold, collecting a penny or two for returning the bottle. This encouraged me to increase my pocket money, by collecting the deposit on many a discarded bottle.

*

Pat (Patrick) had a twin sister named Mary, who died within a couple of weeks of her birth and was similarly laid to rest alongside my own twin. He left school a year after myself to work at Oxford Post Office as a Telegram Boy and junior postie, as our own father had done in Ireland. Located in St Aldates, it opened in 1880. Built in Chilmark stone it displayed a wonderfully crafted coat of arms encased in an arch over the doorway, supported by columns of polished Mull granite. The Telephone and messenger rooms where Pat worked were added later with telegraph messages being conveyed to the Boys' rooms via a pneumatic tube. Outside the front door way were situated three large mahogany style collection boxes which originally hid a large hole that allowed letters to be delivered directly to the basement for sorting. Interesting and historical it may have been but his efforts were ill matched to his low income which was determined by his junior status. However, things later went awry. He found himself training newer, albeit older, recruits who earned more money than himself so he "jacked it in" in favour of a more financially rewarding post at the Cowley works to join Dad and Nicky where he enjoyed a good year.

Within a couple of years, he had met and married Shirley, fathered his first child Samantha, followed by Rebecca and Terry. Workwise, after leaving Cowley he qualified as a bus driver, with a Driver number EE532/73, coincidentally the same

166

work number he had previously been allotted at the post office, which he thoroughly enjoyed.

Pat recollects one amusing story from his bus days. He was driving his bus when he spotted our brother Nicky on the other side of the road seemingly not in full control of his wayward looking bike, which appeared to have a mind of its own and was wandering in a not very straight line from path to road. Pat pulled up his bus alongside, guided Nicky onto his bus and plonked him on a seat before similarly gathering the miscreant bike and securing it by the stairs. He then drove them both back home, in company with the amazed passengers. Whether that was still on the timetabled route or by way of diversion he is not at liberty to disclose.

Our sister, Ann, found herself unmarried and pregnant and although she lived with Mum and Dad for a short period, she had to leave when Mum became unwell and so went to live with Pat and Shirley at the same time as they had taken on a lodger named Leo with Pat working nights on the buses

Shirley then left to set up home with the lodger and Pat was bereft. He joined the Wesleyan General Insurance Company and formed a friendship with the District Supervisor who was a member of the Salvation Army and this proved to be the catalyst that set off a chain of events that would lead to future happiness. He was introduced to subsequently lifelong friends, Lesley and Steve, who looked after him and invited him to stay with them whilst he recovered from the wreckage of his marriage.

Pat was so taken with the support and love received from the Salvation Army that he bade farewell to insurance and placed his future to faith in God. He was ordained as a minister, rising to the rank of Major and this faith in his chosen path guided him to a meeting with another salvationist, Kate.

Kate had served seven years as a salvationist nurse in Ghana before deciding to induct herself into the Salvation Army

College from 1984 to 1986, when she was ordained and returned to Ghana as a Sub-Lieutenant. During an outbreak of Cholera a few years later she was given a booster injection but it transpired that the needle used had been infected and she ended up with Hepatitis. She was very poorly and in early 1989 was sent home to the UK, to the Salvation Army in Oxford where, in another of these coincidences that life throws up, our brother Pat was serving, as if the poor girl had not suffered enough already!

The pair of them met, got on famously and by the end of the year we were celebrating their wedding at The Oxford Citadel, and a son Jonathon followed in 1992. Kate was a well-loved lady and during her service in Ghana she had met the future General of the Salvation Army, Eva Burrows who herself was one of nine children born to salvation Army officers. At a major conference in London the General had stepped down from her platform and made her way through the hall to confront Pat with the immortal words "And what have you been doing with my Sub-Lieutenant"? referring to Kate for whom who she had clearly formed a loving concern. They were both flabbergasted that the Army's highest-ranking officer should not only remember Kate but made a point of checking out her potential husband to boot.

*

One year after Pat, saw the only other red headed Carton join the ranks of the employed. My likewise coiffured younger sister May (Mary) exchanged Edmund Campion for Boots the Chemist in Cornmarket Street. According to geneticists there are more redheads born per capita in Ireland than anywhere else in the world. Both parents seemingly need to possess the gene, which can date back or skip generations. Instead of greying into old age we merely turn blonde or white as I can testify. My own youthful summer mane, decorated to resemble a sunflower, seemed to have a propensity to attract admirers from afar but were, unfortunately, mostly of the bumblebee variety. Although we are said to possess far fewer hair strands this is compensated for by being thicker, in hair growth I hasten to add.

May at one point in her life had flirted with the Baptist Church. In company with Bernadette, a close neighbour, they began to attend church services at the Baptist Church in Wytham Street, enticed by the enjoyable atmosphere and the joyful singing of hymns with uplifting words such as *"Give me love in my heart, keep me singing"*. Regrettably, this came to the attention of Father Crozier who met with Dad to express his unhappiness with the girls' mixing with non-Catholics, resulting in Dad informing his errant daughter that she should no longer attend the Baptist church.

Working at Boots at the same time was one of our neighbours Karen Davis, whose brother Richard and I, armed only with a torch and a net, used to spend many a dark night trying to catch his Houdini like white rabbit that led us on a merry dance across numerous of his neighbour gardens. May was appointed as one of only two chosen sellers of its iconic Cosmetic no.17 Make-Up range which was great news to her proud Mum. She was and remains a dead-ringer for singing star **Lulu**, *the Scottish "Boom-Bang- a bang" winner of the Eurovision Song Contest in 1969.*

May has fond recollections of meeting with Mum for tea and cake in the stylish Cadena café, a venue with an aroma of fresh coffee beans that floated down the Cornmarket. Wood panelled it had wide armchair style chairs surrounding spaced out tables, lit by chandeliers and pendant wall lights. The pinafore dressed waitresses served tea in bone China cups and saucers overlaid on lace tablecloths. A variety of cake-types were often presented on a double-tiered stand whilst live performances of easy listening music resonated quietly in the background. A spiral staircase led upstairs to a luxury restaurant where you could be serenaded by a white suited pianist on a matching piano. Such a difference to today's offerings and how delightful to reflect on the pleasure the Cadena brought to our Mum.

*

Twenty-five years after our parents wedding saw a large family gathering at Littlemore Hospital Social Club, where Uncle Oliver, who worked at the Hospital had hired a room to celebrate their Silver Wedding Anniversary. The room was beautifully decorated in flags, balloons and tinsel, a special cake had been baked and all was ready for a rocking night of reels and jigs, with Oliver himself adding to the fun by playing his accordion. Family and friends had come from all over the country and everything was set for a great gala of celebration to our parents. However, all did not go according to plan for two reasons. Dad had earlier been taken into the Radcliffe Infirmary with a suspected brain haemorrhage, basically he had ruptured a blood vessel in his brain. Mum was distraught but we decided that the event would still go ahead as Dad was receiving the best attention possible. Betty remembers Mum tearfully saying that she had bought this special card and now she might not be able to give it to him. Whether the collapse was due to his heavy smoking or exhaustion or combination of both we would never know but ill he most certainly was and for a few days it was touch and go whether he would survive. Oliver, as usual, was a positive tower of strength portraying all the positivity he could muster and instilling in us his belief that Dad would be ok after some rest, a four-letter word most alien to him.

It was doubly unfortunate that on this night some wretches decided to issue a warning to the police that a bomb had been planted. The building had to be evacuated and searched before we were able to continue. In context, 1969 saw the re-emergence of bombing by the Provisional IRA in pursuit of their aims of a United Ireland through violence. Whoever made the call obviously knew it was an Irish gathering and wished to cause inconvenience to innocent Irish people. The police were quickly on the scene and carried out a diligent search declaring that it was a bad hoax. Despite our best efforts to reactivate the evening into a celebration mode, the incident had imposed a dampener on the night and gradually we all filtered off home. Not quite the expected wedding anniversary that had been planned but there was soon better news about Dad and he would return home and complete a full recovery.

A strikingly similar event occurred later in the year when a number of us were enjoying an evening at the Irish Club in St Clements. Our group comprised myself, Betty, May and her boyfriend Pat and our cousin Ann. After a beer or two for me and Pat, and no doubt a glass or two of sparkling Babycham for the ready-to-dance ladies, we were in the full throes of merriment and dashing into an explosive reel when proceedings were brought to a halt by an almighty crescendo of sound heralding from the direction of the stage. The announcer, clearly not a man to exude peace and calm, leapt onto the podium and hollered somewhat over excitedly "get out everybody, quickly, there's been a bomb". Had he chosen to cause maximum chaos and panic as possible he could not have done it any better. Still not quite certain which way to go, we gathered our few possessions and raced towards the fire exit that was an open window about two feet off the ground. Alongside scores of others', we found ourselves being pushed from behind and pulled from the front before being clasped by strong, sweaty Irish labouring hands and deposited with obvious relief outside amongst the milling crowd, glad enough to breathe in the fresh night air. Another unforgettable evening was added to our life experience. On arrival home and recounting the experience to Dad he "advised" us not to frequent such places again at any stage in the near future and we were happy to comply.

Earlier in that year, July 20th 1969 saw a different form of crash with man landing on another planet as Neil Armstrong set foot on the planet I had observed from a distance since my early years. President Kennedy's vision to land a man on the distant planet within ten years had been nobly achieved. Suddenly, Mum's taunts of being visited by *"the man in the Moon"* for not doing what I was told seemed all too real. I had by now left Oxford County Court to work as a relief clerk across courts in London and the South East. Whilst the world watched in awe and held its collective breath during the Apollo 11 spaceship's wonderous walkabout and its safe return to Earth, I watched the events live in a London hotel.

November saw me celebrate my 21st Birthday with a party held in our house at Vicarage Road. Organised by Betty and my siblings with Mum's blessing the room was decorated with balloons and posters and surrounded by both family and friends whom I had collected since starting work. Since my eighteenth birthday I had enjoyed a rather serious relationship with Double Diamond. Its TV adverts proclaimed *"a Double Diamond works wonders, works wonders."* Well, it certainly had an effect on the stomach and I must have consumed gallons each week so it is quite remarkable to have lived to tell the tale. Most of this consumption took place in local pubs, most notably The Grandpont Arms where I learned the art of beer drinking, being rewarded with a silver tankard to mark my coming of age and, for a number of years, my personal jug hung proudly above the lounge bar. Opposite the lounge, separated by the mahogany wood Bar, was the room commonly referred to as the Irish Bar for obvious reasons and, almost without fail, each Sunday evening would end with bloody noses and an almighty punch up with pints of precious Guinness carpeting the floor only for the combatants to finally shake hands in exhaustion and end their feud with arms draped around each other until the rematch took place the following week. Watching over all of this was the best bar lady in all Oxford, Mrs Gleeson (Mrs G to us regulars), a smiling and delightful Irish lady with a great manner and sense of humour who served us for many years.

*

Oxford had a vibrant night life and was well suited to my teenage self as a member of the so-called generation of *baby boomers*, born between the end of the Second World War and the mid-sixties. Apart from the Grandpont, there were a host of bars in the city centre including Whites Bar, The Roebuck, The Turf Tavern, The Crown and The Chequers that were frequented by our family including myself with Betty and Nicky and his brother-in law Tom. One favourite was The Bear Inn, a small cosy pub where even I, at just over five foot something almost caressed the ceiling. Historically it dated back to the 13th century and exhibited a collection of over 4000 ties. At other times, accompanied by my best mate Neville and an assortment of former school chums and fellow Oxford United football supporters we would spend many Saturday evenings supping pints, discussing pop music, resolving all the world's problems, and possibly creating a few new ones, as we shuffled from pub to pub before ending up at the Indian for a Vindaloo.

Being a mere skeletal seven stone weakling, I must somehow have possessed the constitution of a horse as I rarely suffered illness or missed work. There were exceptions and I vividly recount the night I had consumed a not-too- clever mix of whiskey and beer at the Grandpont. Gingerly making my way back home I would learn to climb a lamp post by the light of the silvery moon but not before I had draped my arms around its slender frame and began a routine that convinced me I was dancing legend Fred Astaire. My cheery dream sequence was interrupted when I heard a voice emanating from an open door and proclaiming loudly "look at that bloody fool" and then the identity of this "fool" dawned on him. It was Dad, standing in our open doorway with our neighbour Jim and he was not best pleased. He grabbed hold of me, yanked me inside and packed me off to bed without another word and minus my bedtime Ovaltine. The next day he informed my swishing head that if I could not hold my liquor then I should not be drinking. Sound advice that was (mostly) well heeded.

This was also a magical time for those seeking to let their hair rock in a different direction to their head and again with family and friends we would dance away the night, especially Saturday nights at Oxford Town Hall where local promoter Adrian Hopkins had a talent for encouraging names such as Simon Dupree and The Big Sound; Andy Fairweather Lowe and Amen Corner on a number of occasions and a host of other star gazed hopefuls into the city before they became household names. Then there was the confined venue of The Stage Club, located in an alley adjacent to The New Theatre where you would have to queue up and be fortunate to gain entry as I once did in 1967 to see and most definitely hear the sound of ear-piercing group, *Pink Floyd,* years before they associated themselves with *The Dark Side of The Moon*, a planet where I am sure their sound easily reached on that night. The Falling Leaves were a classy local band in their own right and who also appeared on TV and also toured with The Beatles and Rolling Stones. Infamously, they were the support act to the Rolling Stones when they performed at the Magdalen College Ball in 1964 for a fee of just £100, a bit before my time. I would join friends and family as we visited St Dominic's where Uncle Michael was heavily involved in the running of the social club. An Irish showband was the normal fare and our Mum would happily join us to enjoy familiar music especially when the performing band was that of our close neighbours, The McCarthy's, with eldest daughter Mary being the lead vocalist.

One notable concert I attended was to see Julie Driscoll, with Brian Augur Trinity, at the Bridge Hotel in Wheatley, just outside Oxford. Her performance of *This Wheel's on Fire*, was unforgettably mesmerising and even today I can visualise her large, dark shadowed, bewitching eyes and chiffon covered fluttering hands seemingly in a trance. I was so captivated that I lost all track of time and missed the last bus back to Oxford. I was rescued by an old school colleague Rory who kindly offered me a helmetless and hair-raising lift back as a pillion rider on his own fiery wheels before dropping me, legs-shaking, at Donnington Bridge. Though immensely grateful to him It was a travel experience that convinced me that four wheels would be better for my sanity.

Chapter Seventeen

Wheels on Fire, Molly Goes to Paris

My own love affair with cars began in 1970 when I became the proud owner of a thirteen years old Trafalgar Blue Morris Minor 1000 with a trillion miles on the clock, purchased from Aldens Cars Lake Street and sold to me by an Arthur Daley lookalike (a dubious car salesman from the TV series Minder) and presented it as if I was buying a Rolls Royce. It cost me the princely sum of £90 with a further equivalent sum for insurance. My slender hands shook as I handed over the hard cash and climbed into my "Rolls", completely unaware of how to start the thing let alone drive it home. Soon I was kangaroo hopping down Lake Street as I tried to steer the heavy machine around a few badly parked cars before cornering into Vicarage Road. Parking up, I strode inside to announce to Mum and Dad that I had now bought a car and the whole family trooped outside to have a gawk.

Leading up to this day, my sights had long been set on learning to drive and own my own car. Depositing the first of my wages safely in the bank I had booked my driving lessons with BSM (British School of Motoring) soon after my eighteenth birthday. Following on from an unfortunate "good failure", as described by my instructor, when a ciggie puffing coalman decided it was a good day to practice annoying a ginger-mopped Irishman, enticing me to blow my horn long after he had turned his smoke emitting chimney on wheels into my path, I finally obtained my licence a couple of months later. The roads of Great Britain would have a new obstacle to overcome once I had purchased some wheels. Having invested my savings and passed my test I was now ready to take to the open road with my new best friend, named "Molly" in honour of dear old granny. Little did I know what adventures we would encounter over the next couple of years. Mum and Dad were very happy for me as I became the first member of our family to own a motor car.

One problem was the absence of any manual for my sturdy friend and many a day was spent trying to work out what did what or should have done had it worked properly. Finding the box was one thing but as I discovered replacing the fuse required patience as the temporary substitute silver paper had to be rolled like a cigarette and contorted into shape to fit its cradle. I had to practice lowering the window in order to wave my intended direction but alas the window had a mind of its own and would either not budge at all or drop completely allowing a howling gale to enter and scatter anything within its path. I would shortly identify its little foibles and over a year or so the Molly would earn her spurs and would take me on a few adventures. She was built like a tank with a heart to match and I became very fond of my new acquisition.

Mr Purvey offered me a parking place in the back yard of his shop which was very noble of him and ensured she was secured out of the street. In the colder mornings I discovered that starting required me to use a heavy metal handle that would be attached to the front of the engine and I had to turn it until the engine decided to crank into life. The challenge was first not to break my arm as the engine kicked the handle back and second to race around to the front of the car, jump in before it stalled, ease off the choke and maintain my foot on the accelerator without drowning the engine. The next stage was to decamp from the car, close the garage gates and re-enter the vehicle, again without stalling the engine.

On a regular basis I was able to take Mum into town or to visit aunt Margaret and uncle Michael in Cowley. My earliest real venture was to take Mum to visit Aunt Mae and Uncle Dudley in Southwold, on the East coast in far off Suffolk.

Aunt Mae (Mary) was actually first of the Carton family to depart for England. Escaping school at 14 she went to work as a nanny for the Bayliss family in Dublin, returning home to recuperate from a bout of rheumatic fever. She was later offered a post as a Governess to Captain Loftus and his family, and in 1946 left home to join them in Bulcamp, Suffolk. By all accounts she wore the full nanny attire donning a uniform that included a starched hat, collar and cuffs and she ruled strictly over her kingdom of the day and night nurseries, allowing a choice of jam or butter-never both, in those days of post war rationing. She was regarded as extremely pretty and had a waist that could almost be encircled by a man's hands as her future husband was soon to discover. It was at Bulcamp that she met with and married Dudley Wythe, a kind and gentle soul who also possessed healing hands and indeed removed warts from the hands of one of my cousins. Sadly, Grandad was unable to reconcile Dudley's religion with that of his Catholic daughter, notwithstanding his willingness to convert, and a short rift developed. Eventually, they married in England in 1951 but Mae never returned to Ireland. During their courtship, which was then a very traditional pastime, she changed her name to Jackie to distinguish her from her mother-in-law who was also known as May.

The newly married pair had a terrible shock on the night of 31st January 1953 when they awoke to see lights flashing in their bedroom window and as they put their feet out of bed found that they were floating. This was the night of the East Coast floods and Captain Loftus had come to their rescue, driving them to safety with my aunt clutching her wedding album as her most prized possession. In contrast, farmer Dudley chose to save his pigs! They subsequently settled in White House Farm where they raised their children, Susan and Russell.

The journey to Southwold with Mum was a marathon effort, unaided by a motorway, and I was relying on a simple AA road map. Considering it was my first major trip it was with some relief that we arrived at our destination safe and sound, stopping en-route for the obligatory tea and cake of course and we enjoyed a few lovely days being looked after and walking around Southwold.

Mae and Dudley were regular visitors to Oxford and we would learn more about their life and work on the farm in sunny Southwold. They owned a small mini traveller van into which Dudley had been known to pack a large number of us children and take us on the odd trip out, most notably to Bourton on the Water. Mae never drove herself but did a splendid job as a passenger driver, amusing us all with her careful directions to Dudley on how the vehicle should be driven and her strictures that on no account was he to exceed the dangerous speed of 50 mile per hour. I am not sure even now where everybody managed to sleep on their visits but as usual our parents managed, helped no doubt by Dudley's calmness and good humour whatever the situation and Mae's willingness to muck in and help out in true Carton fashion.

*

A career move gave me the opportunity to travel frequently with Molly when I obtained a post which took me to county courts around the South East gaining driving and map reading experience whilst covering a large number of miles with visits to Bury St Edmunds in the East to Brighton and Lewes on the south coast and she never let me down. I often worked in courts in central London and one day was startled to be accosted by an Evening Standard seller exclaiming in a very loud voice "what a colour scheme, me old cocker". My sartorial elegance had never been so publicly noted. I had spent the previous evening touring Carnaby Street, home of the "swinging sixties". Encouraged by an impeccably dressed flower pot of a salesman, who quickly identified a lad easily parted from his money, I was convinced that a new look was required for a new age. Smart dark-suited Court Clerk was cast aside. The new me was a colourful rainbow and the reaction of the news seller both pleased and horrified me. I was decked out in a light brown flecked jacket concealing a sun-bright yellow Ben Sherman type shirt over a pair of light blue flared trousers. To top it all, I wore a tie of many colours all vying for attention. I was working at Lambeth Court and I was not sure what the Chief Clerk thought of my new gear but he dispatched me with a mischievous chuckle, to purchase him some cigarettes, treating me more like a messenger boy than a new fashion icon.

Returning home, Mum had to look at me twice before realising it was her newly re-created son, and not some door-to-door hoover salesman, she simply said "well, its' a bit different" I decided that my new look would become my evening alter-ego whilst employing the dark suited style to protect and enhance my career prospects.

*

Having spent a year on relief duties I returned to Oxford on promotion to Senior Clerk. Back at home, my best mate Neville and I decided to drive ourselves to Paris for the Arc de Triomphe, one the most famous horse races in Europe expecting to see Mill Reef, English Derby winner, take on the French on their home soil. Neville was far more experienced than me and he undertook most of the driving.

Relaxing in Paris and taking in the magnificent sights along the Seine, including Notre Dame, and stopping off for occasional drinks, we conversed with waiters, many pleasant but a handful we found truculent and unwelcoming. We were well capable of ordering *deux café avec lait* and *deux bierre s'il vous plait*, but found language more a barrier with staff at our hotel. We did convince some of the waiters that our English raider would beat French filly *Pistol Packer* to win the race and our tip to them was to put their money on our boy. The irony was that when we finally got to the racecourse, we could not work out how to place a bet under their *Paris Mutuel* system so we could only watch in agony as our horse, destined to pay for our weekend away, romped home easily leaving us happy with our experience but financially wondering what might have been. *C'est la vie, mon ami* as the French would have put it.

The journey home proved to be more exciting than we imagined. I negotiated a few short mileage trips despite the irritation of French drivers who would insist on driving on the wrong side of the road. All was going well until within sight of Calais "Molly" spluttered and coughed herself to a standstill. Fortunately, Neville was a competent mechanic. Having peered under the bonnet to diagnose the problem as a faulty petrol-pump he rubbed his chin and he Instructed me to start the engine with my foot on the throttle. He then applied his knowledge and well-honed mechanical skills by delivering the engineering equivalent of an almighty clip round the ear to the pump that shocked it back into life. We sped all the way to the port coaxing Molly along before reaching Calais where we boarded the ferry.

We were on the verge of congratulating ourselves on reaching the outskirts of London when disaster stopped us in our wheels. Molly cried enough, enough and ominously surrendered to an inevitable halt close to London's Elephant and Castle tube station in the early hours of the morning. The RAC was summoned and a young mechanic, clearly besotted with our old metal trouper, initially dampened our spirits explaining that no garage would be open at this time of the morning. Not to be outdone, he said he knew of a car-breakers around the corner and, if we didn't mind and kept it to ourselves, he would hop over the wall and see if there was a suitable petrol pump in their yard. Half an hour or so later, he reappeared with a broad grin and a pump in hand. In no time he had inserted and tested the replacement prior to waving us on our way. We were more than happy to hand him a good "tip" before we set off on the final leg to Oxford with a revitalised Molly. Thus ended one very memorable trip to lovely Paris and the opportunity next day, and forever more, to relate our tale to parents, siblings and friends.

Drinking at the Grandpont was pretty much a daily event. A lad called Chas, from Northampton, used to spend a few weeks at a time working as a Senior Clerk at the County Court and lodged at nearby Yew Tree Hotel (aka Charlie's Porridge House) during the week. We would meet up at the pub most evenings and afterwards he would come back to Vicarage Road for tea and toast. He was a lonely soul and Mum and my sisters had no problem with this arrangement. However, for a short period I started to invite other regular drinking companions as well and we would gather around the glowing embers in the fire, exchanging views on this and that and playing some music. One was Gordon, a bit of a mystery man who we had met in the pub. Always dressed in a suit and tie with a white handkerchief smartly set into his top pocket, he gave little away about himself or his background but was content to be part of our group. Altogether different was "little Mick", another Scot from Glasgow with a loud voice, a happy enough demeanour and wearer of casually thrown together clothes.

This was of course unfair on Mum, and my sisters in particular, who had to go through the room to access the kitchen and bathroom. Mum said very little and I was much too-preoccupied to notice their reaction when we all turned up unannounced. She must have been worried enough to mention it to Dad. After one session too many, he took me aside and pointedly remarked that "this is not a halfway house". Taken aback at first, I soon realised he was absolutely correct (and my drinking companions agreed). Suitably contrite I immediately stopped. Mum and Betty did kindly say that they were happy to have Chas in the house as they had taken a liking to him and he was so very polite. He returned to Northampton sometime later where he died suddenly of a heart attack.

Molly had been a wonderful servant to me, teaching me much about her body parts and her need for care and attention to get her to peak performance. After a couple of years, she was beginning to show her age, with bits requiring a face lift and internal organs ready for renewal at great cost. No dealer was willing to make a decent offer to trade her in for a newer model so, with advice from Neville, I decided to enter her for sale at the weekly Oxpens Car Auction. She attracted quite a bit of attention due to her pedigree and the announcer touted her assets with great aplomb ensuring she was bought by a new fan for the princely sum of £45, half of what I had paid for her but still well ahead of a week's average wage. I bade her one last farewell and strode off in search of Molly mark2 with the words of a familiar song "there will never be another you" humming quietly in my head.

My second motor proved that looks aren't everything. My parents took a liking to her and were happy enough to be ferried around in a bit more comfort. Lime green and stylishly trimmed my new acquisition was a Vauxhall Viva SL Model and was sleek, speedy and reliable enough. She did not require a starting handle to get her moving, was easy to handle and boasted more comfortable seating but she lacked the panache of my first love Molly. She had a couple of fatal flaws in that her carburettor required regular cleaning and her bodywork was prey to rotting, a combination that would eventually see me exchange my rust box for a succession of Ford Escorts.

Chapter Eighteen

The Seventies, All Kinds of Everything

This era is often labelled as the turbulent seventies and with good reason. Following the mildly revolutionary and amiable sixties with its emphasis on fashion, music, free love and hippy culture. The seventies, by contrast, ushered in an altogether a more aggressive decade.

The highlight of the year 1970 for our Mum was eighteen years old Irish singer Dana winning the Eurovision Song Contest when she captivated a massive televised audience of 200 million, singing her ballad *"all kinds of everything"*, which Mum would reprise to herself whilst slaving over a hot stove. Some twenty years later, I would have the very good fortune to meet the lovely lady. I had been entranced when hearing songs on her new Christian album, full of tunes whose lyrics that arrowed directly into the heart. I contacted her at Belfast Opera House. The international superstar threw me into a wild panic when she invited me, with unsupported confidence, to arrange a Christian concert in Birmingham. Thanks largely to my family and the Pastor, Reverend Woodford, the evening proved to be great success. I have often reflected on how delighted Mum would have been to have met such a kindred soul.

The first day of the 70s had commenced with the lowering of the age of majority to 18, opening up a whole new world for my generation. We expressed our views in dramatic fashion, demonstrating our gratitude by turfing out the very government who had so recently empowered us. It came just weeks after World Cup holders, England, sent off to retain the trophy with their recording of "back home" ringing in the ears of an expectant nation, they had instead brought tears and frustration to the country. Having seemingly secured a semi-final place when leading bitter rivals Germany by two goals to nil they surrendered their lead and found themselves inexplicably knocked out.

The inquest in the pub that evening is vividly recalled as myself, good mate Neville and other head-in-hand friends gathered in the bar at the pub. Deploying our skills as experts in match analysis and, in the process, revealing only our own fickleness, we questioned the tactical ability of our hitherto world cup winning manager. In such a doom-laden atmosphere we downed a few pints of gut rot and readily convinced ourselves that the country required a fresh new government to boot, replacing the pipe smoking socialist Harold with Sailor Ted (Heath), an outcome that surprised many. The lesson here is surely never to hold an election during a World Cup campaign, unless you have just won.

Ahead of the election, the then Prime Minister, Harold Wilson, had ended up resembling an omelette after egg missiles were directed at him and his wife Mary whilst on a pr-election "meet the people" walk about that went wrong as even the PMs car was also somewhat comically mislaid. My socialist inclined father, and his brother Michael, blamed the reluctance of the rich and powerful to free up money for investment under a

Labour government but, like football fans, they still hoped for a comeback in the years ahead. Regrettably, England failed to even qualify for the next world cups. For Dad and Michael though it wasn't many years before their election wish was granted but it arrived with a waspish sting in the tail.

Still, it was not all gloom as the first Glastonbury) Festival in September attracted headline act T Rex (Marc Bolan) as concert goers, not a few stark naked, danced joyfully and frolicked happily in glorious muddy pastures. BP (British Petroleum) announced the discovery of major oil reserves in the North Sea amid speculation about a new industrial age where the UK would transform itself into a self-sufficient sheikdom of oil and wealth, independent of overseas producers, with potential for new jobs and prosperity. Worthy of note is, whilst the UK dream of everlasting oil revenues have since largely been dissipated, or squandered, a largely politically-free zone of a music festival has prospered beyond belief.

Concerns of every older generation that the nation was going to hell (again), was provided when the first scantily clad Page 3 girl, a German model, appeared in the Sun newspaper, on a freezing cold November day. This winter wonder simultaneously caused many a young male heart to flutter and some old heads to tut-tut. Sales took off like a proverbial rocket, with older men caught glancing at the paper insisting they had bought the rag solely to study form, as in the horse racing variety, and no doubt causing many a weekly confession to be made to their equally horse mad priest. Many of the girls became household names, including the most popular of them all, Linda Lusardi, who from the mid-seventies went on to become an actress and singer.

The initial expectations and hope gave way to more serious doubts as the advancing year came face to face with crushing reality, and was a precursor to years of strife, incorporating a currency change, power cuts, a three-day week, IRA bombings and a winter of discontent ending with the youth feeling lucky to have any job. De-industrialisation devastated many thousands of manufacturing jobs resulting in high levels of unemployment. Having lived and worked my way through the period I can testify to the fact that it did not actually feel especially awful or worrying as we all lived from day to day as events arose and passed quickly into history. Dramatic and turbulent it may have been in retrospect but when you are concentrating on whatever transpires on a daily basis you do not think about yesterday or tomorrow. My late mother-in-Law, Violet, would often recite, frequently in her own words, the **Lena Martell** song, "*One Day at a Time*", a tune which aptly summed up her approach to life in general.

In similar fashion, my own mother held to her lifetime refrain *que sera, sera*. Asked on one occasion whether she was happy, Mum dismissed any such notion with her retort "I don't have the time to think about that". Philosophers would no doubt spend years debating its merits but just getting on with life may have much to recommend it, neither living in the past nor worrying about an always uncertain future. To be honest, I have to admit that being a civil servant, in a secure post, clearly helped in negotiating a way through the turbulence and I was more than thankful for being so fortunate.

*

In terms of our own family, our respective contributions from the early sixties onward may well have helped but it was still largely left to Dad to cope with financing the upbringing of the family and managing the mortgage and rate payments despite strikes and walk outs especially whilst Paul, Ann and David were still at school at the turn of the decade. Our parents, with patience and determination, accepted their burden without complaint and maintained a monastical vow of silence regarding money matters. I can recall only one occasion when myself and Betty were informed by Mum that Dad was worried about paying the rates. We were happy to help out. When we declined to accept any re-payment Mum typically went out and bought very expensive steaks for our dinner rather than spend it on herself as we had intended.

Dad certainly in his early days at Cowley worked six days a week with only Sunday off. Initially, he worked on day shifts and was responsible for cleaning operations, ensuring all cars left the factory in top condition before working in the Unipart Division. Austin, Morris and Rover cars have been produced at Cowley over the years with the Pressed Steel Company, a subsidiary at the same complex, building the bodyshells.

At its peak, when Dad, Uncle Michael and brother Nicky and his wife Margaret worked at the plant, the beginning and end of the day possibly resembled the scene depicted by *Katie Melua* in her song *"nine million bicycles in Beijing"* as some 30,000 people swarmed into and exited their work abode on trusty and crusty old bikes, rendering the tarmac roads and paths invisible to the eye. The factory was divided into a number of discrete blocks, each responsible for a specific part of the production process with tracks or assembly lines that included body shells, engines and trim shop processes covering interior facias and seating. As previously alluded to, most workers belonged to generations of the same family, from grandparents to parents and their own children and were seemingly well paid. Cowley, and car production, was a changing environment and over many years the once high-quality manufacturing output came under severe strain, leading to frequent restructures and changes of management and direction which all began to take their toll in the seventies.

I knew little of the way the factory operated. Whenever Nicky talked about working in the Trim Shop, I thought for a long time he was employed as a barber. Talk of assembly lines merely conjured up an image of school assembly and visions of the workers meeting daily for a jolly sing along. From later knowledge gained I suspect the singing of *the red flag* might have been the signature choice of some of the senior Shop Stewards.

Dad chose to work at the factory to earn more money than he did at Lucy's, where he had been very happy. Initially, he worked from early morning to evening but soon commenced a near lifetime on night shifts, a move that increased his income considerably but at a great cost to his health as evidenced by his earlier hospitalisation. In the sixties and seventies in particular, there were serious disruptions to the production and he would voice concern that foreign car makers would soon overtake the British. He would work the night shift between around 9pm and 7am before returning home where Mum would be up, fire lit and ready to serve his breakfast. Immersing himself in the Daily Mirror newspaper, Dad would select his bets and retire to bed just as we were either going off to either school or work. This continued year after long year, the spell broken only by a few bank holidays and the annual works break in July, when Oxford would largely be abandoned by the masses. Even then, he supplemented his income by taking on part time work in the local pub and during the summer break would find him, in his baseball hat, operating the turnstiles at Hinksey Pool to earn extra money so there was little or no opportunity for rest. I enquired of family directly involved about the working conditions and industrial relations at the Cowley works in order to understand why our parents had to work so hard.

There was always the continuous smell of tobacco filling the air at home, attaching itself to clothes, and the yellow stained ceilings that reflected the colour of Dad's fingertips.

Unfortunately, at Cowley works there was, amongst some union leaders, a desire to cause disruption for the smallest alleged breach of rules resulting in considerable interruption. Many Senior Shop Stewards were well educated, some at Ruskin College, and possessed detailed knowledge of work regulations and conditions that enabled them to run rings around some managers. They saw it as their duty to look after the welfare of workers when management were seen to overstep the mark or contravene safety. Much of the work was very hard and sweaty and imposed enormous pressures on the workforce. Nicky commented that working in the Glue Room often resulted in fingers sticking together. Many of them joked, with dark humour, that they had to buy more expensive cigarettes as their glued fingers prevented them rolling their own cheaper ones. The summer heat in the Trim Shop glove room was at times reported to be horrendous and smelly and there were apparently times when pots of inflammable glue were set alight by discarded cigarette ends, provoking serious safety risks.

Shop Stewards then seemingly held considerable power and control over work allocation that could determine individual work hours and earnings. The effect of downtime and some working practices resulted in Dad having time on his hands and he started to smoke more heavily. At its peak he said he was slowly killing himself by consuming 60 cigarettes nightly so a fair proportion of his annual earnings were going up in a million puffs of smoke. Being a learned man, perhaps he should have reflected on the words of the Novelist JB Priestly "if God had wanted man to smoke, he would have given him chimneys." My brother Nicky also confirmed the impact of enduring numerous strike periods and his wife Margaret, would rage about the disruptions had on her ability to pay the housing rent and food bills.

Records show that in the period from the late sixties to the eighties there were hundreds of recorded strikes per year.

Whatever the motives, and irrespective of who was responsible, the fact remains that they were difficult times for the workforce, their livelihood and their health. Dad always said management and their inability to understand the feelings of their own pressurised line workers were equally at fault and this was confirmed in reports prepared for the Labour Government. it was not a surprise then that there were so many stoppages but Dad and Nicky were also of the opinion that unions were needed in order to safeguard the workforce. Dad had expressed great hope that the election of two periods of Labour government under Harold Wilson, and later James Callaghan, would lead to better times but he was to be bitterly disappointed. He was an admirer of Barbara Castle and her efforts to improve industrial relations. Her proposed Bill, *"In place of strife"* was bitterly opposed and rejected by the unions. Interestingly, Castle's own diaries subsequently revealed that union officials who had publicly attacked her were privately supportive.

In any event the 1970s ushered in one of the worst periods of industrial strife not only at Cowley but nationally. This would lead eventually to the election of a conservative government under the premiership of Margaret Thatcher. Many, including Dad, confirmed the view that it was Thatcher who reduced the power of the unions and after some turbulence, gave rise to a better future in industrial relations, to the detriment of union power. In common with many others who worked at Cowley, he may have concurred on the disbandment of the "closed shop" and other restrictive practices but he would never bring himself to vote Tory. Mum, on the other hand was very pragmatic and more concerned with feeding and clothing her family and kept any political opinions to herself.

The introduction of Measured Day Working (MDW)) in the seventies was seen as a milestone in industrial relations at the factory. Resisted by an element of Shop Stewards who saw it as a restriction of workers' rights, not to mention their own power, the workers were persuaded to strike over the issue for seven long weeks. The proposal was to replace the system of piecework payment, which handed power to the stewards who were able to determine the cost per job, staffing levels and work patterns. In effect, it was their decisions on allocations that determined how much workers could individually earn and was seen by some as neither consistent nor secure. Fixed hours, by contrast, involved a standard pay rate and was designed to speed up lines and productivity with a more participatory group involvement to the production process but stoppages or interruptions on one part of the line could still halt the whole production. The new system was sold to the workforce on the basis that it would provide better and consistent pay and more security but was opposed by Stewards as they believed it would erode shop floor influence over management decisions. Management concluded that the only way forward was to impose their will and the proposed system was already was common practice at other car plants. English factories were facing stiff competition from car importers and needed to improve technology and productivity to safeguard their own future.

Although a long strike ended in a defeat for union officials it did not immediately end the ongoing disruptions. Cowley workers were paid a varying degree of wages depending on grade, work type, seniority and other variants but were reputed to be well in excess of the UK wage average of £32 when a loaf of bread cost the decimal equivalent of 9p, beer was 20p per pint and a couple of cinema tickets would set you back 90p. The average house price was £4975, around 3 times the annual salary. More pertinently, a new Mini-car could be purchased for around £600. To put all of this into a family perspective and, to the best of my knowledge, Dad had purchased Vicarage Road for about £2200 in 1960, then about twice his income but on terms which are unknown. MDW welcomed by the workforce because it provided a fixed pay rate. A small welcome benefit was that if a line was halted then the workers were able to step outside and have a crafty smoke without incurring any loss of income.

Set against this annual background of strife it is easier to understand how Dad came to smoke so many cigarettes and worked so hard, with the continuous interruptions having exerted severe pressure on family finances.

Away from the turbulence at Cowley, my new role as a Senior Clerk saw me working at Harcourt House on Marston Road, after the old County Court in Castle Street had been demolished to make way for Selfridges in the new Westgate Shopping Centre and Library, together with a host of other famous old buildings including the magnificent G R Cooper Departmental Store; The Paviers Arms, where court staff had held frequent gatherings and Mac Fisheries.

February 15th 1971 saw the death of two familiar friends, Tanner and Bob, who had spent much of their lives nesting in my trouser pockets. Their passing was publicly mourned by Dominic Sandbrook, a writer in the Daily Mail, as the day Britain lost its independence and its very soul. The so named Valentine Day Massacre orchestrated by the Conservative government under Edward Heath, led to the guillotining of our established currency, including my aforementioned companions Tanner (silver sixpence) and Bob (shilling).

The demise of pounds, shillings and pence, (symbolised as £, s, d) seemed a shame and rather unfair at the time especially after all those school years of trying to remember, and getting a sharp teacher stab with a ruler for getting wrong, the number of pennies to a shilling (12); the number of shillings to a pound (20) and number of pennies to a pound (240). We also had silver half crowns (two shillings and sixpence) and in my younger school days we had the loveable bronze Thrupenny Bit (3 pennies), withdrawn a year earlier and the Florin (two shillings) withdrawn in the late sixties. Notes came in the form of ten shillings and five, ten and twenty pounds. Adding up a list of groceries in three columns of pounds, shillings and pence required a bit of mental dexterity without any mechanical assistance. Hence, mental arithmetic was considered an essential skill to be learnt and was drummed into young minds from an early age.

Working at Oxford County Court on *Decimal day* was not as traumatic as were led to believe. Credit for that must go to our genial Staff Clerk, Clive Salmon who arranged all of the training and had prepared well for the day. Under his tutelage it was not long before we discovered that it was a simple enough system to understand. The biggest problem I encountered, in company with countless others for a while afterwards, was trying not to think how much it cost in old money, such as you might do with a foreign currency although it was useful as a check to compare before and after prices, many of which had unsurprisingly been rounded up. Using our office account books was definitely easier with two simple columns based on 100 pence to a pound. French inspired and Napoleonic it may have been but it was easy to operate. Rather like going abroad, shops displayed prices in old and new money for some time. We could still use up any old money but would receive decimal coins in any change. So successful was the changeover that many old coins went out of circulation in six months, well ahead of the scheduled period reflecting the success of the transformation and its efficient introduction. My parents and siblings soon got the hang of this new-fangled coinage and life carried on much as before despite dire warnings of our impending doom from some fear mongering commentators. Indeed, from our collective memories nobody in the family can recall any real problems with the changeover.

Amidst all of this political drama the Minister for Education, one Margaret Thatcher, obtained parliamentary approval, to end free school milk for the over 7s, which many of us Carton's had enjoyed, and she was doomed to be forever own as *"milk snatcher"*. Ironically, it was a Labour Minister, Edward Short, who had himself withdrawn milk from secondary schools three years earlier and suffered less abuse and brickbats, who still chose to lambast Thatcher. Pots and kettles were jibes that sprang to mind and directed in his direction. Alas, such was, and is, the life of a politician.

*

To the utter dismay of our parents, the years following saw increasing troubles in Northern Ireland, with riots, killings and the detention of hundreds. Prime Minister Heath was leading the British Admirals Cup team to victory in his Yacht, Morning Cloud, in August 1971, when the Northern Ireland Prime Minister Brian Faulkner suddenly introduced a policy of internment without trial, on suspected IRA terrorists at Long Kesh. The following January, British soldiers' shot dead fourteen Catholics who were partaking in a protest demonstration against the policy of Internment. The day became known as Bloody Sunday and continues to be a matter of contention and controversy regarding how it unfolded and to apportion blame. An initial report by Lord Widgery cleared British soldiers whereas a more detailed twelve-year investigation, led by Lord Saville, reported in 2010 and found the killings to be unjustifiable. This prompted Prime Minister David Cameron to apologise on behalf of the British State and some criminal proceedings were commenced without any conviction. It was reported that the massacre had resulted in increasing support for the IRA and acted as a recruiting agent, contrary to all intentions.

In the immediate aftermath of Bloody Sunday, the IRA launched a reprisal car bomb attack on Aldershot Parachute Brigade killing seven people, including a chaplain. Ex-Beatle, Paul McCartney, with a new band named "Wings", ventured into this political hornet's nest when he released a single entitled *"Give Ireland back to the Irish"* which was promptly banned by the BBC. By contrast, two of the most popular hit records of this time were *"I'd like to teach the world to sing (in perfect harmony)"* by the New Seekers and "Amazing Grace", performed by the Pipes and Drums Military Band of the Royal Scots Dragoon Guards.

To add to England's problems Ugandan dictator Ida Amin expelled some 50,000 citizens possessing British passports and the government had its fingers burnt during the Cod wars when Icelandic gunboats sank two British Trawlers.

*

Late summer 1972 heralded the most major event in my life with the arrival at Oxford County Court of a vivacious young west country girl, Shirley Baker, driving her maroon Austin A40 whose registration number, RHY746, is still etched in my brain. She revved into the court, also on promotion to Senior Clerk, and into my life, changing it forever and in the process saving me from myself. An endearing memory is of her driving her car with one hand on the wheel whilst the other was busy flicking ash through an open window, in the days when she was an avid smoker.

To say it was love at first sight would be overstating her reaction when we were introduced by Chief Clerk. As she occasionally reminds me, I jumped up like a hopping kangaroo, my Roy Orbison thick rimmed glasses hanging beneath very bushy eyebrows, and held out my long arm to greet her. Her initial thoughts were not "what a wonderful specimen of manhood" but seemingly "Who on earth is this". It may have been brief but was not quite a reprise of the encounter as in the film of the same name. Nevertheless, love and destiny soon won the day and nearly fifty years on we are still going strong.

When she finally joined us on a permanent basis Shirley was staying at Charlie's famous porridge house whilst searching for accommodation. One evening I was with Neville when we bumped into her and another guest from her lodgings whilst watching a game at the White House Ground. We got into conversation and were soon talking about footie and Oxford United. We discovered we had something in common which helped facilitate conversation back at the office. One day my rust box Viva conked out in the office car park and Shirley provided me with a lift home and afforded me an opportunity to ask her if we could meet up outside of work. Thankfully, she agreed and indeed went one better and invited me and Neville to join her, and her best friend Linda, when she arrived to stay for a weekend. On the Saturday evening the four of us enjoyed a good evening out, starting with a drink at our regular haunt before venturing into the city and an evening of dance. Shirley, clad in a figure-hugging orange wool mini skirt, had the most gorgeous warm smile capable of melting an iceberg, let alone me, from a mile away and still possesses that same power today.

Thinking back, we may never have met at all if my application to manage Sunderland FC had been successful. That had arisen after I had watched Oxford beat Sunderland five-nil and sacked their manager as a result. The post was advertised and I decided to apply, citing my fan acquired knowledge as an expert on tactics and my motivation skills arising from my one-year senior clerk experience. Sunderland politely thanked me for my interest but concluded that perhaps a bit of football management experience would help and wished me well for my future civil service career! To howls of laughter, I dined out with my mates on that reply for many months and the letter itself was stationed at the top of a bookshelf. Mind you, had Shirley had her way she would have been an accountant. That would have been her chosen profession and she went for an interview at a firm which promised day-release to obtain qualifications. She was to be disappointed when the interviewer strongly hinted that accountancy was perhaps not a job for a girl, and she quietly acquiesced. My only surprise is that the man escaped with his tongue and head intact for venturing such an opinion, as he surely would not have done had he put forward such a preposterous suggestion a few years later when she had gained some life experience. So, I was put off a career as a journalist and football manager whilst Shirley was similarly denied accountancy yet the Gods miraculously aligned to link us both together.

Back at the office, we were getting on really well and began to meet up regularly. Aside from football, it transpired that Shirley had an interest in horses as well and, as I soon discovered, she was a church going Baptist who had been an active member of her Bible School. I recall Nicky's wife Margaret remarking how fortunate I was to have met somebody with whom I had such shared interests. My sister May and her future husband happened to drop into the King Edward pub one evening where Shirley and I were drinking and, accosting me at the bar, commented "I see you're doing very well for yourself". Both of them were certainly correct in their observations and I knew I was indeed a very lucky boy. More darkly, I overheard one of the office typists express her view, at our office's Christmas party, that lovely Shirley's interest in me must have been "because of his money." Presumably based on her, erroneous, assumption that, as a single man in his mid- twenties, I must have been rolling in the green stuff and, perhaps more understandably, being perplexed as to why such an attractive young lady would fancy me!

Shirley, the eldest of three children, still had to face the ordeal of meeting with my rather large family. First introduction was to Mum who immediately took to her. Shirley was seated at the corner of the table with a chirping budgie caged behind her and with me opposite. Present and correct, eager to meet Shirley, were most of my sisters and brothers. I suppose it would have helped had I arranged for us all to have name badges as poor old Shirley must have been a bit befuddled but she captivated the lot of them with her easy manner. She was after all the daughter of Alf, an amiable self-employed painter and decorator, and a mother, Violet, who worked as a cleaner at Weston Hospital. Our families thus shared a similar council house background and education. In her younger days Shirley worked with her mum with cleaning and collecting glasses at the Imperial Pub to ensure there was enough money coming into the house to keep them all clothed and fed, especially when her dad's work dried up. She endured cold days and nights at home and often had to forage for firewood in dark woods to ensure there was at least a warm fire in the evenings. It was not surprising that, religion apart, we had much in common.

After a couple of hours or so in our house on that initial visit I decided that it was time to rescue Shirley and for us to get off to the pub for a well-earned drink. Returning home later that night, I was greeted by a smiling Mum who chatted away about how nice it was to meet her. One thing that equally appealed to Mum and Shirley was their shared bond with being reared close to the sea and the sound of crashing waves. Thereafter, we spent a lot of our time together especially after Shirley had moved into a flat on Banbury Road, in the north of the city.

New Year's Day 1973 still required us all to attend work and at the court it was a solemn occasion when the cash ledger books had to be balanced with individual record cards of debtors, a process referred to as "agadashing", although agonising would be more accurate. Shirley, and May's boyfriend Pat, had stayed overnight at Vicarage Road and it is still a mystery to me where everybody slept. Anyway, Shirley and Pat, reaping the reward for over celebrating the new year, were still under the weather and remained at our house, fed soup and kindness by our patient non-drinking Mom.

Months before I had met Shirley, Neville and I had booked a trip to Austria for the beginning of February, which was to be my skiing baptism. The magnificent alpine scenery was an instant attraction but it was not long before I discovered that the apres-ski was far more enjoyable than trying to flip flop over snow on a pair of oversized knitting needles. The first day on the nursery slopes saw me failing even to manipulate the wretched poles onto my feet which somehow ended facing in different directions and resembling actor John Cleese on one of his silly walks, except in my case it was unintentional. The old joke that skiing is the only sport where you spend an arm and a leg to break an arm and a leg seemed only too plausible and I soon retired unhurt to the safety of the bar. Neville, being a seasoned skier, was happy to glide his way over the snowy mountains without having to play nursemaid. In any event, I was missing Shirley, writing to her regularly, and Neville agreed to cut short our holiday by a few days.

On my arrival home, late in the evening, I found her drinking in the King Edward Pub down our road, in the company of my sisters. In league with my wibbly-wobbly legs I was delighted to see her and that great big smile as I entered the bar. Later in the year, in contrast to snowy Austria, we went to nice warm Greece for a couple of weeks with her sister Corinne and best friend Linda. Shortly after, to the delight of my parents, we became engaged and celebrated the occasion with family and friends at a dinner in a Chinese restaurant in Summertown. Even now, the delight of the occasion is tinged with a bit of regret on me having to go around the table after dinner to collect money to pay the bill but that is how it was, with money tight and everybody being in the same position as the country was in the grip of conflict and disruption.

A family highlight of the year was the summer wedding of my sister May to Pat Curley, brother of Paul with whom I had shared the same school class as well as a few years working at the court before he decided he would rather be a policeman. They were supported on the day by family and bridesmaids whose number included our Ann, dressed in long and flowing lemon. For our proud Dad, this was another first. Dressed in his new dark suit with navy tie and white shirt, he beamed broadly as he escorted May down the aisle as *Father of the Bride* at the Holy Rood Church before *giving her away* in the traditional manner and handing her to the care of her husband.

Our shy Mum, who had been enjoyably active in helping May with her choice of dress, flowers and invitations, was regally attired in a mix of pale and dark blue. Buttoned to the waist she wore a pale blue dress, with dark blue collarettes and matching waist belt. Atop she sported her co-ordinated dark blue Panama style hat with pale blue band and below strode out in her equally styled blue shoes. The wedding, attended by scores of aunts and uncles from far and wide, provided a welcome day of fun and relief at a time of continuous national strife. The reception was held at The Civil Defence Social Club near Vicarage Road.

*

In the summer, the only surviving twins in the family, Paul and Ann, left school to set out on their much divergent roads. Ann found work at Littlewoods store for some years before transferring to the Co-op, where she worked as a sales assistant. She was thrice a bridesmaid to May, Betty and Shirley but sadly, never the bride herself. Her life was difficult and within five years she found herself pregnant by her then boyfriend who offered little in the way of support following the birth of her son Kieran in December 1978. Pat Curley recounts with some mirth the day he took Ann to hospital to give birth and, on being guided into the ward, was informed by the midwife of his full fatherly rites on the mistaken impression he was the father. On leaving hospital Ann went home to live with Mum and Dad but she had to leave when Mum was taken ill and was no longer able to cope with the presence of a young child. In the interim, Pat and his wife Shirley provided her with a home.

Sometime later though, Ann had the good fortune to meet with Mick Walsh, a thoroughly decent man as well as being a first-class carpenter and with whom she gave birth to two children, Nicky and Scott. Mick also took young Kieran under his wing and looked after him to the extent that he regarded Mick as his dad and often referred to him as such, as indeed he does to this day. They were awarded a council house in Bayswater Road, Headington not far away from my brother Nicky.

They prospered well enough with Mick earning good money in exchange for his skills. Some of his clients, who were well known Oxford names shamefully took advantage and failed to pay for major work he had undertaken in fitting kitchens and bedrooms, leaving him stressed and short of cash at times to support his family. Being genial he was reluctant to chase them for payment. He suffered from high blood pressure but continued, like Ann, to enjoy a drink and a lot of smokies, until it all came to a sudden and tragic end. Ann suffered a brain haemorrhage which resulted in her having speech, mobility and other problems that required support and assistance from Mick and family. Disaster struck one afternoon in 2004, with Ann by his side, Mick collapsed and died of a heart attack at the wheel of his car, colliding with a wall at Bayswater School, just around the corner from their home.

Ann and the children were devastated and never fully recovered. She remained at the Bayswater home doing her best to look after her family. Despite concern and further support from brothers and sisters she struggled to cope, despite strong support from Kieran and she continued to require help and support with her speech and physical abilities that were still mildly affected. In 2007, she had a stroke and was admitted to the John Radcliffe Hospital. Her general demeanour and irrational behaviour caused some of the nursing staff to ridicule her causing Betty to intervene and explain that her unfortunate state of health was primarily the result of her earlier brain haemorrhage. Unbeknown to family, she had been dosing on paracetamol to ease the pain of constant headaches and this had inflicting permanent liver damage. Quite simply, her vital body organs were shutting down.

Ann died two days after Betty and myself had visited her. Strangely, she had then been sitting up in bed and talking away merrily, seemingly without a care in the world and, perhaps mercifully, oblivious to her plight. Her death shocked her children to the core and she was laid to rest with the caring Mick.

*

Paul, by contrast, followed a different life path to his twin sister. Leaving school, he worked for Oxford instruments, renowned worldwide for their design and development of magnetic resonance imaging (MRI Scans) and a succession of innovative medical and industrial equipment. He worked here for a number of years before moving to a number of jobs that took him across the pond to America, before setting up his own management consultancy, the aptly named RESOLVE.

I am not sure how many times my brother visited County Cork but he must have been upended for a long time and his lips sufficiently suctioned to the Blarney Stone to gain eloquence sufficient to persuade hard-nosed industrial managers, and indeed government departments, to part with generous sums of money in exchange for his sage-like knowledge.

His gift of the gab also seems to have enabled him to acquire a collection of young ladies, a few of whom accompanied him when he visited our home in Birmingham to attend wine and dine concerts.

Aside from May's wedding and school departures, this was the year the UK and Ireland joined the European Economic Community (EEC); VAT was introduced; Mainland bombings by the IRA escalated once again, especially in London; Rail and Civil Service Unions caused disruptions and in May over 1.6million workers went on strike. Shirley and I celebrated our engagement at around the same time as the Arab-Israel war that resulted in a huge increase in world oil prices. This was compounded by the impact of rising coal prices in the UK caused by dwindling supplies arising from strikes by both miners and electricity workers. The Government warned of a tough Christmas, declared a State of Emergency and imposed restrictions on power usage, directed a closedown of 10.30pm for television, set a maximum 50mph speed limit on all roads and announced the imminent imposition of a three -day working week to conserve supplies. Power cuts had become a feature of our daily lives at home and at work but we carried on regardless, even enjoying the chaos, as the country responded in positive fashion. Sales of candles and paraffin lamps hit record highs. We would meet, sit and chat amiably in semi- darkened homes or pubs. Perhaps it was not just coincidental that a baby boom followed nine months later. The pop group Slade caught something of the national mood with their cheerful rendition of their song *"merry Christmas everybody"*.

We believed 1974 would see a renewed spirit of hope and optimism. As it happened, the year would see three more family weddings being celebrated within a few months of each other.

Chapter Nineteen

Three Weddings and a Miracle

The 1974 New Year was formally celebrated as a public holiday for the first time ensuring there was no more working to *agadash* the annual court accounts, whilst still under the influence of the previous evening's indulgence. There was little else to celebrate at this time as the three-day working week became operative and lasted until early March, with the government considering coupons for petrol rationing but I have no memory of ever seeing them and did not find petrol especially difficult to come by although some queues formed at forecourts.

Shirley and I were able to spend some time wandering around Oxford, described by Matthew Arnold as "The city of dreaming spires". We visited many university colleges, taking in the historic buildings, frequently adorned with scary and ugly looking Gargoyles, designed as a water sprout to divert water away from the building. The most memorable of our hand-in-hand walks was around Christ Church College and Cathedral, an area steeped in history, and from there we would follow paths through the squirrel filled gardens and meadow to Rose Lane and beyond to Magdalen Bridge and College, where C.S Lewis the author of Narnia Chronicles was a Tutor. The Cathedral itself had its origins in the legend of St. Frideswide, later declared Patron Saint of Oxford. As a notably pious young princess she desired to be a nun but was pursued by nobleman who, with the King's permission, wished to marry her causing her to flee to Oxford, where he found her. Allegedly arriving at the city's Boundary Walls, he was struck blind, he sought and obtained forgiveness in exchange for her release, whereupon his sight was restored. She went on to establish Frideswide Nunnery on the site of the present Cathedral.

Barely a month into a new year the Conservative Prime Minister Edward Heath, chanced his arm by calling an election in the midst of the three-day week in an effort to break the impasse of the concurrent miners' day week and asking the question "Who Runs the Country"? He received a ripe old raspberry in response, "Not You," with voters dramatically swapping the sailor hero of the Admirals Cup in exchange for the return of a hung parliament. This led to the return to power of Harold Wilson as Prime Minister, with Dad hoping that the perennial smoker might use his pipe as an instrument of peace. The election reflected a deep split in public opinion on how to deal with the miners and the incessant strife. Dad was perfectly happy with this outcome and predicted that Harold and the trade unions would reach an agreement. He was correct on that score as the government did indeed settle the dispute by offering a massive 35% pay rise to be repeated 12 months later but this merely postponed the lingering problems that eventually recur. The ending of the three-day week in March instigated a return to normal life patterns. I could not help but reflect on the fact that at the court we had achieved in three days what had hitherto taken five, a somewhat massive improvement in productivity that has probably never been bettered.

In company with our friends, Shirley and I went to watch Oxford United play Manchester United at the manor the day after PM Heath had called his election. In a momentous match Oxford won one nil, with an Alamo style defence where they held out for 89 glorious minutes after scoring in the first. The game has gone down in folk-lore and brought huge enjoyment to the city in torrid times. Shirley did come to a few more games but she had also developed a love for horse riding, joined a riding school and would spend many a Saturday galloping across fields on her favourite grey horse Chevette.

The national madness continued when an attempt was made by a gun toting Ian Ball to kidnap Princess Anne, only months after her royal wedding had grabbed the attention of the nation. The no nonsense princess steadfastly refused to get out of the car as he demanded and is reported to have retorted "not bloody likely". Three people, including the bodyguard and chauffeur, were shot during the attempt which ended with the mentally ill Ball being caught off guard by a passing boxer.

Betty and me had already seen our younger siblings Nicky, Pat and May follow Mehael into the wedding stakes. Mum and Dad must have had a bit of a surprise when we both announced our weddings would take place in the same month of April. To be fair, Betty and Mick had been courting for several years but their relationship was complicated due to Mick being already married, though separated. By coincidence, Shirley was the court clerk on the day his divorce was finalised a month or so before our own scheduled wedding. Betty had always said she wanted an Easter wedding and the earliest Easter date available was just one week before ours. So it was that Betty and Mick, fixed their wedding for two weeks before Shirley and myself.

Their wedding day went with a bang as it synchronised nicely with the Eurovision Song Contest from Brighton, won by a group named ABBA, singing *Waterloo*, who would go on to achieve worldwide fame. The Civil Ceremony at the Register Office in St Giles, with sister Ann as bridesmaid, was followed by the reception held at the Civil Defence Social Club in Gordon Street. Mum was overjoyed to see her eldest daughter finally happily married, a sentiment echoed by the rest of the family, and the wedding afforded Mum another opportunity to obtain a stylish new outfit, as befitting the mother of the bride. Granny unexpectedly hot footed over from Ireland at the last moment to join Betty's celebration.

We continued preparing for our own wedding during the bombings and industrial unrest or rather Shirley did. Extremely proficient at making her own clothes, sewing and an assortment of other arty skills, she designed her own dress as well as that of the three bridesmaids comprising her sister Corinne; my youngest sister Ann and her best friend Linda. She not only sourced the material but made all dresses herself. The flowers were prepared by Mr Dale, father of Shirley's sister-in-law Judith, so it was a real family affair. My main contribution was to attend the church for pre marriage lessons with the vicar, Mr Gathercole. On frequent visits to Shirley's parents in Weston-super -Mare we became regular attenders at the local Baptist Church where Shirley was brought up and attended regular Sunday School and Bible Class. On my initial church visit I was enthralled by the joy and informality displayed as compared to the more staid and rigid Catholic approach beloved by Mum and Gran.

I had got on well with Shirley's Mum and Dad from the beginning and during our visits Alf and I often spent an evening or three at the Borough Arms discussing football and other worldly affairs, not that it did us much good. Alf was a keen

Bristol City supporter and we would go to as many games as we could, especially if they were at home on Boxing Day and whenever they played my Oxford boys, stopping occasionally en-route to pick up his brother Ted. Vi, like my Mum, liked to bake pies, using home grown apples and gooseberries. I soon developed a particular liking for her coconut cake. The main shock to the system was their dog, Suki, a big hairy rough collie. We had never owned a dog at home and I knew little about how to deal with her but she was friendly enough and after my initial wariness our association proved a good training ground for the years ahead when we would have our own four-legged friends.

The run up to the wedding saw both parents get together when Alf and Vi came to Oxford for the day in his Morris Marina and, Dad apart, we spent an amicable afternoon out at The Cotswold Wildlife Park at Burford. Mum was thrilled to visit the park, was especially taken by the antics of the Chimps, I suspect because they reminded her of her children, often referred to as little monkeys.

Prior to the wedding, Dad quietly raised the issue of Gran attending the wedding and asked if I would be happy to have a priest present. My emphatic answer was no, as this was Shirley and her Mum's home church and I was more than happy with the wedding service. The thorny issue of who was to choose as my best man out of my brothers was resolved when Mum suggested my best mate Neville, which was an eminently sensible and acceptable solution.

The big day soon arrived, April 20th. Travelling down to Weston super Mare the night before, Neville and I stayed with Shirley's brother John and his wife Judith. On the day itself we settled ourselves in church and met some of the family as they gathered and we set up the equipment for the audio recording of the service as this was in the days before video and mobile phones. An organ failure as a symbolic precursor to marriage is not recommended but happen it did. We were just into the first rousing hymn when it gave way. Not to be outdone the sprightly vicar announced to some amusement that "it was always good to have a second string to your bow" and deftly provided a Chopin-like substitute. Nevertheless, the day was joyous and the reception at Grand Central Hotel, situated on the sea front, allowed our limited number of guests to sample the sea air and enjoy the views.

Not for the first, or last, time in our lives we owed much thanks to our parents for their contribution to the wedding. To Alf and Vi for their wedding and reception arrangements and my own father for gifting a sum of money that provided drinks at the bar, courtesy of him having successfully wagered a sum of money on the Irish horse Captain Christy, winner of the Gold Cup a few weeks earlier. Even better, our respective Grans got on like a house on fire and, as an added bonus, our staunch Catholic Granny Carton commented on what a lovely church service it had been. After an overnight stop at the hotel, Alf kindly drove us to Bristol Airport for a lovely honeymoon in the sun at Torremolinos, Spain. On our return, he picked us up late into the night as we had been delayed by a bored customs officer who singled us out and proceeded to give us a right earful, accusing us of letting down the side for sinning against the limit on importing cigarettes.

Unbeknown to us but whilst on honeymoon in Spain, further strikes were taking place at Cowley. Carol Miller, herself a part-time cleaner and wife of an assembly worker, led 150 wives of workers to protest against a strike by drivers at the factory. They complained bitterly at the consequent loss of wages, setting out their clear purpose as "all we want is to keep our husbands in work so that they bring home a weekly wage", echoing the same sentiments of Nicky's wife Margaret and a thousand others no doubt. One Newspaper, the Sun, typically, headlined the action as "Sex ban for strikers", ensuring maximum publicity and causing counter demonstrations to be held in support of the strikers in order to strengthen their case against management.

Returning to Oxford, after lunch with Mum at Vicarage Road, we immediately went to the Letting Agency who had promised us that they would have accommodation available for us to live in before finalisation of our mortgage in a few weeks hence. We were as shocked as the biblical Mary and Joseph to discover that there was nowhere available and were left apparently homeless. Once again family came to the rescue. My very kindly and considerate brother Nicky, and his wife Margaret, with two young daughters Nicola and Lisa to care for, on hearing of our plight, immediately offered to accommodate us until our own home was available, despite their own problems with on-going strikes and layoffs. Furthermore, Eric Hewlett, the Chief Clerk at the Court who lived at Brighton, but rented a flat in Oxford during the week, generously allowed us free use of this at weekends. How blessed we were to have such generous family and colleagues.

After six weeks our mortgage was finally approved, contracts were exchanged and we proudly took possession of our own financial millstone enabling us to move into our very own home at 20 Minchery Road, Littlemore. That we were able to afford a deposit on our house at all was due to Shirley exchanging her pension for a marriage gratuity.

The spring weddings were followed by a short period of relative national calm before the arrival of a small miracle on the family scene, courtesy of a boy named Kevin, born to my sister May towards the end of the month of the same name. She had been hospitalised in the John Radcliffe for some three months due to blood pressure complications. The concerned medics decided to induce the birth and Kevin was duly born one month premature with a collapsed lung that resulted in him being immediately whisked off to be placed in an incubator in the Special Care Baby Unit (SCUB). After just three days he endured an operation to help with his breathing and was so unwell that May and Pat were advised to arrange his Christening. Medical expertise and care combined with his own fighting spirit to ensure that, against all the odds, the little battler won his fight for life to the relief and joy of a jubilant family. A real-life miracle had been acted out in front of our very own moist eyes when we visited the following week.

Mum was driven to the hospital by uncle Oliver to observe the screened off recovering miracle boy. On May informing her that she had received an epidural injection to assist in the original birth process our dear Mum, no stranger to the pain and dangers of giving birth herself, retorted somewhat matter of fact and tongue in cheek "oh, you don't know you've even had a baby then!". A comment that raised laughs loud enough to have burst any stitches May might have received.

*

As Spring opened the door to summer, Shirley and I received our first Mr and Mrs Carton invite and made our way South for the third wedding of the year, that of my cousin, Ann Carroll, who had displayed her liking for a man in a smart uniform by throwing herself at the mercy of the police. I had known Ann since my early visits to Aunt Peggy and Uncle Tommy as they moved around the country. At one point she had taken up a post at Catering College in Bushey, North of London. Driving cross-country, I happily collected her from the college and she spent many a week-end at Vicarage Road, sharing boozy nights out in the city of dreaming spires and endless vintage pubs, some with Betty or other family members.

It was whilst working at the college that she met her uniformed beau. Bewitched by the sight of his flashing blue lights and charm, the sturdy Hendon based policeman, Michael Hoy attracted her attention and before long she allowed herself to be gently handcuffed and carted off to official matrimonial harmony, celebrated at the Catholic Church of St Benedict's in the lovely Dorset village of Gillingham, where her parents had moved only a year earlier. The couple moved to Southampton before crossing the water to live in Bembridge on the of the Isle of Wight. Mike, having passed his Serjeant's exam became Police Liaison Officer for a number of police stations and was based at Parkhurst Prison. The family, now including Caroline, settled into the sea life and enjoyed days sailing around the coast and out on the Solent. Years later, Mike unfortunately succumbed to cancer but not before we had a great day out at Sandown races on Betfred Gold Cup Day in 2009. I remember it well. I had backed a horse called Briery Fox who was ten lengths ahead at the final fence, only for that Irish jockey genius McCoy, to conjure up a whip driven finish from his mount, Hennessy, to snatch the race on the line, much to Mike and his brother-in-law Pete's delight. As for Hennessy, I don't think he ever won another race except for a couple of Point-to-Points before his retirement.

There must be something in the blood that attracts the Carroll's to a uniform. Years earlier, with Betty for company, I attended the wedding of Ann's sister Maureen to Pete Townend. They had met in Worksop where I think she was working in a garage and he, by all accounts a dab hand with a spanner. Perhaps realising that he would have to earn a proper living to gain her father's approval to wed his love, he enlisted with the RAF in the year England won the World Cup, starting as an Aircraftsman before gaining promotion to Serjeant. They enjoyed a steamy spell in Singapore where Maureen says she spent half her life cooling in the shower. After running a number of enterprises and working for Radio Lincoln, they eventually retired to Ireland where Pete then exchanged his RAF uniform for that of a Sea Captain, after they purchased their very own Prosecco fuelled boat and now spend many a day cruising happily along the Shannon.

Less happily, 1974 spawned further IRA bombings in both Dublin and London, including the Houses of Parliament and the Tower of London. A second General Election resulted in a small Labour majority, there were prison riots at The Maze prison and murder suspect Lord Lucan disappeared off the face of the earth. To prove to the established order that the country was spiralling into a dark future, McDonalds opened their first UK restaurant. The English Football Association sacked the only England manager who had ever actually won anything and the infamous Brian Clough, said by himself to be in the top one of great managers, disproved the point by being sacked after only 44 days at Leeds United. Inflation topped 17%. The Chinese Government sent two real cuddly Pandas to Britain in sympathetic response.

We were hurtling our way towards the year's end when the IRA launched what became known as The Birmingham Pub Bombings, killing 21 people without warning. It was not a happy time for Irish people in Birmingham or elsewhere as the public mood turned into anger. Thankfully, English people are immensely tolerant, in my opinion, and recognised that these actions were not supported by the vast majority of ordinary Irish people, most of whom worked in the big factories and hospitals and had integrated happily into English life, much like our aunts, uncles and parents in cities such as Birmingham and Oxford. Our parents were aghast at this turn of events. Most of us in the family had long lost our strong Irish accents in any event but it was certainly a sobering reminder of how events could spiral out of control.

It seems strange to reflect on these events that occurred within the year of three marriages and a miracle birth. Watching reviews and newsreels being wheeled out years later, and even today, the impression is that that we all lived in total daily terror and fear with constant turmoil. The reality is that events were more sporadic and indiscriminate. Buses and trains and even life itself continued as normal as possible in a mood of defiance. No doubt that was helped by the absence of a huge and hungry 24 hour a day media competing for attention. More significantly, there was no internet or twitter so a daily diet of fear did not dominate the airways or our minds. Naturally, there were many victims of the bombings and shootings who would be scarred, mentally or physically, for life and for them it truly was and will remain an awful time.

Musically, we enjoyed the introduction of Abba, Charles Aznavour singing "She", the ever popular squeaky clean The Osmond's plus the Three Degrees and the final concert tour of Rod Stewart with The Faces. Top selling albums featured The Carpenters, Elton John's "*Goodbye Yellow Brick Road*", John Denver's greatest hits and Paul McCartney and Wings with *Band on the Run*. The year that commenced optimistically with Slade singing *"Merry Christmas Everybody"* ended with Mud's *"lonely this Christmas"*.

Chapter Twenty

Mrs Whatyamaycallit –
Pets, Family and Tragedy

Christmas at Vicarage Road would never have been described as lonely despite Mud's mournful offering. For as long as I could remember they have always been joyful occasions with plenty of food, drink and merriment on offer. There were visitors galore incorporating family, friends and neighbours. That was equally true of the rest of the year as our house was rarely without someone calling in for a cuppa or, like cousins Sean and Ann Carroll, staying a weekend or longer. Uncle Peter would signal his Sunday arrival by turning up unannounced, via train and taxi, from Birmingham, accompanied by wife Agnes and later on their sons Paul and Mark. This once prompted Dad to ask him if they had such a thing as a telephone in Birmingham! Perchance, years later I was very grateful to Peter and Agnes for accommodating me, over several weeks, after my transfer from the London to Birmingham Crown Court, before moving to our home in Hollywood. Even without a warning smoke signal from Smethwick, Peter and Agnes would always be welcomed and Mum would do a compelling reprise of Jesus's parable of feeding the five thousand. Loaves were not much of a problem as she always had one ready baked but fish replacement came in a tin caught at the local Spar. School chums of all ages, workmates and neighbours were often entertained and fed at our house as well as those who attended to do work, read meters, deliver post or generally pass our way it seemed. Observing Mum's oft repeated expression to "put the kettle on", now a catch phrase used on the Ken Bruce Radio 2 show to announce the *Popmaster* quiz, was ingrained into all of us from a young age and activated on observing a new entrant into the house.

Humans were not the sole species to benefit from the open-door house policy of Mary. We had never had animals at home until one sixties day when a four-legged clump of hungry fur meowed her way into Mum's heart. She simply tiddled her way into the kitchen and refused to leave until she had devoured a saucer or two of unfrozen milk and repeated the exercise daily until she was soon staying overnight, in a warm bed with full board and lodgings. Mum named her Tiddles and the pair became constant companions, with the lodger curling up on her lap in the evenings.

Cats of course are independent and, once she had her paws under the table, she was soon off out into the night hunting a mate. One Christmas time, I noticed Tiddles jump into the lounge linen cupboard but thought no more about it until hours later when Mum enquired as to her whereabouts. I opened the cupboard and Tiddles jumped out with a tiny piece of blood covered fluff in her mouth and we noticed there were a few other kittens neatly laid out on top of some soft blue sheets. Surprised, and awe struck at her efficiency and motherly care, we fetched a large cardboard box, bedded it with more clean linen and patiently transferred half a dozen tiny bundles into the comfy nursery box, where they remained for a couple of weeks.

Over time we gradually accustomed them to outside conditions and the usual hygiene needs. For my part, with my, now well-honed DIY skills, I managed to transform an old armchair into an outside bed chamber of sorts using wire surrounds to ensure they were safe overnight. I made a fatal mistake however when I decided they all required a tub wash and in an exasperating episode I found myself being given a good run around as the kittens dashed hither and thither to escape their bath and my feeble attempts to dry clean them resulted in blood being spilled, mine. Having so many kittens around was unfair on our elderly neighbour, Mr Walker. The poor man had always had an aviary full of budgies at the rear of his garden and spent many hours down there talking to them and caring for them. He must have been mortified but he never complained.

When the kittens were several weeks old a decision was made to hand them over to the RSPA for rehoming, including Tiddles herself, as it was pretty certain that we would be overrun again unless she was neutered before being re-adopted. Mum took a keen liking to one of the kittens, black as the ace of spades save for a white blaze under his head, whom she called Smokey, and decided to keep him. He did have a very dangerous habit of testing the theory of nine lives by prostrating himself on lit fireworks but survived for many years before giving way to Mum's final adopted cat, Cindy. My young brother David reminded me that feline Cindy was outed as a Tom when sent to be neutered and immediately dispatched home. David wanted to call him Tigger but Mum decided as he was used to responding to Cindy, she would retain the name. so, as David joked, he became the cat equivalent of *"a boy named sue"*.

Our birdman neighbour presented Mum with a lovely budgie called Snowy and he lived for years on a ledge next to the old wireless and above a storage-cupboard and happily chirped his way through life until the day I sat down for breakfast and found him flat out on his sanded floor. His replacement was Joey, who was apparently found near the local railway line, and yet another stray, somehow ended up in our house for the remainder of its comfortable life.

*

By Winter 1974, Shirley and I were now well settled into Minchery Road, a former council house with wide open spaces and a garden that backed onto a school playing field, providing an open sunny aspect. The inherited love of a potato led me to turning over part of the sandy- soil garden to provide a mini allotment sufficient to supply us with fresh potatoes, carrots and green vegetables. We continued to meet friends at the King Edward pub in Vicarage Road most Sundays, stopping off to see Mum, at the now much quieter old house, when we handed over some of our homegrown produce.

Workwise, Shirley and I were permitted to continue working in the same office against the normal Civil Service rules that applied at that time. Not surprisingly, being the son of a strong-minded Labour supporting father with many similarly inclined aunts and uncles, I had recently taken on the role of Branch Secretary of the Union, the County Court Officers Association (CCOA) and soon rubbed a few people up the wrong way. I circulated my virginal letter to members telling them that "if they allowed themselves to be used as doormats, they should not be surprised if management walked all over them". Cue, an attack of the vapours from an assortment of the disgruntled who objected to being described as doormats. On the plus side, I had learned how to provoke a reaction and grab attention. Now, being selected for an official Union position does not imply any specialist skill as the candidates are few and far between since most sensible people have better things to do with their life than ponder over policy and archaic rules of engagement or quite frankly to be able to keep their eyes open long enough. I found it rather fun for a while as meetings were usually held in the pub to entice people to participate and it was something new to do. Ironically, one of the "disgruntled" turned out to someone I would happily work with many years later.

Much of the then political discourse with management at this time revolved around pay. Inflation was 24% and years of pay restraint had resulted in Civil Service pay falling behind the cost of living. A few months after settling their dispute with the coal miners, every other public body sought parity, even as unemployment spiralled towards 2.2million. The IRA continued sporadic deadly attacks including the shooting of Ross McWhirter, co-founder of the Guinness Book of Records. The Balcombe Street siege, a six-day December stand-off between the Provisional IRA and police ended with the IRA surrendering and the release of two hostages, watched remarkably, live on television.

All of these issues lurked menacingly in the background in the midst of the red- hot heat and drought of Summer 1976, where temperatures soared in to the eighties from March to September ending only when the government appointed Dennis Howell as the Minister for Drought. Alas, it was not long before the heavens opened and he was soon nicknamed "Minister for Floods". The summer had brought us water shortages illustrated by the sight of scorched greens, hosepipe and car wash bans and humorous adverts, posterboards and T-shirt stickers exhorting the nation to "save water, share a bath with a friend". Personally, this was somewhat difficult as Shirley was heavily pregnant and three in a bath did not work quite so well. Newspapers and an assortment of bleating experts over-excitedly proclaimed this was a forerunner to the future and recommended that we all build swimming pools.

Betty, with exemplary planning, gave birth to her first two children Christopher the year before the heatwave and daughter Louise the year after. Shirley was not so fortunate and spent a large part of her blazing summer pregnancy laid out on a camp bed in soaring heat with what little breeze there was wafting into the house from the local sewerage works. Mind you, a certain Mr Fox chose one summer night to investigate the cage, where our rabbit was languishing in the heat, before being spotted by Shirley. She took off like a sprinter, raced down the stairs and out into the garden and so terrified the Fox that it fairly flew over the hedge, minus its potential dinner and was never spotted again.

The episode failed to spark any premature baby contractions so some weeks later, after a long and difficult day and night, she gave birth to Julie on a roasting 16th August, by Caesarean Section, thanks to the skill of staff at the John Ratcliffe Hospital. It was the next morning before I was able to hold lovely baby Julie in my delighted arms and able to pass on the good news to Shirley's excited parents, and a few days later they bombed their way up the M5 in their pot of custard on four wheels dubbed a Morris Marina. I did what all men do on these occasions. Leaving the hospital in the early hours I headed home for a quick sleep before stopping at Mum's to deliver the news and we shared a celebratory cup of tea whilst she cooked me breakfast. At the same time Stevie Wonder released a song called "Isn't she lovely" to celebrate the birth of his own daughter and we happily adopted it as our own theme song as an expression of our own feelings.

Now, this was an occasion to savour because Mum had not many weeks before been released from hospital herself. Earlier in the year, she had been suffering from stomach pains. Nobody realised the full extent of her plight until one day, May, being several months pregnant with Michelle (born in December), was having a check-up when their shared GP, Dr James, enquired of May how she felt about Mum's stomach cancer. Well, this came as a severe shock as Mum had only days earlier been sitting happily in the garden with children and grandchildren and had not mentioned anything about cancer to anyone.

It was not long before the dreaded news had spread around the family despite Mum's reticence. Shirley and I, amongst others, visited after she had undergone an apparently successful operation to remove the cancer. Typical of Mum, with more concern for others, she instructed Shirley that she should not visit again in her heavily pregnant state. Fortunately, Mum was shortly back home to receive a host of cards and good wishes from far and wide as she slowly recovered from her operation. Happily, sister May safely gave birth to her daughter Michelle just days before Christmas, thus adding to the festive celebration.

In a wider context, our parents were happy to see the emergence of hope in Northern Ireland when some 10,000 women marched for peace in August followed by another 25000 in Derry just a month later. Betty Williams and Mairead Corrigan were awarded the Nobel Peace Prize in December "for their courageous efforts in founding a movement to put an end to the violent conflict". Sadly, it was be many more years before peace was finally agreed.

At times like these the nation often relies on its sporting heroes to cheer us on and up stepped two totally different characters. Mum was a big fan of the ice dance skating and loved to watch it live on television. Her biggest delight was to watch when the shy and poetically diffident skater John Curry entranced her by winning the Figure Skating Gold Medal at the Winter Olympics in Innsbruck. She also had a fancy for the odd wayward character battling against the odds and the charmer James Hunt was one such character. Almost the total opposite of John Curry in stature and lifestyle, James Hunt, the hard drinking larger than life racing cavalier, defied all the odds to plough through torrential Japanese rain to become Formula 1 World Champion to the absolute delight of Mum and millions more watching at home, on our black and white screens.

Around November time, I obtained a post as a Departmental Training Officer, based in Russell Square, London meaning we would have to leave Oxford and find a new affordable home nearer London. Dad, conscious that Vicarage Road was old and rambling and was now going to prove too much for Mum to cope with, decided he would like to buy our home in Littlemore, with its fitted kitchen and easily managed garden, a house Mum visited often and would be only too pleased to live in. This may have had something to do with an evening visit she had made in company with her visiting sister Bridgie, on holiday from Wexford. In any event, with Shirley unable to spend time on a property search I eventually chose a home in Stevenage from where I would be able to catch a daily 30-minute commute to London for the next four years. We moved early in the new year allowing Mum and Dad to sell our old Vicarage Road home to a cash rich Irishman for an undisclosed sum but barely a fraction no doubt of its current estimated half-million-pound valuation. Accompanied by Paul, Ann and David they settled into a new life at Littlemore.

Mum still treasured a signed photo from her all-time favourite, Val Doonican, when she met him way back in 1965. In later years many international appeared in Oxford so Mum was especially delighted to see folk singer George Hamilton amongst others. During her recuperation, Betty and May took her to the New Theatre where she laughed her way through the pantomime Aladdin that starred Freddie Garrity (Freddie and the Dreamers) and Lulu. Later on, she was made-up to see one of her other all-time romantic folk heroes, Slim Whitman, whose album "Red River Valley" topped the charts for weeks.

She had always loved music, often singing along to familiar tunes on the radio and, during her illness and beyond, she loved listening to programmes that reminded her of the old country, such as that of folk singer Finbar Furey, who hailed from a musical family in Ballyfermot, Dublin where our Aunt Lizzie lived and that earned him extra kudos in her eyes. In the seventies he became lead singer of The Fureys and they played regularly on the radio and achieved huge success with songs exemplified by *"When you were Sweet Sixteen"* which she sang along to whenever it was played, topping the Irish charts and being 14th in the UK in 1981, a year that would have great poignancy for all of us. Mum also adored Eamonn Andrews and was an avid fan of his show *This is Your Life*.

The lovely village of Dawlish, in the warm South West, played host to Betty and Mick and their children, Christopher and Louise when they took Mum on holiday in the summer of '78. Located on the English Riviera it still boasts one of the most scenic railway views in the country as the railway line almost caresses the deep blue sea before disappearing into a row of tunnels as it races on wards towards Paignton. A week of fun and sun followed but and included a rather bizarre encounter with a fortune teller.

Mum sent postcards back home to Paul, Ann and David. Nothing unusual in that except on this occasion she asked them, to "keep these cards" and "have the tea ready about two or so on Saturday". One of these rare hand written cards from Mum, is especially treasured and is now in Betty's keeping. Strangely, it seems the cards were written after an encounter with a Gipsy lady offering to tell them all their fortune, a common feature at many resorts. Bearing in mind Mum was still recovering from her operation, she reluctantly looked at the lady who clasped her hand, stared Mum in the eye and with a mournful look quietly announced "I can't" before promptly turning on her heels and walking off. Had our mother discerned some meaning in the actions of the fortune teller and decided that a happy holiday memory of her enjoying family time would be a fitting memory? In July of the following year, Betty gave birth to Caroline to complete her family. Mum wasted little time to visit, welcome and cuddle her latest grandchild.

*

In the meantime, Shirley and I had settled into Stevenage as I began a four-year spell as a Departmental Training Officer and mad London commuter, probably not unlike Leonard Rossiter in the TV series *Reginald Perrin.* I would invariably sit in the same seat in the same compartment, alongside the same identikit dummies as we clutched our briefcases to emphasise our importance and guarding their contents as though they contained national secrets rather than our mundane sandwiches.

The daily commute was interrupted with the birth of our second child Andrew, born in Hitchin Cottage Hospital halfway through my London stint, following another long labour and difficult birth that again resulted in a Caesarean Section. Shirley had to await the arrival of the senior consultant from nearby Stevenage and once again I was unable to be present though I was also looking after Julie at home on extended special leave as Shirley was hospitalised a week before Andrew's birth and a further two weeks afterwards due to complications. Whereas Julie entered the world in a quiet slumber, Andrew announced his presence by loudly bellowing his way through many hospital nights that had nurses eagerly awaiting the dawn of a new day. Appropriately perhaps, the loud and rocking major hit film *Grease* was released within a week of his birth with the rhythmic hits *Grease, Summer Nights and You're the one that I want* providing a musical backdrop as Shirley waltzed whilst

I Dad-danced around the living room to encourage our new-born to sleep! Despite, or maybe because, of our musical efforts, he turned out to be somewhat averse to sleep until a miraculous conversion as a student some later years. Andrew was a welcome addition to the family, with blonde hair, sharp eyes and a handsome look that one nurse prophesied would break a hundred hearts, so clearly did not mimic his father in that direction. In any event, following two such difficult caesarean births we concluded our family was complete.

*

Mum had not returned to Ireland since 1958. Her cancer proved a catalyst for a long-awaited visit. Shortly after the first General election victory of Margaret Thatcher, she and Dad, whether by shock or coincidence, concluded the time was ripe for a well-deserved holiday back in the old country. They enjoyed time in Dublin with Lizzie and Bill before catching the diesel train through Wicklow and the mountains on route to Bagenalstown, welcomed by the perennially genial Anthony and Eileen, who hosted them at Kilree Cottage for a week of tea, cake, laughter and chats over old times. They enjoyed time visiting our former neighbour's such as the Hughes, Dillon and Furlong families. Nostalgic walks took them around the almost unchanged Streets, conjuring up a scene from the distant past, and popping into shops with some still familiar faces despite the long passage of time. Mum recounted to us her emotional walk along the River Barrow, the crowning jewel of the town, reminiscing of the times she had taken us children on the same route to the swimming pool and the McGrath Park. Evenings, after a hearty meal, often ended with a game of cards or a visit to the corner pub. She may not have been a drinker but Mum enjoyed listening to the live Irish music whilst Dad would enjoy his Guinness over chats with old pals, none more so than his lifetime friend, Bill Power.

By all accounts they both had a wonderful time before moving on to Mum's home town of Wexford, where they stayed for a second week with Bridgie and her family. Mum was overjoyed to be back with her sister who had moved from her country cottage at Crosstown, which Mum would have known well from her younger days, to live in a small cottage in St. Mary Street in the heart of Wexford Town. The two-bedroom cottage is set in a sloping one-way street and though small and somewhat archaic in appearance was very cosy and comfortable. Not far away lived her nieces Nellie and Kathleen with the latter owning and running a pub with her husband Jim. I visited Wexford many years later when the cottage was owned by another niece, Beth. Shirley and Julie stayed with Beth whilst Myself and Andrew boarded at Kathleen's old pub. Julie remembers, on a visit to the pub, she got into conversation with a man who, on discovering she was Paddy Carton's granddaughter, immediately offered to buy her a drink. Clearly oblivious to the fact she was still a teenager it said all we needed to know about the man's feelings towards Dad. Beth eventually moved into a care home where she ended her days in comfort but the old cottage remains in family ownership through Beth's daughter Nicola, who herself lives in Australia, and it is currently occupied by her brother Fergus.

One of the highlights of our parent's holiday was the day Mum set foot on the sweeping sands of Curracloe Beach in Wexford Bay, brought to world attention many years later when used for the filming of the D-day landing scenes in the film *Saving Private Ryan*.

Mum confided to Betty that her first return walk along the almost empty sands accompanied by Bridgie, Simon and her nieces Nellie and Kathleen, had brought tears to her eyes and a lump to her throat as she once again cast off her sandals to feel a million grains comfort themselves between her toes as she trod the sands. It was as though the spirit of the forceful westerly winds had sensed her presence and the vibes of her inner feelings. The sight and sound of the crashing waves released a torrent of emotions that swirled around her and returned her momentarily to her earlier peaceful and carefree days when all of life lay before her. That walk alone was said to be worth the trip and had sunk indelibly into her holiday memoirs.

Not far away, she revisited Screen cemetery. Opposite the familiar sight of her now revamped childhood school, she slowly moved amongst the grey stoned graves, of old friends and distant relatives, before coming face to face with those of the father she had never known and younger siblings. Walks around lovely Blackwater reminded her and Dad of their courtship days, meandering alongside familiar flower-adorned streams, and of her time working for Sinnott's and Dad's time as relief postie. Stopping at one pub, Dad was astonished to hear a voice of an old friend he had not seen or heard for over forty years booming out the words "Paddy Carton, what'll you be having to drink", as if he had never been away.

All too soon it was time for them to take the return trip home to Oxford but they did so with a mountain of memories that brought back a spring in Mum's step and a joy to her heart. She took home as a present for Betty an early recording of Irish Singing star Larry Cunningham, which she still possesses, singing the beautiful "Lovely Leitrim", a big hit in the sixties when he sang with The Mighty Avons Band.

Mum, although wistful once again to leave behind her beloved Ireland, was also pleased to return to her Oxford family and recount tales of her joyful adventure. Clearly it had meant a great deal to her and the whole family rejoiced to see that the experience had rejuvenated her spirit.

She returned home to her work at Annabelinda. Previously, she had worked for the Council for a number of years as a Home Help, undertaking domestic duties for the elderly and disabled in their own homes, with her customary good cheer. The Job had, however, taken its toll on her physically and one day she informed Betty that she was finding it difficult to cope with its demands. Coincidentally, the upmarket dressmaker Annabelinda was looking for someone to undertake light domestic duties. Our Aunt, Helga, worked there as a high-class Seamstress and recommended our Mum. She was immediately taken on and, although there may be differing recollections about dates, one thing we are all certain about is that she absolutely loved working there.

The story surrounding *Annabelinda* is in itself somewhat extraordinary with background of colourful characters sufficient to grace a number of books. The name itself was formed when Belinda O'Hanlon combined with Anna Woodhead to open a clothes shop in Park End Street, in Oxford, selling ball gowns to the rich students. They were approached by Howard Marks, a former university acquaintance, who informed them he had inherited a large sum of money and wanted to help them develop their business, providing funds to purchase larger premises, in Gloucester Green, from where they would trade for the next 40 years.

Completely unbeknown to them, he would actually become one of the most wanted drug smugglers in the world. He used the upper floors to establish an international drug network but his masterplan to open further shops never materialised. Apparently, he used over 40 disguises and amassed a small fortune before being caught and sentenced to 25 years in an American jail, obtaining parole release after just six. This enabled him to commence a new career by writing his huge selling autobiography **Mr Nice Guy** and becoming something of a celebrity, selling out venues across the globe, and added lustre to his fame by claiming he worked for the secret services, which was denied. He was regarded as charming by those he was involved with, even his captors, hence the title of his book.

Mum was a welcome sight at the workshop. Belinda was married to Redmond, having met at university. Resembling a delightfully eccentric professor, he was very colourful, charming and extremely intelligent. Coming from opposite ends of the social and religious spectrum, where Mum's working-class Catholicism sparred with his strong atheist inclinations, they formed a unique bond. He related to Betty that he always knew when Mum was on the premises as *"she was always singing and was a ray of sunshine"*. One of the songs she would have showered upon Redmond was her rendition of Irishman, Johnny Logan, singing his 1980 Eurovision winning *"What's another year?"*, a rather prophetic title bearing in mind the events that followed.

Coincidentally, there was another Redmond O' Hanlon that Mum may have recalled on joining Annabelinda. He was an Irishman who lived in the 17th Century and regarded by some historians as Ireland's answer to Robin Hood, who reputedly extorted money from British landlords to give to Irish peasants after he had witnessed his family being evicted from their homes. The present Redmond has achieved great fame as an author and intrepid explorer and adventurer as recounted in his books "Into the heart of Borneo" and "Congo Journey". Mum would certainly have been very proud of such achievements and honoured to have known such an adventurous soul.

Some of Mum's expressions may have baffled Redmond with loads of "for sure", "sure you know what I mean", "ah, go on with you" and "go way with ye" amongst others. But her favoured expression was "whatyamaycallit" when she couldn't quite remember an exact person or event and this greatly endeared her to Redmond, so much so that he wrote on her birthday card signed by all the *staff "and lots and lots of whatyamaycallits from Redmond xx"*, surely a lovely and fitting reflection of their friendship.

Mum's years of this happy employment came to a shuddering halt late in 1980. May lived in Walton Street and used to walk to Annabelinda to see Mum and then have tea. On this occasion she was met by Belinda who informed her that Mum was feeling unwell and May took her home. She told May that she was feeling a lump in her throat prompting an immediate call to her GP who placed her on medication whilst ordering a series of tests to identify the cause. On another day when out with Betty she explained how very tired she was whilst waiting for the bus home at Queens Lane, causing deep concern for her plight. Subsequent blood tests confirmed her worst fears and disclosed that her cancer had returned in a more virulent form that required immediate treatment. Needless to say, the whole family was devastated but remained hopeful that she would respond to treatment and recover.

The following months seemed like years as she undertook chemotherapy which initially seemed to signal improvement but as the months passed Mum became steadily weaker. The news that the cancer had spread to her liver and bones was a shocking blow and, in the absence of any prospect of successful surgery, she returned home.

Mum was looked after on a daily basis by Dad who would sit with her be it night or day as they steadfastly supported each other as they had throughout their married lives. Brother Paul was immense in his care and devotion as he held Mum's hand as he sat by her bed. David, the youngest of the family provided much welcomed assistance, with Betty, May and Ann visiting regularly, whilst the rest of us could only offer distant support and sporadic visits home.

Mum's medical needs were provided through the care of a McMillan Nurse, responsible for daily Diamorphine injections of increasing amounts, who by all accounts was an absolute wonder of tenderness and love. Myself and Shirley, together with five-year old Julie and three-year old Andrew, last visited Mum a few days before Christmas in 1981. To them, Mum was known as Cat Nanny, to distinguish her from Granny and Grandad Baker, Shirley's parents. After seeing Mum, a mere shadow of her former self, Dad asked what she had said to us. She simply said "goodbye" I replied. We then made our way to Weston -super-Mare where we spent Christmas with Shirley's parents.

28th December and still in bed. Betty phoned to say Mum had died. Shirley relayed the message to me upstairs and, for the first time in my whole life, I simply collapsed between the sheets and sobbed uncontrollably for some time. Recalling the moment even now arouses similar emotions.

Paul was with her when she died but according to David, he had some difficulty in persuading Dad to accept the fact, probably through shock. The next morning our sister Ann and her son Kieran arrived to see Mum and also would not accept that she had died so it was a very traumatic time for him in particular, as he also took charge of arrangements for involvement of the doctor and the undertaker.

Once I had sufficiently composed myself, I set off on the train to Oxford, which had battled through the prevailing wintry weather conditions. Shirley drove me to the station and offered to come with me but for some quite unfathomable reason I declined and set off on my own, a decision I soon very much regretted. The journey was a weird mixture of sadness and anger. Sad, at the undeserved death of Mum, aged just sixty-three. Anger, as I sat seatless on the corridor floor, that my fellow passengers should be so unconcerned as to be chatting away, merry and full of the Christmas spirit. Did they not know that my mother had just died! How dare they! Such irrational and unexpected thoughts, were my dark companions for the rest of my journey.

At Minchery Road, I met with Dad and all my devastated brothers and sisters as we exchanged thoughts and reminisced about Mum. Betty succinctly summed up our mother's character, informing us what Mum had said to her barely twenty-four hours earlier:

"I am sorry to have spoilt everybody's Christmas".

Even at the end, tired and pained, her thoughts were for others.

Mum's funeral took place in January 1982 at Our Lady Help of Christians, Cowley. Myself and Shirley had travelled up from Weston the previous day. We stayed overnight with May and Pat and joined close family for the traditional short service of reception at the church, said to reflect the fact that a life member of the church is not brought into church in death.

The next day, family and friends from all over the country and Ireland gathered to pay respects and say good bye to our much -loved mother. The sombre mood matching the cold, dull-grey day for the most part, in keeping with the winter reported by the press rather excitedly as *The Big snow of 1982*. Certainly, a severe spell with heavy snowfalls had swept the country from early December and lasted well into January. Such conditions failed to prevent the arrival in Oxford of the considerable number of aunts, uncles, assorted nieces and nephews who defied the cold and turned out in huge numbers. Offering condolences and engaging in teeth chattering small talk we gathered outside before we allowed ourselves to be quietly ushered inside to take our appointed seats, in a church packed to the rafters.

The service followed the usual catholic tradition including the saying of Mass, the singing of hymns, such as *Ave Maria, How Great Thou Art and Amazing Grace,* and the taking of

Communion before the final blessing of the coffin. It was at this moment that something most wonderous and awesome occurred. Whereas many in the congregation solemnly lowered their heads I became transfixed. The white and black cassocked priest, took hold of the Thurible, suspended from chains, extravagantly cast its incense contents from side to side in the direction of and around Mum's coffin, while his fellow patron sprinkled holy water. Suddenly, a sunbeam burst through the stained-glass window from high above the altar, casting a shaft of golden rays to cascade downwards before alighting on the coffin, as if drawing out Mum's spirit to join the heavenly hosts and transporting her to another realm. Uncle Michael, who had also watched the scene unfold, commented to me afterwards "did you also see that?" I could never forget such a spiritually uplifting moment, reminding me of Shakespeare's phrase in Hamlet "There are more things in Heaven and Earth than are ever dreamt of…".

The blessing was followed by the organised procession out of the church whilst the choir empathised with departing mourners as the church echoed to the uplifting words of *"I watch the sunrise"*, as we tearfully departed.

> *"I watch the sunrise lighting the sky, casting its shadows near;*
> *And on this morning, bright though it be, I feel those shadows near me.*
> *But you are always close to me, following all my ways*
> *May I be always close to you, following all your ways Lord."*
> *(Words and music © by John Glynn and Colin Murphy, reproduced by kind permission)*

In a convoy of cars, we then made our way to the Headington crematorium. A few Catholic relatives were initially reluctant to enter the crematorium as this was not in keeping with their beliefs but were readily convinced by their younger offspring to join the rest of the family for the short service and the final good bye to Mum, whose ashes would subsequently be placed in the flowered memorial garden. The day was rounded off with a traditional reception at the Dominic's Social Club, allowing time for reminiscing over old times, chatting, eating and drinking in time honoured Irish fashion.

Not surprisingly, Mum's illness and death impacted on us all. Some were unable to reconcile Mum's faith, and her belief in a benevolent God, with the pain and suffering inflicted upon her over the past years, each person has to deal with these matters from their own perspective. Irrespective of any religious belief, we could all agree on the kindness and generosity of spirit that pervaded all of Mum's actions. This was probably the greatest gift bestowed to us, to rest forever in our hearts.

So ended an era.

Chapter Twenty-One

Dad and Life Without Mum

Mum and Dad held an unshakeable trust and belief in each other with clearly defined roles that might be considered old fashioned by today's standards but worked for them and us. Mum largely looked after the home and cared for the day to day needs of us children. She ensured we were fed, washed and clothed and cared for physically and emotionally and she herself undertook work to supplement their income at Lyons bakery, spent time as a Home Help before finally working for Annabelinda. Dad was chiefly the bread winner, often taking on extra work in pubs, acting as gateman at Hinksey Park during holidays or when the Cowley works were on strike. Pillars of strength, they stood solidly together to fulfil the destiny they had decided upon, to ensure us children would have a better future, putting aside any personal fears and enduring hardship and exhaustion. None of us can remember them exchanging strong words or being ill tempered with each other and any doubts or concerns were well hidden.

Mum was undoubtably the soft-spoken mother who would leave it to Dad to advise us strongly when she felt we needed to be spoken to or were taking them for granted. Personally, this included an occasion when I had spent time in hospital and was reluctant to go back to school, making excuses each day to prolong my holiday. It fell to Dad to instruct me that I would be returning to school the next morning and that was that. Similarly, when I had used the house as an interim pub stop for friends, it was Dad again who advised me of the error of my ways as he advised me on the need to remain in control of how much you drink. A clear unofficial demarcation line was established and I believe we all knew where we stood.

Mum's illness and ultimate death foreshadowed a new structure. In a strict role reversal, Dad had to become a carer to Mum and learn to do household tasks that had hitherto escaped his attention, such as learning how to operate a washing machine and hang clothes on a line for starters. His culinary skills had previously been limited to carving the Christmas Turkey on his slightly inebriated return from the Seven Stars pub, just prior to listening to the Queen's Speech. Suddenly, he was a changed man, turning his attention to gardening, sometimes seen on his knees thinning out the weakling carrots from their better endowed neighbours with some gusto, steeping himself in the art of cooking the chosen ones in a pot of boiling water before discovering the delights of using a soap wire-made pad to cleanse the victims' pot.

Betty helped out with changing the bed linen and there were two brothers still living at home after Mum died. The house had been purchased in cash and as far as we were aware there were no heavy financial outgoings, apart from the rates and fuel bills. Dad was in receipt of his works pension but was still years off receiving his state equivalent.

Two brothers still lived at home, providing Dad with moral and financial support, Paul was then working for Oxford

Instruments and David, the youngest of the family had left school just four years earlier.

Leaving with his clutch of CSEs and an O level in History, David achieved a pass rate of 99%, despite his teacher having doubts he should be taking the subject and following two days of *I'll show them* revision. Selfridges offered him a post as a sales assistant and he relishes the story that unfolded in his early days. He caught sight of a strange looking man enquiring about binoculars and entered into conversation with him about the intended use of the binoculars before completing the sale. A week later the Store Manager informed David that the *strange man* was in reality the Chief Buyer, acting incognito, who had been most impressed by the young sales assistant whom they promptly enrolled on a two-year managerial course, incorporating law and accountancy. He conceded it was a lovely place to work but left when Cavendish Woodhouse, in recognition of his skills and potential, offered to almost double his money and, at the same time, delighting our Mum by significantly increasing his contribution towards his keep. She was as pleased as punch, as much for the fact that he was getting on so well as for the additional money.

David then followed a more nomadic route. Moving first to work for Dixons, before spending short spells at, among others, Tenancy Purchase, Swindon Automobiles and SEMA (Dept of Social Security) before working for I.T company EDS (Electronic Data Systems) prior to taking redundancy. He met Sue in 1985 and they married two years later to live in Swindon, a railway town housing the Great Western Railway Steam Museum. Nowadays, aside from fine parks and museums, it has earned fame as the home of The Magic Roundabout, which links together five mini roundabouts in a wonderous circle, named after the children's television series. A studious feat of ingenuity and planning it may be but a joy for a traveller such as me it most definitely is not recommended.

Following Sue's untimely death after a fall, he unceremoniously, and in his own words, "turned down the advice to sue the hospital as some ropey cheque was not going to bring her back".

*

Dad was a traditional hard working labour supporter all his life. Nevertheless, he was not surprised when Margaret Thatcher swept to power in 1979 after years of strikes and public disorder. The Falklands War of 1982 ensured she stormed to a second term, with a massive 144 seat majority, notwithstanding 3 million people being unemployed, leaving Dad's bedraggled Labour lagging well behind and causing opposition leader, and cousin Fiona's former walking companion, Michael Foot to resign. Public opinion is often as fickle as the weather, bending to the wind of change as one crisis leads to another, and throughout the eighties, opinion polls often veered between predictions for a massive Labour victory followed by an equally clear Tory majority. Dad was happy enough to discuss the merits of each but any suggestion of voting for the blue bloods would not ever be contemplated.

Following their massive election win the government found themselves in dire straits for the following few years. The 1984 Miners strike invited easy media headlines depicting violent clashes, with pitched battles between police and miners in many mining communities as one side fought to preserve law and order and the other sought to preserve their futures. Privatisation of some National Health Services were announced including cleaning, catering and laundry services, much to the dismay of Violet, my mother-in-law, for one. She had seen herself as part of the hospital and was absolutely dedicated to ensuring *her* hospital ward was spotlessly clean. She lamented the fact that so much of the camaraderie and care was lost in this process and has probably never been replicated. This was a lesson I took to heart when I became a staff inspector in later years, having observed at first hand the benefits of all workers, being treated as an equal and important cog in the NHS machine. National turmoil continued when riots broke out in a number of inner-city areas aggravated, it was suggested, by high unemployment and perceived lack of opportunities.

By the end of 1985 it was perhaps somewhat bizarre that the Christmas number one song was *"Merry Christmas Everyone"* sung by Shakin' Stevens.

*

1986 offered up something more optimistic for the nation and for me personally as an Oxford United fan. Our boys in yellow defeated the mighty Aston Villa over two legs to march into the final of the League Cup at Wembley and against the odds won our first ever major trophy beating Queens Park Rangers three nil in front of ninety thousand fans at the glorious sun decked Wembley Stadium. This was our best team ever, assembled by manager Jim Smith, featuring big names like John Aldridge, Ray Houghton, Jeremy Charles, the meanest "they shall not pass" defensive pairing of Captain Shotton and Scary Gary (Briggs) alongside the mercurial Irish right back Dave Langan. Manager Jim Smith had resigned a few weeks earlier after a dispute with infamous owner, Robert Maxwell, and in a sad irony, he was now in charge of our opponents in the final with Maurice Evans taking up the role for Oxford. It was great to share the day with so many family members, and friends, as we joined together for a wonderfully entertaining couple of hours and basked in the joy of our lads holding the trophy aloft before the parade around the pitch.

Tens of thousands of supporters, more than three times the average gate attendance, had turned Oxford into a deserted city, donning yellow shirts, scarves and hats as they travelled by car, train, coach and bus to the pinnacle of football. Together with Andrew, then just seven years old, I drove our old escort down the Motorway from Birmingham to an outlying tube station before joining up with the rest of our clan for the day, sweeties and drinks packed into my rucksack. Shirley and I were also celebrating our wedding anniversary, so a real day to remember and savour. We qualified for a place in the UEFA Cup but were unable to play in the competition because English teams were banned from Europe following the Heysel Stadium disaster. A great day out and one to remember for life.

This was also the year that the Republic of Ireland introduced one Jack Charlton, as English as they come with a broad Northumberland accent, to be their new manager and much to the utter consternation and head shaking amongst some of Irish sportswriters, many aghast at the very thought of an Englishman leading their national team. The Irish FIA reasoned they needed some experience and landing a world cup winner with a management pedigree to boot was seen as a defining moment of change. They had big dreams and a vision for the team and argued that they did not come bigger than "Big Jack".

At this time Ireland itself was in the doldrums, with continuing conflicts with the IRA, the national debt had doubled and there was a huge problem of emigration of the young and talented. Jack's task was to take Ireland into the finals of the 1988 European Championship and the 1990 World Cup and to provide an uplift to the nation. He not only achieved this but in 1988 he achieved saintly status when his underdogs team beat England one nil in Germany on their debut match at a major international championship. Expectations were low and playing with pride was the main pre-requisite against an all-star England team, led by Bobby Robson, who were expected by many to win the tournament. To cap it all, the goal scorer was Glasgow born Ray Houghton who had played for Oxford before being transferred to Liverpool. That one big win started a golden age of international football for the Republic. More importantly though, the team's success caught the imagination and support of the populace. Suddenly, there was an outpouring of national pride that would have massive implications for the way the country saw its own future.

Jack's style attracted many vociferous opponents within the country but he ignored them all. His mantra was simple "you do it my way or you don't play." His straightforward high energy direct football befuddled his classier opponents not only in 1988 but also at the Italia 1990 World Cup where the team reached the quarter finals, earning Jack the title of Honorary Irishman. The no-nonsense management style, combined with his easy nature, won over Irish hearts as they followed the team across continents, fuelled on the nectar of over achievement. Irish pride in their own nation and their national flag was rekindled and a new wave of optimism swept the land, brought about by a belligerent but humble and humorous Englishman. Strange how seemingly small decisions, matched by vast enthusiasm and determination, has the capacity to transform a nation without any political input. In any event, Dad was just as eager to follow the Irish fortunes as were the rest of us and jack's mantra of being *just a hard-working lad from a northern mining village* struck a chord with him.

Football aside, there were major changes to the sedate life at Minchery Road. Following Mum's death, Paul spent some spells working in America in various jobs and returning home around 1984. Along with his latest girlfriend, he visited our home in Hollywood, not the sunny celebrity decked Californian resort alas but the Birmingham version, and we would enjoy several weekends visiting the Night Out Cabaret Club.

In the mid-eighties he met the love of his life in Tracy, a seemingly super-sonic saleswoman, and they lived with Dad for a few years, celebrating the arrival of their first child, Emma, in February 1987. Quite surprisingly, to my sisters in particular, were the newly developed skills that Dad displayed, even extending his repertoire to nappy-changing, a chore studiously avoided in the previous half century and proving that you can teach an old (Gran)dad some new tricks.

Emma's arrival opened up new frontiers. Paul and Tracy had agreed terms with Dad to buy Minchery Road, their ownership maintaining the family connection, and they soon set about enhancing its value, enlarging and modernising the kitchen where they entertained family members on many occasions. Within a couple of years, they decided to sell up and move to Long Hanborough, where Tracy gave birth to their son Maximillian. Tracy had qualified as a Horticulturalist and garden designer, applying her skills to buying, renovating and re-selling properties. Her first venture brought her to the attention of the Oxford Mail who heaped praise on herself and Paul for transforming an old run-down country cottage into a very desirable home.

They had invited Dad to join them at Hanborough and he did seriously consider such a move, going so far as to visit the area and cast his eye over prospective social venues. He opted to stay in the familiar surroundings of Littlemore, renting a compact one-bedroom, upper floor flat still within walking distance of the Royal British Legion Club, where he was most welcomed as his own father had fought with the British in France. He had after all invested much of his time over the years socialising with the legion of locals, enjoying a drink and playing card games and bar billiards. Lorraine Whip, current Secretary and now Chairperson of the Oxford Cribbage League, credits Dad with being the one who first taught her how to play and she considered our dad, whom she calls Pat, to have been a lovely and popular member. Selling on his home to Paul provided him with a significant cash injection that enabled him, courtesy of rail and sail, to journey back and forth to Bagenalstown, staying with Anthony and Eileen and meeting up with long-time friend Bill Power for nightly chats as they sought to resolve the world's problems assisted by downing a pint or more of brain enhancing Guinness, supplemented with a drop of whiskey or two.

Dad was beginning to feel the effects of a lifetime of hard work and smoking as his health deteriorated, made bearable through the infusion of drugs including dollops of rat poison, branded more ethically as Warfarin, designed to reduce blood pressure and open up his clogged heart veins. He was provided with a new companion, a walking stick, as he made his way to the shops and, more importantly the Legion Club, for his nightly medicinal intake. Mind you, stubborn as he was, he did continue to ride his old bike from his flat to the Legion as often as he could with rumour suggesting he was even more stable in the saddle on his return journey.

As time swept swiftly on, he was seen by an assortment of medics, after developing an aneurysm that was hindering his daily activities and one that could conceivably burst at any time. Hope of an operation that might afford some health improvement was canvassed but accompanied with warnings of inherent dangers, given his overall state of health. He opted to take his chance and the operation was scheduled for the Autumn of 1991. Beforehand, there was the serious business of an August family wedding to attend in the north of England, where most of his brothers and sisters would be present and this was one event he was not prepared to miss, although he did his best!

I collected Dad from Oxford so he could stay with us on the Friday night before travelling north for the Saturday wedding. There was a bit of a panic as he could not find his blood pressure tablets and would not manage the weekend without them. Shirley made urgent arrangements for him to be seen at our own surgery early on the Saturday. Our GP very helpfully authorised a weekend supply and off we went in time to book into our accommodation before joining all the other guests at the happily sunlit church. Unpacking his suitcase at the hotel, lo and behold, out fell his own missing supply of blood pressure tablets!

Uncle Oliver and Aunty Helga, on holiday from Australia, ensured the day got off to a humorous start. Looking around the church we were surprised that they had not yet arrived and indeed it was about ten minutes into the service when they breathlessly ushered themselves into the rear of the church. Oliver later sheepishly explained, to some amusement, that they had been to another church. Direction wise, they were slightly lost when they spotted a veiled bride in a wedding car ahead of them and in true keystone-cops style decided to follow it and hurriedly made their way into the church before her. They realised their mistake when they discovered there were no other Cartons to be seen and when the groom turned to face the bride as she marched down the aisle, guarded by complete strangers, the penny finally dropped and they hot footed it to find the correct wedding not far down the road.

One photograph of the day stands out. This depicts Dad and his brother Michael flanking his younger siblings- Peter, Ado, Peggy and our man from Oz, Oliver. Smiling warmly, they look really pleased to be re-united for the first time in many years. Dad, outwardly looking well nourished, was dressed in his smart dark suit and white shirt and sporting his Guinness tie (now in my possession). The sole indicator of any discomfort was his need of a walking stick for support

What followed was a traditional Irish evening of song and dance, with guests inebriated with beer, Guinness with whiskey chasers and wine for the so inclined. Tales of days long past were resurrected from distant recesses of ageing minds and expanded with some relish to the delight of us in the younger generations. My favourite was the tale involving an irate milkman.

Dad, recounted the tale of the milkman and his horse. Near Bagenalstown, there lived a farmer who also delivered milk, housed in a large tank located on his horse driven cart. He was always giving out that people, armed with their pint-sized ceramic or tin jugs, would be late arriving at his cart causing his round to be extended. One day he lashed out at one poor woman jug carrier bellowing into her elderly ear "I suppose you expect me to bring my effing horse into your effing kitchen to get your effing milk". To teach him a lesson, Dad and a few others took him at his word. They arranged for him to be distracted by fellow conspirators by taking him for a drink at the pub. As best as I can recall, Dad took up the story.

"We then walked his horse and cart to his own cottage, not far away. It had stable-like doors that led into the scullery. We stuck a quantity of hay in a bag and tied it round the old nag's head before we unhitched the big bugger from his cart. A couple of big, strong farm lads took off their tweed coats, rolled up their sleeves, spat on their hands and unhinged the wooden doors, casting them aside before forcing the bogey through the doorless opening into the kitchen where we re-hitched the still scoffing beast to his cart. The lads replaced the doors and we returned to the pub.

The milkman had had a few beers by now and asked about his horse and cart. We told him they were safe and sound at his home and off he went, with the rest of us following behind. Nearing home, he could not see his nag nor his milk chariot. When told they were safely tucked up in the kitchen he roared heartily and slapped his own window to find the assembled horse and cart standing in his kitchen. "You effing buggers, what have yuse done" he screamed as his laughter turned to anger and we left him there scratching his head and effing away".

Ado, listening to Dad's now expanded tale, interjected with a story about her successful days playing camogie (like Hockey) for Bagenalstown ladies where she informed us that camogie legs with huge bruises were quite a common feature of the game, decrying any suggestion that they were simply genteel ladies playing for fun. Winning is a habit that is not easily surrendered and tallied with Dad's own motto "if it's worth doing, then it's worth doing properly", including beating up your opponent before exchanging pleasantries and handshakes it seems. On a more sombre note, our dear aunt recounted an incident of being burgled whilst living at Stanley Street, conveniently located within staggering distance of the Railway Club. It badly upset her to think that somebody had entered their home and been rummaging through their personal belongings. This soon led to a discussion on the merits of various penalties that should be inflicted in the unlikely event that a culprit was ever apprehended.

I informed the gathering of a day when I was working as a crown court clerk. The judge I was clerking was normally very lenient and considerate to young criminals, believing their mostly unstable upbringing was largely responsible for their criminality. Defence barristers were happy for their clients (now more grandly titled as customers) to appear before His Kindness. One day, however, a string of startled burglars found themselves dispatched immediately to prison, wide-eyed, open-mouthed and with their feet barely touching the floor of the dock. Surprised by this sudden change of approach, I mentioned to His Honour that this day he was not exactly full of the milk of human kindness. Whereupon he informed me, with steam blowing out of his red ears, that his mother-in-law had been burgled the night before! Hell, it seems, hath no fury for a judge whose own family had personally experienced the reality of being a burglary victim.

I also recalled an encounter I had with a barrister. Sitting in court, and clad in my newly acquired white wig, the arrogant legal eagle, clearly sensing that I was ripe for a bit of fun, asked of me in condescendingly superior tone of voice, "And where were you educated, my boy". To which I replied, truthfully, "Oxford" and left it at that. His colleagues rolled over in laughter on the bench in front of me as the now dumbfounded legal brain box could only mutter "oh, Oxford" and immediately sat down on his deflated posterior. Had he been half as good a barrister as he thought he was, he would have asked "where?". He didn't and I saw no need to enlighten him, of either the ability to form a quick retort or the merits of an Edmund Campion Catholic School. Unsurprisingly, in the few years our paths crossed I never did have any more trouble with him. Assembled family members and Dad giggled approvingly.

After the evening of celebration, and storytelling, we gathered the next morning for breakfast before collecting our belongings. We sought out and bade our traditionally drawn-out Carton farewells with fellow guests exchanging hugs and kisses. Dad, perhaps more tensely, exchanged best wishes and goodbyes with his brothers and sisters as they again implored him to reconsider having his risky operation. He had set his mind on proceeding and the outcome would be evident to all in the months ahead.

I was now working as a Regional Staff Auditor (Inspector) covering the Midlands and Wales, recruited by John Selch, head of the national unit who had been my senior officer at the Crown Court. The job was Birmingham based so it avoided any need to move house, especially as we were all settled in Hollywood although the job involved a deal of travelling and overnight stops. The real benefit was being largely my own boss, with an office in central Birmingham.

I am not sure that my labour supporting father was entirely convinced about the post but as I pointed out it was better to have me doing the job than some external management consultant with an eye on his next lucrative contract. I had after all worked in the courts all my life, knew how they operated and understood the problems from personal knowledge. Additionally, I had worked as a Trade Union Branch Secretary as well as having a spell as being Chairman of the London Branch.

Mind you, he may well have been justified in his concerns after my first inspection, undertaken at the Royal Courts of Justice in London, accompanied by northern colleagues John and Malcolm, as well as experienced London inspectors. I was allocated the allegedly straightforward task of auditing the four ladies in one section of the typing pool. I reported back to my astonished colleagues that pool only required one typist, not four, and immediately earned myself the title of *"the mad axeman"* as they fell about laughing at my decision with veiled threats of being brought before the highest judges in the land to explain to them that they would no longer have typists available to help them with their administration. In comical *"yes, Minister"* style, it was conveyed to me that on reflection and in consideration of all the facts, not to mention the wrath of the judiciary, I of course would recant of my error and offer a true and fulsome apology to all concerned for any perceived suggestion that the hard working and loyal typists were not fully and gainfully employed. The truth of the matter was simple. The typing ladies, unbeknown to me, were all part-time, working equivalent hours to one full typist as suited their personal lives in respect of childcare and flexibility. Oops, my error indeed and a lesson in checking facts that would stand me in good stead in future assignments. That did not exempt me, even to this day, from the goading humour of former colleagues with the reminder of my *"mad axeman"* title. My father laughed at my tale, recognising, correctly as it happens, that every typist in the whole of the country would be safe from my over keen inspection from then on!

The flexibility of the Staff Auditor job certainly enabled me to visit Dad several times between the August wedding event and his operation, to which he remained steadfastly committed.

The operation was scheduled for November and it soon became apparent from discussions with my siblings and doctors that Dad would afterwards require some period of convalescence as he lived alone in a one roomed upstairs flat. The Civil Service had an excellent welfare service and I was introduced to a lady from the Benevolent Fund, a society that provided assistance to civil servant members including accommodation at care and convalescence homes. In the run up to the operation, She and I met a number of times to consider options for helping Dad in his recovery.

The operation went ahead as planned and Dad, much to our relief, appeared to be coping with its rigours. In company with Betty, I went to see him several days later in the renowned John Radcliffe Hospital when he confided that it was much harder than he expected, as he struggled and grimaced in pain and exhaustion whilst pulling himself up in bed via large straps hung from the ceiling akin to those on a tube train. We explained that he had come through a major operation but it would take time for him to recover but that there were homes available where he could recuperate once he was able to leave hospital and I was in the process of locating one. He probably really just wanted to go home but that seemed somewhat implausible in the circumstance.

16th November, 10.30am. Days after my visit I was in my

office with the Welfare Officer when the phone rang. It was my brother Pat and he had bombshell news to relay and his words still reverberate down the years.

Pat: "hello Peter, the old man's gone".

Me: somewhat shocked- "gone, gone where?"

Pat: "he's dead, died this morning"

Me: "Dead, what you mean Dead?"

At this point the welfare officer quietly absented herself

Me: "Why, how? What happened- I thought he was recovering"

Pat: "Had a major stroke and they couldn't save him. Sorry".

Me: "Ok, I'll see you later".

I phoned Shirley and passed on the grim news before informing John (Selch) of the situation. Typically, John offered his condolences and gave me permission to do what I wished. I sorted my desk out and left for home, before travelling to meet my siblings in Oxford as we gathered at Dad's flat. His end came after he suffered a slight stroke whilst in recovery but this was later followed by a second massive one that had left him without any hope of survival. Betty, who had not long left the hospital after a visit was hurriedly recalled with others as doctors expanded on the dramatic, though not unexpected turn of events, and the inevitable prognosis. He had decreed that in the event of such an eventuality he did not wish to be resuscitated with a lifetime of impairment and disability.

So, fate had decreed that barely three months after that wedding gathering in Durham County, we would reconvene to say goodbye to a much- loved father and grandfather, brother, uncle and friend. In retrospect, how thankful we were that his final outing had been in the company of so many of his family including his brothers and sisters, leaving him and us with a fond and lasting memory. Of the six brothers and sisters in the photo taken in 1991 only the non-smoker and teetotaller Oliver is still with us and, with his twin Liam, are the sole survivors of that generation. The latest to pass on was Peter, departing in some style, as the curtains drew on his life in 2022, with the crooner, Val Doonican singing Peter's own mantra for life, "walk tall, walk straight and look the world right in the eye".

Dad's own funeral took place, as Mum's had ten years earlier, at Our Lady Help of Christians in accordance with pre-ordained Catholic traditions, although Dad was not especially religious. His brother Michael played an appreciatively large part in the organisation of the service. I read a verse from the bible and distinctly recall the departing hymn, *The Old Rugged Cross*, as it was belted out with some gusto in the manner of a beer fuelled Christmas carol, a fitting accolade to a man who liked a Guinness or two. There was the usual large gathering of family and friends from far and wide added to by an influx of former workmates and friends from the British Legion. We then made our way to the crematorium for the final goodbyes before retiring to Dominic's Club for the traditional Irish celebration of his life.

Our younger brother Pat sighted a forlorn looking figure at the funeral whose presence encapsulated our father's strength of mind and his belief in honesty and principle. He had been great friends with this co-worker from Cowley works and Pat was friends with his son. Dad was a strong Trade Unionist and acted upon many requests for strike action to resolve disputes, though not without some misgivings. On one occasion, however, a strike was called that he fervently disagreed with, considering it was not merited, was out of order and as such he could not, as a matter of principle, support it. For the first time in his life, he made clear his intention to cross the picket line. His very good friend personally sought to persuade him to change his mind but to no avail. Dad crossed the picket line and ended a great friendship which was never restored, a very sad long-term casualty over a strike that itself was soon settled, rendering the break-up wholly unnecessary.

Pat clearly recognised the solemn tear-faced man across the road as being Dad's old pal. Their eyes briefly met and the, now sad, old man raised a limp hand and Pat graciously nodded in acknowledgment.

Finally, a few weeks later, in a simple close family ceremony, Dad's (Paddy) ashes were re-united with those of Mum (Mary), his loyal and devoted wife. Symbolically United again, forever in eternity. Two souls who had braved new horizons for the benefit of us children and committed themselves so faithfully to their chosen cause, were now resting jointly at peace. So ended their earthly journey, their legacy passed into the hands of us remaining siblings.

Chapter Twenty-Two

The Legacy

November 4th 2008. Dressed in light blue jacket and matching trousers, a yellow shirt and tie that matched the sparkling sunshine of the day and accompanied by Shirley, herself dressed immaculately in turquoise with a matching fascinator, I had to pinch myself. We were standing in the packed stands at Flemington watching the Melbourne Cup in Victoria, Australia. A race that always stopped the nation in its tracks and is as famous as own Grand National. This had been my dream since reading a book entitled *The Old Mare's Foal*, whilst holidaying with Aunt Peggy and Uncle Tommy. We were hosted by our cousin Oliver and his family who lived in that great city, the Cartons having fortunately planted themselves in exotic locations across the world. We had a grand time staying at their home and attending the races, without winning a bean, and I declared that the next time I attend the Melbourne Cup it will be as an owner of a horse running in the famous race. I am still waiting for that opportunity to present itself.

We first visited Australia in 1989, accompanied by Julie and Andrew and were welcomed to Perth by uncles Oliver and Liam and their family. The trip gained added significance in enabling us to meet with two of Mum's nephews, Nick and Aidan. We caught the Mr. Prospector train for a delightful seven-hour trip from Perth, across wild parched bushland and yellow desert, to Kalgoorlie, a standout town with homes and businesses that would not have looked out of place in a Hollywood cowboy film. We enjoyed a weekend with Nick and his lovely wife Maureen, who took us deep into the bush for another unforgettable two hour treat, ensuring we were never far from the car, water or each other. Aidan joined us overnight and we all spent an evening reminiscing about their time in Wexford with Mum. The next day, Aidan took us on a personal guided tour around the goldfields in his massive truck. Our, once in a lifetime, visit culminated in a tour of a real deep gold mine. All very memorable and how lovely it was to meet Mum's nephews and family, some ten thousand miles from home. Dad was very glad to hear news about Mum's far away nephews and really pleased we had met with Nick and Aidan.

One thing is certain, without the hard work and support of our now departed parents, none of this would have been possible. In common with my siblings, I have been very fortunate to have been employed all my life and been supported considerably by Shirley, with a very similar background. Prior to establishing her successful Solicitors Costs Drafting business she supplemented our income by cleaning windows and homes and even selling carpets from our garage home, all very much in the tradition of our respective parents.

My brothers and sisters have equally reaped the benefit, perhaps to different degrees, arising from that decision to emigrate, taken all those long years ago, in November 1958. Myself and Mehael, Betty, Nicky, May, Paul and David have become well-travelled. This is something that would have been alien, and totally unaffordable for our parents. Ann, as has been written about earlier, died far too young. She was much less fortunate but remains in our thoughts. Salvation Army Major, Pat, found his vocation after meeting Kate, a Nurse Lieutenant and have added one family addition, Jonathon, to those from Pat's first marriage to Shirley; Rebecca, Samantha and Terry. Together they managed Hostels, caring for the less fortunate in this world, before Pat suffered a stroke and they retired. I hasten to add, the consequential poor eyesight and physical impediment has not in any way diminished Pat's own special brand of humour.

Nicky was widowed in 2003 when his wife Margaret succumbed to Emphysema. Explicitly timing their arrival, six robed monks decamped from a taxi and strode purposefully into the crowded cremation service, totally unexpected and all the more poignant for it. It was a mark of respect for the woman who had catered for their domestic needs, at Blackfriars in St. Giles, over a number of years and underlined the rapport between them. All the more remarkable given that Margaret was not in the least bit religious and was very forceful in expressing her opinion. The monks clearly saw through the smoke clouds of doubt to love the real person within.

Recovering from this sudden tragedy, Nicky visited Wexford frequently and over the years spent time with his cousin and good friend, Jim Kinsella, attending race meetings and travelling around the country on coach excursions. During one such trip he met Ann, a church going larger-than-life and enthusiastic bundle of joy, never short of a word or three, who remains his partner to this day with the blessing and goodwill of all his family. He continues to enjoy his frequent travels between England and Ireland to meet up with Nicola and Darren and family, and a host of grandchildren, having sadly lost Lisa to illness in 2019.

In yet another twist of fate our youngest brother David was also widowed, not once but twice. Years after Sue died, he met Therese, a mother to a daughter Catherine from a previous marriage. She was working as a training officer at the Bristol hospital where he was engaged as a Microsoft engineer. Circumstances bonded them together and their relationship soon developed with David being Incredibly happy to meet such a new inspiring love. Unfortunately, Therese, the love of his life, was all too soon diagnosed with cancer, leaving David distraught. They married, celebrating in front of a large gathering of family and friends, at Eastwood Park in May 2011. A few months later, the family had gathered again as Therese lost her battle for life.

Widowed for a second time, David later visited Nicky and Ann in Wexford where he received support from a kindred soul. Encouraged by Therese's sister, Mel, he eventually decided he would retire, sell up and move to Ireland. Guided, perhaps, by an inner light he found a home close to the village of Blackwater.

A fitting finale, and a tribute to our mother, rests in the fact that Widower's Nicky and David have now returned to live in Wexford County, to reside near the very same town where Mum had grown up. David, despite being the sole brother born in England, has expressed a strong affinity with the county and now feels very much at home. He has enthusiastically embraced the local culture, joined local clubs and a ukulele band and is very much part of the local scene. This is not altogether surprising as he possesses a fine artistic vent, which manifested itself on a cold February day in 2018. He posted an evocative and sublimely written poem, on the Nostalgic Oxford website, recalling the days of his youth, which clearly struck a chord as it garnered him over three hundred *likes* from his new found fans, with one zealously nominating him as Official Group Poet.

He has once again found love and companionship, with a lady named Mary, living in the same area as Mum had in her before meeting Dad. For both Nicky and David, life has turned full circle. Strange are the seemingly co-incidental, and mysterious, workings of the world.

And finally, this book would not have been completed without the help of two of the most influential people in my life, my wife Shirley since we met in 1972 and my eldest sister Betty who has been a constant presence since birth. Betty has been the focal point for the Mary and Paddy family, particularly since Mum's rather untimely death. Ably supported by her husband Mick, she is often the first line of communication between siblings, conveying news, exchanging views and always willing to offer advice and encouragement to others. Having been married within two weeks of each other in 1974 we have retained strong bonds ever since.

I believe that is fitting that I conclude this book by reference to a joint holiday trip we made to Australia in the spring of 1998 as it is a worthy illustration of the legacy passed on by our parents. Steamy Singapore was our first stop-over and, to the eye rolling astonishment of Shirley and Mick, Betty and myself wasted little time in stepping out into the scorching heat in a bizarre search for a cup of English tea and a slice of Victoria sponge. After a weary sponge free hour or so we admitted defeat and alighted at the famous Raffles Hotel and were soon hydrated back to life with a comforting gin and a few cocktails. After a few days sightseeing of temples and the wonderous Botanical Gardens we flew on to Perth, where we were welcomed by Oliver and Helga, Liam and Hannah and their families and again met with Mum's nephew Nick and his wife Maureen at a BBQ held in Oliver's lovely flowered garden and we generally toured around for a week.

We next headed some 600 miles North to Monkey Mia Conservation Park where we walked among wild female dolphins. We stayed in a Denham beach resort with fantastic sunsets and an enormous Moon that seemed to caress the silent Indian Ocean in scenes of wonder and awe. On route, Mick decided to step out of the car to take a once in a life time photo of the eternally straight and red sandstone road. A fatal mistake as it happened as he was soon colonised by hundreds of flies seeking to create a toupee on his bald head and eager to sample some live British beef to boot. He quickly retreated to the car, whilst hearing our unsympathetic laughs at his plight. To assist, we gathered all the fly spray cans available and he was thus showered for his troubles whilst the enemy dripped onto every available bit of space. An emergency stop was made in a shadier spot to remove the dead bodies of the fallen.

Returning to Perth, Shirley and I departed for a week in Cairns on the East Coast where we visited Cape Tribulation, the Great Barrier Reef and the mountainous retreat of Kuranda with its scenic railway before flying on to Sydney to meet up again with Betty and Mick. We all enjoyed our hotel overlooking the harbour which we sailed around, visited the Opera House and Bondi Beach and engaged in the other usual touristy trips. Mick was made of sterner stuff and bravely and enjoyably fulfilled a personal wish to walk the mighty Sydney harbour bridge. Our homeward journey included a stop at smog laden Los Angeles where we window shopped in expensive Beverley Hills and toured the Hollywood homes of the famous. More than anything else, the holiday afforded us the time to reflect on how blessed we all were to see and do things that each of our parents could barely have imagined possible, even in their wildest dreams.

I believe the trip provided a fitting legacy to the question posed by Mary and Paddy (Mum and Dad Carton)-was their decision to move to England worth it? I think we all agreed it certainly was and I like to think that we have honoured their efforts by writing this book.

In the words of Mum's favourite Irish presenter, Eamonn Andrews, I say:

"Mary and Paddy, this is your life". Thank you and God bless.

Acknowledgements

I wish to thank my sisters Betty and May, brothers Mehael, Nicky, Pat, David and Paul, my wife Shirley, children Julie and husband Paul, Andrew and Bex for their advice, support and provision of anecdotal recollections, personal memories and their input in proof reading and amending of manuscripts.

I am grateful my cousins Paul and Mark Carton and family, Andrew and Siobhan Carton, Maureen Townend, the late Sean and Maria Carroll, Ann Hoy, Gerard and Viv Carton, James Carton and Marie Knight, Fiona Cummins and Susan Clark for their factual input, advice and comments.

I am indebted to late Uncle Anthony and Aunt Eileen, Uncles Peter, Liam and Oliver, together with their respective families, for providing memories of their own childhood.

I thank Pauline Verity for her proof reading, advice and comments.

Thanks to my publishers Matador/Troubador including Hannah Dakin, Beth Archer and their colleagues for their advice and support and guiding me through the whole process.

I acknowledge that the words from the song "I watched the sunrise" are copyrights © John Glynn 1970, the music © Colin Murphy 1970. I am grateful to them for permission to reproduce the words in the context of this book.

Photographs and images

My grateful thanks to all family members who have kindly searched their archives and provided photographs from their own collections, dating back many years, for either inclusion in this book or as background information. This has added immeasurably to that available from my own collection.

Credits

Anglesey Information. Maritime History and Chronological List of Ships (October 2019).

Muckross House Research Library, Trustees of Muckross House (Killarney) CLG. For permission to use extract from Library article, "Ireland in the 1930s and 1940s".

Dr Ida Milne for permitting me to use short extracts from her research into the social and health impact of the Spanish flu epidemic in Ireland and Wexford in particular.

I am obliged to Padge Quirke for allowing me to include information from his recording of The History of the Quirke's of Clonasheogues, ("Family of the Fairies") which has proved so valuable in understanding the history of my mother's family.

Football Association of Ireland (FAI). History, The Charlton Years.

For exclusive discounts on Matador titles,
sign up to our occasional newsletter at
troubador.co.uk/bookshop